# Afterlife,
## Interrupted

# Afterlife, Interrupted

## Helping Stuck Souls Cross Over

A CATHOLIC PRIEST EXPLORES THE INTERRUPTED DEATH EXPERIENCE™

NATHAN G. CASTLE, OP

FIRST EDITION, SEPTEMBER 2018

Published in the United States by Fluid Creations, Inc. d/b/a C2G2 Productions, 2018.

The Library of Congress has cataloged this edition as follows:

Castle, Nathan G., 1956, March 12 –
Afterlife, Interrupted: Helping Stuck Souls Cross Over
A Catholic Priest Explores the Interrupted Death Experience™/by Nathan G. Castle, OP
– 1st U.S. ed.

ISBN: 978-0-692-18753-1

New Revised Standard Version Bible, copyright 1989, Division of Christian Education of the National Council of the Churches of Christ in the United States of America. Used by permission. All rights reserved.

Book cover and interior design by Doreen Hann
Rani, *Afterlife* assistant editor
Betsy Rapoport, editor
Laura Dunham, copy editor
Cathryn Castle Garcia, publisher

# Gratitude

Lots of people in the Catholic Church, which is my spiritual home, are understandably guarded where dealings with spirits are concerned. Sometimes I'm asked, "What does the Church say about the work you're doing?"

The Catholic Church has nearly 1.4 billion members. Within that large body, I live a vow of obedience to my religious superior, Father Mark Padrez, OP. He is the provincial of our Western Dominican Province.

I'm very grateful for his fraternal support, as expressed in the following statement:

"Father Nathan has written from his deep experience of prayer, faithfulness to the Church, and dedication to his ministry as a priest. He has the profound desire to bring reconciliation and healing to those most in need."

Very Rev. Fr. Mark Padrez, OP
Prior Provincial, Province of the Most Holy Name of Jesus
Oakland, California

# Table of Contents

> "I do not occupy myself with things
> too great and too marvelous for me."
>
> Psalm 131: 1b

## Preface:

# In Truth and Love

You're reading the preface of my book, maybe because you're considering whether or not to invest the time and energy to actually read about my experiences helping "stuck souls" cross over into the next phase of the afterlife. Let me supply a few words that might help you decide.

Though it's true that I'm a Catholic priest, this is not a doctrinal book. I'm not trying to persuade the reader to agree or disagree with Catholic Church teaching about the afterlife.

This is not a book on "how to contact the dead." It's not to be understood as an encouragement to seek out conversations with the dead.

Are you familiar with the word *necromancy?* It is the practice of calling forth someone from the dead to declare future events or to reveal hidden facts for the benefit of the one doing the calling forth. That is not at all what I do. You will not find that here.

The motto of my Dominican Order is *Veritas,* which is Latin for *Truth.* We understand truth to be something that is, at the same time, possessed and sought. There are truths that we believe are unchanging and reliable, like this one: *Human beings are both mortal and immortal at the same time, but in different ways.* But there is so much that we don't know or that we know imperfectly. And so, we seek the truth.

The modern research university can serve as an example. In the morning you might find a professor, an expert in her field, at the front of a lecture room providing information proven to be true to her students. In the afternoon, you might find the same professor in the laboratory coordinating the work of students in the search for the truth of some disputed or unexplored question.

The Catholic Church of which I am a member and in which I serve as a priest, asserts many things to be true about the afterlife. It does so with conviction and humility. We know some things to be true, but infinity includes much for us to learn.

Why do I do this work with stuck souls? Because I believe the Holy Spirit whom I serve has asked me to. I believe the same Spirit has equipped me for this work and supplied wholesome companions to assist me. It has been a privilege and a joy. This all came as a surprise to me.

Why am I telling these stories? Because I believe the Spirit has called me to contribute them in support of what the Church calls the Easter Proclamation: Jesus is risen from the dead! He is not the One and Only. He is showing us what we all are: eternal persons who can always say, "The best is yet to come."

I also hope to contribute my experience and the experiences of those I've served to the expanding academic study of human consciousness. That we survive our death needn't be thought of as a uniquely religious idea. Many of the stories you'll find here involve persons who practiced no religious faith.

St. Paul of Tarsus wrote a beautiful description of love that is often proclaimed at Christian weddings. In it, he spoke of flashy, miraculous spiritual gifts. It seems that some in his Corinthian community had been given gifts of prophecy (as I believe I have) and were arrogant about it. He wrote that no such gift has value in the absence of love:

*If I speak in the tongues of mortals and of angels, but do not have love, I am a noisy gong or a clanging cymbal. [2] And if I have prophetic powers, and understand all mysteries and all knowledge, and if I have all faith, so as to remove mountains, but do not have love, I am nothing. [3] If I give away all my possessions, and if I hand over my body so that I may boast, but do not have love, I gain nothing.*

*[4] Love is patient; love is kind; love is not envious or boastful or arrogant[5] or rude. It does not insist on its own way; it is not irritable or resentful; [6] it does not rejoice in wrongdoing, but rejoices in the truth. [7] It bears all things, believes all things, hopes all things, endures all things.*

*[8] Love never ends. But as for prophecies, they will come to an end; as for tongues, they will cease; as for knowledge, it will come to an end. [9] For we know only in part, and we prophesy only in part; [10] but when the complete comes, the partial will come to an end. [11] When I was a child, I spoke like a child, I thought like a child, I reasoned like a child; when I became an adult, I put an end to childish ways. [12] For now we see in a mirror, dimly, but then we will see face to face. Now I know only in part; then I will know fully, even as I have been fully known. [13] And now faith, hope, and love abide, these three; and the greatest of these is love.*

You will find truth and love in these pages. You will also find the search for truth and wounded, flawed souls exploring new ways to become more loving in an afterlife expanding out infinitely before them.

Godbless,
(Father) Nathan G. Castle, OP

# The Story of Ray, the Perfect Gentleman

What did I do today? I went to the dentist for a routine exam. I shopped for groceries on the way home. I bought some laundry detergent because it was on sale. When I got home I warmed up leftovers for dinner. Then I returned a phone call.

Many days are so ordinary that when we're asked, "What's new?" we reply, "Nothing much. How 'bout you?"

And then there are days like the one where the other second grade teacher comes running into your classroom and shouts, "The president's been shot!" Or the day when you stand with your cafeteria tray looking for someone to eat with, and an acquaintance introduces you to the guy who will become your best friend.

Or the day that turns your entire life upside down. In fact, this day wasn't even a day. It was night. And I was asleep. I often remember my dreams. I'll never forget this one:

*I had just finished a round of golf with my priest–friend Michael. We were in the 19th hole, what golfers call the bar. We were having a drink, standing among donated items at a silent auction, a fund–raiser for some charity.*

*Across the room I spotted a large piece of framed art on the wall. I couldn't read the details from so far away, but I knew that the scene it portrayed was ghastly. I said to Mike, "Look at that godawful thing. Who in the world would donate that to a charity?" It was so horrific that I had to cross the room for a closer look. As I walked toward it, the whole thing lurched toward me. Everything inside the frame started moving like a video. Though still asleep, I could remember thinking, "This isn't my dream anymore. Someone's trying to show me something important."*

*A young white male, maybe twenty years old, was facing me. He was sitting on the radiator of a car, one of those from the late fifties with the fins and lots of chrome. The hood was up, and the guy's feet were on the bumper.*

*Suddenly he burst into flames and started screaming in agony at someone just outside the frame toward the lower right, where an artist's signature goes. The poor man was a screaming ball of fire. I awoke.*

*I felt the way you might when the phone rings in the middle of the night. I've had to sleep with a pager on the nightstand, in case there was a hospital call for a priest. This felt like that. Someone was calling, just not on the phone.*

My name is Nathan. I'm a Catholic priest. I became one when I was twenty-nine. Before that I was a college student confused about what I was going to be when I grew up. Before that I was a lonely teenager. And before that I was a bookish little kid growing up in a Catholic family. But at the moment I'm describing to you some eighteen years ago, I was a half-asleep, forty-four-year-old guy leading a spiritual retreat for some folks up in the mountains. Blinking through the fog in my sleepy head, I tried to focus on the burning, screaming guy.

I knew right away someone had come to me needing help. Then a feminine voice inside my head said, "Be careful. This one has not yet chosen the Kingdom." When you answer the page, you're immediately talking with someone at the nurses' station who's giving you needed information. This felt like that.

By now I was wide awake. I went into prayer in the Spirit. I made the Sign of the Cross, calling on the protection and wisdom of God as Father, Son, and Holy Spirit. I called on St. Michael the Archangel, too. He keeps me safe. "It feels like I just got called to help somebody," I said to them. "But it seems like he's somebody that already died." Then, trusting that the burning guy was still present and could hear me speak to him, I said, "Hey. My name's Nathan. I was sleeping, but then in my dream I could see you on fire." I scrambled to find pen and paper on the nightstand. I wrote down all I could remember and asked the burning guy and my guardian angel, Phillip James of the Line of Michael, to help me recall anything of the dream that might be fading away. I dedicated the remaining hours of the night in prayer to the burning man and eventually fell back to sleep.

I've been blessed over the years with faithful prayer partners. With a partner I can speak aloud to God and ask for whatever I need. That might be something about my own heart's desire, or it might be an intercessory prayer in which I ask for the good of another person. A prayer partner hears your heart and accepts you without judgment. In the morning, over coffee, I sought out a dear friend who was also my prayer partner. "Something strange and important happened last night," I told her. "I had this dream. I think someone is asking for our help. Would you help me pray for him?"

Afterlife, *Interrupted*

She agreed right away. We found a private place and prayed silently for some time. This prayer was contentless. Sometimes it's called "waiting on God." It's really just being spiritually still inside. It's not speaking; it's listening. Eventually my friend said, "Whoever he is, he wants to talk to you. Would that be okay?"

I knew my prayer partner had a gift of prophecy, for facilitating sacred speech. Though uncommon, it's mentioned in the letters of St. Paul in the Christian New Testament, for example, in 1 Corinthians 14:3, where he defines the role of prophecy as to "speak to other people for their upbuilding and encouragement and consolation." I told her about the feminine voice that had said, "Be careful. This one has not yet chosen the Kingdom."

*Safety first!* sounds like a good motto. But I follow Jesus. He often warned his followers he was taking them into danger, giving them plenty of chances to turn back. Besides, this guy was on fire! Sometimes people run into a burning building to save someone. This seemed like that kind of action moment. I've been trained in theological reflection: first, act as God's servant. Later, in prayer, reflect. I said a quick prayer to St. Michael the Archangel (considered an angel of supreme power and the leader of God's protective army) and to Holy Mother Mary and invited the burning man to speak through my friend to me. If this was a bad idea, I trusted that my heavenly helpers would see that the process would go no further.

Quite quickly, the dead man began to speak through my prayer partner's voice.

Nathan: What's your name?
Burning Man: *Ray.*
Nathan: I saw you sitting on a car radiator. Then you burst into flame and died horribly. Did I get that right?
Ray: *Yep. That's how I died.*
Nathan: Why were you sitting on a car's radiator?
Ray: *I was in my shop. I was having a fight with my friend. We'd had a little too much to drink.*
Nathan: It looked like a car from the late fifties when I was a little boy. Do you remember what year it was when you died?

Ray thought for a moment.

Ray: *1960.*
Nathan: Oh. I was four then. How old were you?
Ray: *Twenty. I'd gotten my girlfriend pregnant in our senior year. We got married. The baby was a year old. I went in with my buddy and started a car repair shop in the garage of our rented house.*

Nathan: That's a long time ago now, more than forty years. What've you been doing since then?

That's when Ray got angry. My prayer partner's brow furrowed, and her voice came out practically in a bark.

Ray: *Who the hell does He think He is taking me just when my life is gettin' good?*
Nathan: Huh?
Ray: *Who the hell does God think He is taking me just when my life is gettin' good?*

Well, I thought, at least he knows there is a God. But he thinks God set him on fire. No wonder he hasn't chosen the Kingdom!

Nathan: Hey, Ray, how did you find me, anyway?
Ray: *I don't know. Somebody brought me here.*
Nathan: Okay. Tell me how we can help you. What do you want?
Ray: *I want to be with my wife when she passes, and I can't the way I am now.*
Nathan: Oh. Well, then we need to figure out what there is about you that would prevent your greeting her, don't you think?

Ray kind of growled, like he didn't want to think about much of anything; he didn't want to change. Sometimes, people want the world to change around them without changing themselves. I've seen that often enough in others and in myself. It looked to me like Ray might be a tough nut to crack.

Nathan: So tell me about your wife.
Ray: *After I was gone, she married again. She married UP. Moved to South Carolina and married her a lawyer. They didn't have more kids. Look, I got nothin' against that man. He did a good job raising my son. But now she's dyin' of cancer, and I want to greet her when she passes.*
Nathan: Yeah, I got that part. Look, Ray, here's what I see. You've spent the last forty years without much to show for it. Cancer's got its own schedule, and it's not going to wait on you. If you want to see your wife when she passes, we might have to work fast. I might have to be hard on you, and I don't think you're gonna like it. Do you think you're up for it?

More muttering from Ray. Change is hard.

Afterlife, *Interrupted*

Ray: *Okay.*

Nathan: All right. We've gotta go right now. How about we meet up soon and get to work? Good. See you later, Ray.

My friend and I had never done anything quite like this before, but it seemed like the Spirit's work. The fact that something happens in this spirit–realm doesn't mean it takes precedence over every earthly thing. We were faithful about our regular commitments but scheduled a time a few days later when we'd go back into prayer and try to help Ray. He stayed on my mind and heart in the meantime.

When we had a next opportunity to talk, I thought maybe we should get straight on some basics.

Nathan: Ray, you know you survived your death, right?

Ray: *Yep. I didn't think much about stuff like that until that day.*

Nathan: And you trust that your wife will survive her death, too. That's good. Lots of people are unclear on that. People think it's all about religion. God created physics, too, and I think this is physics. We were made to be the kind of beings that live in a body for a while and then out of that body after it dies. So how did you know about God anyway? Who taught you about God?

Ray: *My mother. She made me kneel next to my bed, and she beat me while I said my prayers.*

Nathan: Good grief! Why'd she do that?

Ray: *I don't know. She just did.*

Nathan: Was she also the one who taught you that when people die it's because God takes them?

Ray: *No, that was Brother James.*

Nathan: Who's Brother James?

Ray: *Our pastor.*

Nathan: Well, Ray, I think Brother James may have meant well, but I think he was full of shit. I've known God all my life, and God is my friend and God doesn't set people on fire and take them just when their life's getting good. Ray, did anyone ever say anything about you that wasn't true, even if they thought it was? Well, do the math. We're small; God's huge. If people say some untrue things about us, imagine how many wrong things get said about God all day every day. Do you believe everything everybody ever says, Ray? Would you be willing to consider that maybe you were given some wrong information about God?

Ray: *But he was our pastor…*

Nathan: Yeah, and I'm a pastor, too. So what? And I'm a Catholic priest, and—

Ray: *You're a Catholic priest! Shit!*

Nathan: Well, yes, I am, and they make us go to school forever and ever to become one. Ray, do you know I'm a freakin' Master of Divinity, and I have the diploma to prove it. Imagine that—<u>mastering</u> Divinity! I couldn't fix a car to save my life like you could, Ray, but I know an awful lot about God. You've spent decades being mad at God and where has it got you? Ray, would you consider that maybe people just die and it's nobody's fault? I'm sorry you didn't get to be with your wife and son for very long. And I'm sorry that you died in a fire. I wouldn't wish that on anybody. But remember what we're doing here. You want to greet your wife, right? Just think about it.

My friend and I needed to bring the session to a close. I'd come to realize that Ray hadn't been with anyone since his passing because that's the way he wanted it. He lived outside of time, we discovered. He wasn't being punished; he made that clear. "Somebody brought me here," he'd explained to us, so we knew we were part of a Spirit–led team. He wouldn't have said he was in purgatory because he'd told us he was a Baptist from Georgia, and they don't do purgatory. He just isolated himself because he was angry and hurt. Because he was so skittish and alone, it seemed like getting someone to keep him company would be a good place to start, if he would invite it. I didn't want to leave him that way for another week, or until we could meet again. I had an idea.

Nathan: Ray, you know how at the front of the Bible, God says, "It's not good that the man should be alone?" I think that's true. You've been alone too long. What if we asked someone to come and be with you? (I thought of his mother first, then nixed that. The mom who beat her praying boy might not be the first face he should see). Ray, what about your Dad? You never mention him.

Ray: *I didn't really know him and was kinda afraid of him. He died when I was ten. He died in the war.*

Nathan: Vietnam?

Ray: *No, Korea.*

Of course. Ray died in 1960. I got my wars mixed up there for a second. In counseling, oftentimes when people go dark on someone and the relationship isn't great, I like to ask if there's ever been a moment when hearts met.

Nathan: Well, think for a minute. What was the very best time the two of you ever spent together? Did you ever have a really good time as a father and son?

Ray thought for a moment.

Ray: *Once we went and looked at cars.*

Doesn't that sound like a guy thing? Asking in the Spirit for Ray's dad to come keep him company seemed like a no-brainer.

Nathan: Ray, would it be possible for you to arrange your surroundings, whatever they are, so that you can let someone come near, but not too near? If I ever enter a room where I might be afraid, I stay near the door. Or maybe if I'm a little afraid of an encounter, I limit the time. I tell the other person, you can come but you can only stay for a few minutes. Maybe this could work for you. What if we ask for your dad to come but not to come too close or to stay too long? Would that be okay?

There was a pause. He was thinking.

Ray: *I could do that.*
Nathan: Okay, good. Then is it okay with you if I ask for him to come?
Ray: *Okay.*

So I quietly said a prayer. I believe we all live inside God. I believed Ray's dad would hear me if I called out for him. I don't have to know how it works. I just know that it does.

Nathan: "Ray's dad, would you like to see your son?"
Ray: *Ohmygod, there he is over there!*

I didn't see anything.

Nathan: Does he look scary?
Ray: *No, he just looks like my dad.*
Nathan: Is it okay for us to leave the two of you together? We'll check back with you soon.
Ray: *Okay. Thanks. See you later.*

Another week passed. Ray stayed on my mind and in my prayers. So did his dad and the dying wife in South Carolina. My friend and I set a time to get back together. We went into prayer, again within the Holy Spirit and with the protection of St. Michael the Archangel and Holy Mother Mary. Ray showed up quickly.

> Nathan: Hey, Ray. How'd it go? You were with your dad. Did he stay long?
> Ray: *No, we went and looked at cars.*
> Nathan: Which cars, Ray? He died in the early fifties, and you died in 1960. How does it work? Did you have to choose which time to go back to?
> Ray: *No, we went and looked at the new ones.*

So, somewhere on God's green earth, Ray and his dad had some father–son bonding time at some car lot. *That's good*, I thought. *Ray's not isolated anymore.* He knew he could be with other people if he chose to. But we still needed to get him ready to greet his dying wife.

Of course, there wasn't any textbook to follow in helping Ray; my prayer partner and I drew on our education, upbringing, and intuition. My prayer partner had room in her heart for Ray from the start. She, too, had been taught cruel, untrue things about God that had to be unlearned before a new truth could be known. I think her personal résumé made her a very good candidate for this kind of work: she had endured a lot of suffering. Her childhood had been harsh, and its bitter fruit followed her into adulthood. She had made that decision so many must make: *Do I let suffering make me bitter, or do I let it make me compassionate?* She had chosen compassion. We both knew the importance of dying to our own egos and knew Ray would have to do some of this in order to get to greet his wife.

We worked with Ray a little like a physical therapist might. The therapist might have to lead a patient through painful exercises on the way to healing, but the patient remains in charge of his own health. We were careful not to always assume we knew what was best for Ray. We would propose a plan, explain it, and ask for Ray's permission to proceed. We sensed his isolation was no longer helpful. He wanted to leap into greeting his wife, but he'd been by himself for so long it seemed like we should try to help him make smaller first steps. That's why we got him to agree to reuniting with his dad first. As a counselor, I don't tell others what they should do. I just try to suggest what seems like a positive option. When I think of Ray now, that's what I admire most about him. His love for his wife gave him the strength to grow and change in ways that caused him some pain, at least in the short run.

My prayer partner and I often met in her home. She had recently adopted an abused shelter–dog. When I'd come over, he'd run and hide in his crate. Over time I earned his trust by getting down on his level, lying on the floor, and speaking in soothing tones. I wouldn't make sudden moves. I'd let him sniff at me to get my scent. I tried to do something similar with Ray, while at the same time trying to move the process along at our next session.

Nathan: Okay, Ray. Today we figure out why you can't be with your wife when she passes, as you said, "the way I am now." I think I know what the problem is, Ray, but I don't think you're gonna like it.

Ray: *What's that?*

Nathan: You're a caveman, Ray. You were with this woman for two or three years out of sixty–something, and you sound to me like you think you own the exclusive rights to her. I think when you see her, you might just drag her away by her hair.

My prayer partner grimaced, eyes narrowing. So Ray didn't like to hear that. Who would?

Nathan: I'm just trying to help, Ray. You can get rid of me anytime you want to, but your wife's cancer has its own timeline. I'm not being blunt without reason. Here's the deal, Ray. This woman has lived more than sixty years. She will have been loved by lots of people—parents, siblings, friends, people she met only after you'd passed. I don't know how all of this works, but don't you suppose there are lots of people who love her in different ways? Some of those will have passed before her and, like you, are eager for a reunion. So there's probably going to be a group. Now, she only had two husbands, and you're the only one of those who has passed, right? And she only had one child, and that was with you. That's huge, Ray. You're probably very important in her life. I think you'll belong there when she passes, Ray. I think she'll be happy to see you. Why wouldn't she? Just have a little humility, Ray. Don't be a caveman.

Ray, to his credit, endured my little sermon. The three of us got together the following week, this time briefly.

Nathan: Hey, Ray.

Ray: *Hey.*

Nathan: So what's new?

Ray: *Big news, that's what.*

This was the most excited I had heard him sound.

Ray: *My wife passed. And I got to be there when she crossed. And you would have been proud of me. I was a perfect gentleman.*

Nathan: That's great, Ray! That's terrific! I knew you had it in you! Good job! So I guess our work here's done, huh?

Ray: *Yeah, I guess. Thanks for your help.*

Nathan: You're welcome. Thanks for putting up with me and for working so hard. One thing before you go, Ray. Now that you're an official afterlife greeter, and you're not all alone anymore, what would you say to being in the welcoming party when it's my turn to pass?

Ray: *It would be an honor, sir. Just look for the perfect gentleman.*

I'm not much of a crier, ever. But Ray almost made me cry. I had one final question for him.

Nathan: Ray, why do you think people die?

Ray: *I don't know for sure. I could be wrong.*

With that, Ray went on his way. It felt strange to part with someone I'd never even seen, except in that fiery dream. As he left, my friend and I said a little prayer Christians call a doxology: *Glory be to the Father, and to the Son, and to the Holy Spirit, as it was in the beginning, is now, and will be forever. Amen.*

Ray was able to get himself unstuck because he shifted. We all have to go through some shifts in life if we're going to grow. He was willing, begrudgingly, to reconsider long–held ideas about God. He was willing to think again about why he had died at all. He was coaxed out of his crate by the presence of a father he felt he barely knew. Ray did all of this because he was a man on a mission. He loved his wife and was determined to greet her when she passed. When I asked him why he thought people die, Ray shifted from his earlier certainty that God "took him" in a fire to an agnostic position. He was willing to say, "I don't know for sure. I could be wrong." When's the last time you said that of anything important?

Sometimes we think and behave as though we're the center of the universe, especially when we're younger: *Everything revolves around me.* Ray, who died at twenty, had a lot of that going on. But with only a little input and persuasion, he was willing to shift his understanding. He was willing to acknowledge that he was not the unique center of his former wife's universe. Ray humbled himself and took his place in a constellation of love of those awaiting his beloved's arrival.

I never really planned to stay in touch with Ray, except to call him to mind and pray for him from time to time. Then the concept of this book began to take shape. It felt like another calling.

For forty years I've belonged to an 800–year–old, semi–contemplative religious order, the Dominicans. One of our mottoes is "Contemplate and give to others the fruit of your contemplation." Contemplating involves slowing down and breathing deeply. It means listening to the Spirit. That process can yield insightful lessons and new questions.

In trying to give you the fruit of my contemplation of the story of Ray and all that surrounds it, I'm trying not to load you up with all the fruits in the produce section of the supermarket. What follows here are what could be called the first fruits; more will come later.

Do you remember the scared little boy, Cole, in the 1999 movie *The Sixth Sense*? His mom and teachers concluded that he was disturbed enough to need a child psychologist. After experiencing more and more ghostly phenomena, Cole decides to trust this helpful man and confides in him, revealing his secret: "*I see dead people.*" So, I'm trusting you with my secret: "I see dead people, sort of." At least I see what they show me in a dream. I hear them, too, when in protected prayer a faithful companion with the appropriate spiritual gift allows them to speak through. I have been given that prophetic gift, too, and use it to give those who are otherwise voiceless an opportunity to express themselves.

There was no way I could have known at the time that Ray was just the first of many folks who'd find their way first into my dreams and then into my heart. Night visitors kept coming, about three times a month. Since meeting and helping Ray, I have been visited by more than two hundred fifty others who got stuck on the way through their death experiences—a lot more than that if you count the ones who showed up in groups. Most of these stories are of individuals, but sometimes stuck souls seem to gather with others who died similarly traumatic deaths. And sometimes my prayer partners and I help them move on in a group.

Why did I decide to gather these stories into a book? Because I'm a follower of Jesus. I was born and raised and have chosen to live my life as a Catholic Christian. Easter is our most important day of the year. Here is the joyful Easter proclamation: "Jesus is risen from the dead!" He has taught us that we're indomitable. Death is not the end of us. We'll survive our deaths, too. That's the most important thing I can think of to share with people, that however good or bad the present moment is, the best is always yet to come.

But we're not just happy for Jesus. We believe him to be the first fruits and strongest evidence of the eternal life offered to all of us. In his life before and after dying we see the pattern. To be human is to be the kind of being who lives for a time in a body made of flesh; after our deaths we live in another form. My Catholic tradition calls this form "the glorified body." This is who we are. From the moment we came to be, we have been eternal.

That is about as preachy as I intend to get here. I am a preacher, but the One I love and follow spent very little time in places of worship. In fact, he was thrown out of them. And for centuries, people who have seen and spoken with Jesus after his death have been willing to tell their stories. They overcame fear, in some cases even the fear they would be put to death, to tell their stories.

I'm willing to share these stories because I want people to be happy. I think we're happiest when we are free. We are freest when we are not afraid. When we know that death is not the end of us, there really is no stopping us. We are free to love, not only until death do us part, but even after. Even ever after.

So what have the experiences I'll share here taught me? I'll summarize a few here and expand upon them later via the stories of some of my afterlife friends.

- Most people who die traumatically quickly complete their transition into the afterlife. Only a few need the kind of assistance my prayer partners and I have been asked to provide. I once dealt with a group of twenty people who died instantly in the same airplane crash. Nineteen passed completely without incident. Only one had what I call an "Interrupted Death Experience" (IDE).
- All human beings who die survive their deaths. *You are eternal. You always have been since you came into existence. You will always be.*
- Your individual consciousness will survive. You will still be recognizable as you. You will have your memories. Your life will continue.
- No one dies alone. At your death you will have supportive companionship. You weren't born alone; you won't die that way, either.
- You will be greeted and welcomed by loving helpers. God/heaven/the universe will provide the ideal loving guide even if you weren't religious or a believer in an afterlife.
- Your freedom will be respected. You will not be forced to do anything you don't freely choose. If you prefer not to go with the program right away, you may choose to wait until you are ready.
- You will be respected. You won't want to disrespect yourself or anyone else.
- You will leave behind all physical pain. Any emotional or spiritual pain will heal as you allow it to.
- Time will behave differently. You'll be outside of it. There will still be sequence, things happening after and as a result of other things, but they will occur in what is always now. A few of those I've met keep track of earth-time; most remember it but have to work to recall the specifics of ages and dates.
- There are infinite opportunities to learn in the next life. When you arrived here as a baby you quickly set out to learn to crawl, to walk, and to talk. You learned about dinosaurs and numbers and letters. The afterlife is full of things to learn. Others may enjoy learning with you.
- You'll have some kind of body that others will recognize as you. You may prefer to be an earlier version of yourself. How you present yourself is changeable.
- You can visit or look in on loved ones here on earth. You just can't be creepy or obsessive about it. How to do that is one of the things you can study.
- Some things are not to be known just now.

These stories are highly personal, perhaps too personal to share, but sharing this message of faith, hope, and optimism has felt like the most important part of my mission on earth. But did I have the right to share these stories? I expressed this concern with a friend who asked, "What if you got their permission?" What if I went back into prayer in the Spirit and asked if Ray was still available? If he was, maybe he'd say yes to letting me share his story.

I didn't know if it would work, but it did. I don't spend my days just chatting up the dead. That you *can* do a thing doesn't mean you *should* do a thing. My Catholic tradition cautions against conversing with the dead as it could invite dark spirits. I get that. I didn't have any unholy intentions. I wasn't asking for tomorrow's lottery numbers or seeking any personal power or advantage. So I did ask the Holy Spirit to help me speak with my old friend Ray because I had an important question to ask him.

Happily, Ray came through right away and told me he was happy to have his story shared here. He could see that his story might have the power to save someone who's still alive on this earth from the kind of trouble he'd been through.

We didn't talk long; I'll save that for the afterlife. But I did ask Ray, "What's new?" Ray told me that once he learned, when his wife passed, how to be an afterlife greeter, he wanted to learn more about how it all works. On earth, Ray didn't like school, and it didn't like him. He wasn't being taught the things he really wanted to know about. Once he found questions he really wanted answered, he discovered he was a good, motivated student. There were other people interested in learning some of the same things he was, so instruction was organized into something like a school. "No one I've run across in the afterlife ever makes you feel dumb," he told me. "People are always kind."

Does that make sense to you, the existence of some afterlife academies? It does to me. I was taught as a little kid that heaven would contain every good thing. I think schools are good. I've always enjoyed learning. Maybe when my time comes, I'll be greeted by my old friend, that perfect gentleman, Professor Ray.

I didn't talk to Ray for years after that. Our lives intersected for a while and for a specific purpose. Many relationships are like that, don't you think? I did ask him to hover over me as I was writing and help me recall our time together. He's even praying in his own way that our book gets published and widely read.

Once Ray showed up, a door opened to me for a new way to serve. Was I ready for it? In a story about Peter as a young disciple, he sees Jesus in a storm standing on the sea. He asks Jesus to call him to walk upon the water, so Jesus calls him. Peter manages to take a few steps on water. Then he gets ahead of himself, looks up, notices the forceful storm clouds, and begins to sink. The story reminds folks to take one faithful step at a time. No need to see several steps ahead. Just take the next step. That's what my prayer partners and I have been doing, with the help and protection of the Spirit. We could have wondered if we were getting into something over our heads. We didn't do that. We didn't turn away because Ray needed help. We probably wouldn't have chosen ourselves to do this work, but it seemed clear that the Spirit had chosen us. We had made ourselves available to God's work in whatever form that might take, however strange.

Thirty–nine years ago I joined The Order of Preachers, the Dominicans. I lay prostrate on the floor of St. Albert's Priory in Oakland, California, with arms outstretched in the shape of a cross. I consecrated my life to the Spirit's purposes. I gave my body, mind, and spirit, and especially my voice to God's project. I am God's instrument. I allow the night visitors I'm given to help borrow the voice God gave me just long enough to say what they need to say. I believe this work is led by the Holy Spirit and consistent with my Christian faith. Some may disagree, but I'm hoping they will listen respectfully to what I have to say.

My prayer partners and I have chosen, from among more than two hundred fifty of these stories, a few which we think illustrate the phenomena of what I've begun to call the "Interrupted Death Experience." Each one causes questions to arise. I'll share the ones that came up for us. There are also many sweet surprises. Even though these earthly lives all ended tragically, you'll hear afterlife stories of great resilience. I hope you'll find them inspiring. I have.

What you will not get in this book is a guided tour of the afterlife. I believe life is a mystery. Love is a mystery, too. Life and love are not whodunits that tease us with easily overlooked clues, daring us to arrive at the only right conclusion. Many of the things of God and of all that is are not knowable to us here and now.

But for now, I invite you into the lives, and the afterlives, of some of the most beautiful, courageous people you'll ever meet. As you listen to their stories, I hope you'll delve more deeply into your own. These people have allowed me to share their stories with you so that, when the time of your death comes, you may flow easily from one manner of being to the next, without interruption.

When I've mentioned this work to friends and family, people ask, "Why do they come to you?" Here's my short answer to a lot of questions that you may have as you read this book: *I don't know.* Early on I did ask the visitors how they found me. Most of the time I've gotten this reply: *I don't know; somebody brought me here.* One visitor said he'd been told that when I'm asleep I can receive a signal, like a satellite dish. Once I heard a reply I thought was really cool: *Your light was on.* Remember that Tom Bodett Motel 6 ad tagline: *We'll leave the light on for ya?* So, is my bedroom a cosmic cheap hotel room? *I don't know.*

*I don't know* is really only half of the thought. The rest is: *But here's what I think.*

And here's what I think. I learned to open my mind, heart, and spirit to God a long time ago, very early on, when I was a little boy.

## Chapter One
# Pray, Pray, Pray

Have you ever asked yourself, "How did I ever get here?" Life can be such a wild ride, with so many unexpected twists and turns. If you choose to read the stories I will tell, you might wonder how I came to be involved in something as unusual as helping people who've died, but who aren't exactly resting in peace yet.

To try to help you understand life as I've experienced it, I'll have to go back a long way, even to the womb. I'm sixty–two as I write this.

Let me ask you this: You know that phrase, "inner child?" It was very overused for a while in pop–psychology. Is the childhood version of me hidden within the adult me that I show the world? I'm not sure, but I know that the experiences I had as a child were stored in the categories and the vocabulary of the little guy I once was. Here I'm going to do my best to let him speak and tell you things that might help you to get to know me.

My mom and dad were devout Catholics. They had two children before I was conceived, and they'd suffered one miscarriage. I came upon the scene in 1956. Mom was thirty–five as my birth approached. But there was trouble. I had never been born before—as far as I knew—and I was doing it wrong. You're supposed to be upside down, head down, feet up, when it's time to come out. I was the other way, and they couldn't get me to turn. And that umbilical cord thing isn't supposed to be wrapped around your throat, because it can strangle you while you're being born. Who knew?

Fortunately, my baby doctor did. His name was Doctor Robert. He was trying hard to help my mom get me here safely. Mom had this good man helping her on earth and another one helping from heaven. His name was St. Gerard. When Gerard was alive on the earth, he collected up thrown–away young women, pregnant prostitutes on the streets of Paris whom other people mistook for trash. He helped these pregnant women in difficult circumstances bring their babies safely into the world. Catholic people think that when people love doing something and are good at it, they can find a way to keep doing it after they die. Mom believed this and believed that St. Gerard could hear her when she prayed to him inside the Body of Christ. She asked St. Gerard to help Doctor Robert get me here safely. It all worked out well in the end. My dad, who piloted ships, told me I entered the world "stern first." My backside smiled at the world before my face did. Mom recalled the thirty–six hours of labor and kept a promise she'd made to her helpers on earth and in heaven. They had me baptized and gave me the name Robert Gerard. Doctor Robert joined St. Gerard in the afterlife the next year, but I still think of both of them as part of my posse.

As a little boy, I learned that I had a mom and dad on earth and another pair in heaven. All of them loved me. After I brushed my teeth and got into bed, Mom would help me talk to my other family. We'd do a series of "God–blesses." She'd list family members one at a time, and I'd repeat after her and ask God the Father to bless them, which meant to give them something good that they needed even if you didn't know exactly what it was. God would know what they needed most, Mom told me. I learned that you could God–bless anybody you wanted to, and it didn't matter if they were alive on the earth or had already died. God the Father lived everywhere, so anywhere there were people, God was with them. The ones who had died would get their blessing, like a present you sent to them. Blessings were a way to send love to other people and praying blessings was something even a little kid could do.

When I was four, my parents built a new home for our growing family on a lot behind our house; Mawmaw and Pawpaw, my dad's mother and father, moved into our old house. At sixty–three, with no previous construction experience, Mawmaw, born Anna Lee Alloway, began tearing into their new place.

Mawmaw could do things other people wouldn't attempt because she always had heavenly helpers. If it wasn't Sweet Jesus helping her paint, it was St. Joseph the Carpenter helping her remodel her house. St. Joseph, Jesus' foster–father, wouldn't have done electrical wiring in first–century Palestine, but he and Mawmaw rewired that old house together. They had the help of diagrams in the Time Life do–it–yourself books she got in the mail. They knocked down walls and added a bathroom in the garage so she wouldn't track dirt in the house. That was important, because she was on to a next passion: gardening. She learned about composting and roses. God knows who she had helping her with grafting different kinds of fruit trees together. She created all these cool little trails lined with stones that curved and intersected through her elaborate gardens.

Mawmaw gave St. Anthony of Padua the run of the place. He was everywhere, always involved in whatever she was doing because they were such good friends. I don't know how they became such a pair. She had lived for many years in a parish named for him; maybe that was it. St. Anthony was the patron saint of lost things, and he was especially devoted to sick and poor people. She tried to get me to be friends with him, but I never really did. He was her saint friend.

One day I came upon Mawmaw down on her old-woman knees pouring cool, gray cement into square wooden forms she'd placed on the ground. As the cement began to harden a little, she let me pick a piece of broken bathroom tile, whatever color I wanted. She showed me how to press down on it to imbed it in the wet cement. The next day it would all be dry and solid, and we'd have a bit more of the landscape of the patio that would lie beneath the grape arbor she was creating above it.

When I try to think of her now I think of that patio, simple materials arranged in a creative way. It was the shapes and colors you noticed against the coarse, gray cement. But there was really more of the gray.

Don't you think our way of seeing and knowing people is like that? We see the icy tip that pokes above the water line, not the much larger berg that floats below the surface. Sometimes we forget and think that what we see of another is all there is to them. I want to show you Mawmaw, as best I'm able. The result might be an abstract mosaic: colorful shards of tile, mostly bright, some dark, all small parts of a beautiful, if mysterious, whole.

Out of the sea of gray that was her childhood, a few things are clear. There was an oil boom raging in swampy southeast Texas. Roughnecks came from all over to work in the oilfields and the refineries that were quickly springing up along the recently dredged waterways. Mawmaw, then ten-year-old Anna Lee Alloway, was a drudge, Cinderella before the prince and the ball. Her parents divorced at a time when hardly anyone did that. There were whispers of abuse. That's all a part of the gray background.

Young Anna Lee cooked and cleaned and did the laundry around the boarding house her mother ran for the young working men far from home. As part of a fifth-grade family genealogy assignment, I asked her to tell me about her childhood. I got the message: she hadn't had one.

Anna Lee never did get her handsome prince. Aubrey Maxwell Castle, my grandfather, whom we called Pawpaw, was fourteen years older, the eighth child of a poor Kentucky family. There'd been no record of his birth: more gray family background. His dad died when he was four. Several siblings died as babies.

They married in 1914 when she was almost seventeen; he was thirty-one. I can't remember ever seeing a wedding picture. Tucked between the pages of her crumbly family bible I found a small envelope. On the outside, in fine cursive, were the words: "Pictures Dad carried when he was in France, 1918." It was several poses of his young wife and two little daughters all dressed up out on the lawn.

Mawmaw told me he came back from the War to End All Wars different. He seldom spoke. He'd been in the terrible trench warfare where they were using tanks and grenades and chemical weapons for the first time. For a while he owned a bar. Prohibition took it; he was not compensated. A business partner cheated him out of money. His service station burned down. During the Depression he was out of work for eight years, much of my dad's childhood.

The family crowded together and sublet a bedroom to boarders who helped the little family of five make the rent. Mawmaw did their laundry and mending; she was an older Cinderella now with hungry mouths to feed, my father and his two older sisters.

Is that why two of her three children have mostly harsh memories of her? Those were hard times. At least she had one treasure, her middle child and namesake, young Anna Lee. Why is it that sometimes hearts only have room for one? That's what it felt like to my dad and his older sister, Edith Mae.

These pieces of a family held together. The girls each became Catholic nuns. Edith Mae became Sister Maximus to honor Max, her dad. Young Anna Lee became Sister Leona, to honor her mother. To be a nun was hard and you needed a heavenly helper, so they chose one and received that saint's name. Sisters Maximus and Leona both taught first grade and loved kids.

When I entered their Dominican order decades later, Maximus confided that she'd entered the convent "to get away from Mama." Still, she stayed. Whenever Maximus and Leona visited from the convent, they always came with a gaggle of other white-robed nuns who oohed and aahed over the blossoms and sampled the fruit preserves from Mawmaw's little orchard. Sister Maximus's life blossomed into more than seventy years of beautiful service. From her I learned that if you wait to have absolutely pure motives before acting, you might end up doing absolutely nothing.

One day when I was about six, Sister Maximus taught me something very seriously. I was about to make my First Communion.

"I want you to know something," she told me. "God loves everyone and hears everyone's prayers. But God especially loves children. Children's prayers go straight to God's heart. The prayers of children are super-powerful. And you won't be a child for very long, so don't waste your short childhood. Pray hard about everyone and everything you can think of."

Well, that made sense to me. Everything I was learning about heaven and heaven-on-earth was that the last were first and the least were really the greatest. Why wouldn't the prayers of little kids have a big impact? So I got very busy. I was getting to be too big to be tucked into bed at night by my mom. And besides, I knew how to pray on my own now. I'd gone from tricycles to training wheels to a big-kid bike. I was a child in motion and a little praying dynamo.

On the wall above my bed was a picture of a guardian angel. Maybe you know this painting; it's pretty common. A young boy and girl are walking on a rickety footbridge above a swiftly-rushing creek, oblivious to the inherent danger. Above them floats a radiant guardian angel, wings outstretched. The picture was there to remind me that I came to earth with an invisible angel to guard me. Your guardian might save you from an accident like falling into a creek. At the end of the day it was important to thank your angel for getting you through the day safely. When it did come time for you to die and go back to God they'd help you do that too. They didn't need money or things, but you could pray a blessing for them, and they'd receive it as a gift.

We were being taught in Catholic school about what happens when people die. It seems they all have to decide whether or not they want to live with God and the holy ones. Though it could get complicated, the rules came down to this: loving God and loving everyone else. That's all. Just love all the time, and you're good. Treating everyone the way you'd like to be treated was simple enough, but easier said than done. We were taught that anyone could make wrong choices, or even get in the habit of making the same wrong choices over and over. Some people hardly knew anything about God at all. We were taught about people's particular judgments. People who died weren't kept in suspense wondering if they'd get into heaven or not. Some lived such good lives that their getting into heaven was, for God, a no-brainer. Maybe some would choose eternity away from God and go to hell. But we were reminded that this was all a mystery and that the only way we'd know if a particular person was in hell was if God told us they were there. God had never revealed the name of anyone who was in an eternal, no-turning-back hell. Not even Judas or Pontius Pilate or Hitler or anyone you'd like to send there. I didn't really believe that God had created an eternal torture chamber where bad people had to stay locked up forever. It didn't make sense to me. When people asked Jesus this kind of question, he pretty much told them to mind their own business. Maybe there was something like an eternity time-out where people had to go to their room and stay there until they were ready to behave themselves, and the rest of us would be kept safe from the trouble they'd cause. But I just couldn't believe God would just give up on anybody completely and forever.

Heaven involved being perfectly loving, like God. But most people weren't perfectly loving or perfectly anything at the exact moment when they died, especially the ones who died suddenly in car crashes or who dropped dead of a heart attack. The Catholic ones could've gone to confession, but what if they didn't confess their sins in time? These people ended up in purgatory, a kind of in-between place. We knew the Protestants didn't believe in purgatory because it wasn't in the Bible exactly, but it made sense. Purgatory was more good than bad, closer to heaven than hell, and once you were in it you were safe. It was a place to rest and get cleaned up after you died. The people there suffered. They learned how things they said or did hurt other people, and they were given the chance to become better people. They could hear heaven's music but weren't invited into the dance, at least not yet. They had to wait. If they'd done a lot of wrong things, they might have to wait longer.

In the classroom, when we did very well on some math or spelling worksheet we sometimes got a prize: a holy card. It was a small colored picture of Jesus or Mother Mary or one of the saints. On the back there was a prayer you could say. At the bottom of the prayer *in tiny italic print* there might be the phrase "100 days indulgence." Ice cream on a hot day is an indulgence, especially if someone else pays for it and gives it to you for free. The idea was you'd pray this prayer and offer it as a free credit to someone's purgatory account. You could tell God whose time in purgatory you wanted shortened. It could either be someone you'd known who had died, like my godmother or my Baptist piano teacher, who wouldn't have believed in purgatory, but I prayed for her anyway, just in case. If you accidentally prayed for a soul in purgatory who wasn't there, God would credit that prayer to someone else who needed it. Prayers never went to waste.

I used to go to the bank with my dad sometimes. You almost always had to wait in line. The bank people even planned to make you wait in line and had these zig-zaggety velvet ropes that kept everyone in their place as they waited for their turn. I thought that purgatory must be like that, because lots of people die on the same day and their pictures are in the paper. Some were from devout Catholic families like mine who had lots of people praying for them. But some didn't have anyone praying for them and had to watch new arrivals cut right in front of them because they got more prayers. At church, old people, especially old church ladies, would pray out loud, "For all the poor souls in purgatory, especially those with no one to pray for them." What a concept! The italic 100-days-off prayer on the holy cards always struck me as a little silly, like clipping coupons to use at the grocery store, except these were for getting into heaven faster. Praying blessings for people didn't seem silly at all, though, and praying blessings for the people in the purgatory line seemed to me a good thing to do. No one likes waiting in lines and certainly not for something as important as getting into heaven.

I remember being taught that, if your prayer was the one that sprung someone into heaven, that person would be eternally grateful to you. You really would have friends in high places! And they'd start praying for *you* and sending you blessings.

So if there's a line and some people are moving quickly, maybe there are some who are right on heaven's threshold but nobody's praying for them. Wouldn't they be like low-hanging fruit? One little prayer from me might spring them into heaven. I'd fall asleep at night, not wasting my short childhood, praying for the next person who only needed one

Afterlife, *Interrupted*

prayer to get into heaven. And once they were safely in, the whole line would move up one space, and I'd pray for the next person. And so on.

But then I'd tire of that and think of the poor soul who had just died and was all the way at the back of the line with no one praying for them. They'd be next. Then I'd ask God to pick someone at random, someone in the middle of the line; the next prayer would be for them. Does this sound exhausting? I didn't care. Eventually, I'd fall asleep. The next night I'd repeat the whole process. No one was going to be stuck waiting to get into heaven. Purgatory was going to have prompt customer service if I had anything to say about it.

At our school every classroom had the American and the Texas state flags and pictures of the Trinity on the wall. Not the Father, the Son, and the Holy Ghost, but Jesus, the Pope, and President Kennedy. He was the only Catholic president there'd ever been. Most presidents were old, but he wasn't. His children, Caroline and John, were younger than me. That summer Mrs. Kennedy had baby Patrick, who was born sick. We all prayed for him, but he lived only a few days and then he died.

It was a Friday afternoon in November and we had just come back into our classroom from lunch and big recess. Suddenly, Mrs. High, the other second grade teacher, came running in, screaming, "The President's been shot!" We quickly knelt beside our desks and prayed children's super-powerful prayers for President Kennedy to be okay. The teachers were too upset to keep having school, so they sent us home early. Before we left, the principal, Sister de Pazzi, told us to, "Pray, pray, pray for the President!"

He was dead by the time I got home. Somebody shot him in the head while he was riding in a parade.

I remember my dad holding my mom while she cried. I didn't cry. There was nothing on TV for days except news and pictures of more people crying. People in foreign countries were crying. They showed home movies of when the President was still alive, riding on sailboats with his kids. They both had birthdays the week after their dad got shot.

That long weekend was sad and scary. The President got shot in the middle of the street in the middle of the day with police all around on motorcycles, and nobody could keep him safe. On Sunday we were playing football, but we came inside to see the man they blamed for shooting the President get shot, too. Somebody shot him in the stomach right in the police station while he had police standing on both sides of him. They couldn't keep him safe, either.

One of my Louisiana cousins told me it was my fault the President was dead because I was from Texas. Little John-John was holding his mom's hand and saluting his dead dad with the other hand. They showed that a lot. In the funeral parade there was a horse with a saddle but nobody riding it, which was a symbol that the President was dead. At his grave they lit an eternal flame that would never go out to remind people that his soul was still alive, and I wondered how they could make sure that the fire didn't ever go out.

Have you noticed I haven't said anything about praying for the President yet? I think it was the night after his funeral, when things were starting to get back to normal and there was school the next day, that I got back to saying my regular souls–in–purgatory prayers before going to sleep. Instead of thinking of all the people in the line like I usually did, I thought I'd just pray, pray, pray for the President. I wondered how he was doing and what it felt like to die so suddenly and not be with his family and not be president anymore. I started praying for him.

This next part had never happened to me before. I was awake saying my bedtime prayers for the President, but I could *see* him. I wasn't just thinking about him. I could see him, and I could feel some of what he was feeling. Maybe you don't believe me because sometimes kids just make stuff up to show off. I'm telling you the truth. I could see the President. He was all alone in a gray place. The ground was like the gray modeling clay we made things out of at school. It wasn't an indoor or an outdoor place. It didn't have furniture or trees, only gray space. It was a lonely place but not a punishment. He was sitting on the gray clay ground. He wanted everyone to go away and leave him alone. I could feel his feelings, and he wasn't angry about getting shot. He was very sad about disappointing people. He felt like he had let people down. I don't know why; he just did. He looked up at me, and we nodded at each other but we didn't say anything. I knew he didn't want company so I didn't keep looking at him. I just prayed blessings for him that he would feel better soon.

I wasn't scared about seeing the President. I didn't tell anybody about seeing him because I was afraid they'd make fun of me and say I made it all up. But I didn't. I really did see him and feel his heart. It changed me. After that, I didn't think of the poor souls being in line like at the bank anymore. I supposed they could all choose their own kind of place to wait until they could get into heaven like the President did. He was in crowds all the time and even died with lots of people watching and taking his picture. He just wanted to be alone and sad for a while. Getting to feel the President's heart that night made me pray, pray, pray for him, all right. I've never really stopped. We've become friends. He's in my posse, and I'm in his.

When I was about twelve, something started happening in the Catholic Church. Some people noticed how the stories in the Bible about Jesus and the Holy Spirit had lots of miracles being done by ordinary people. They started asking the Holy Spirit to talk to them plainly and to give them spiritual gifts, like speaking in tongues and healing. They weren't afraid if it made them look weird. In our local Catholic weekly paper there was a young priest who did these things and wrote a column about it. Mawmaw clipped these out and pasted them in a black–and–white–speckled notebook. When I'd visit, she'd get it out and read these stories to me. I didn't understand a lot of it, but I could tell that it was all very important to her. She didn't have anyone to talk to about it except me, her young grandson. I was it. So I listened. I remembered that notebook at different times in my life when the Spirit did new things with me, like when Ray and the others began showing up in my dreams.

The vines of the grape arbor above the multicolored patio began to produce. Mawmaw learned winemaking, pressing and bottling her very sweet red vintage. She was nearing seventy by then; I was big enough to lift the heavy bottles and vats in her backyard winery.

While we worked, Mawmaw taught me about praying to St. Joseph the Carpenter, who, as it turns out, was also the patron of a "happy death." You don't often see those two words side–by–side, do you? A happy death was one you were well prepared for. If you were in a state of grace and right with God, it didn't matter if your death was expected or sudden; you'd go straight to heaven. Nobody really knew how St. Joseph had died, but he'd gone before his wife and son. If he had a sickbed, he must have had Jesus and Mother Mary hovering over it, taking care of him, which was about the happiest death a pious person could ask for.

Mawmaw leaned close to me to whisper to me. "Robert, would you like to know the secret of the happy death I'm asking for? Pawpaw needs me, and he's much older, so I need to outlive him." But not by much, she told me, because then her main work would be done. Once he had died, she said, "I'll be ready to go, too, right behind him."

I didn't know then that part of my mission would be to help those souls who didn't have a happy death.

All my life I've prayed before sleep. When I joined a semi–monastic religious order, which prays together morning and evening, I learned that what I'd been doing all along is what Catholic contemplatives call "compline." As you can tell, the word is related to "complete." It's the last prayer of the day for monks, when the day is complete. But our lives are never completely complete, not even when we die. While we're asleep, at midnight, a new day will begin. In compline, we imagine handing our consciousness to God, maybe for safekeeping, or so that God can accomplish something in us that's more easily done in the night.

When I was little, I used to fall asleep listening to the radio while saying my purgatory prayers. So much of our country's midsection is flat without mountains to block radio waves. Sometimes in southeast Texas where I lived I could pick up baseball games from St. Louis and even Chicago. It would be crackly if there was lightning somewhere and the signal might fade in and out, but that sound would never have travelled that far during the day. I'm always teaching people to remember that because God is everywhere, God is also where you are, even within you. But because God is everywhere, God is in St. Louis and Chicago and every other distant place.

At some point, people in faraway after–death places heard me or I heard them. Or my light was on. How does it work? *I don't know.* In the end, it doesn't matter. We end up together with important work to do.

## Chapter Two

# Borrowing My Voice

Imagine walking into a crowded room where you don't know anyone. You begin scanning around, hoping that maybe there'll be someone you recognize.

I was having a late lunch on a class day in the cafeteria of my college residence hall complex. It was the second semester of my freshman year. Holding a tray of food, I noticed most people were finishing their meals. Then I saw Michelle. We weren't friends, really. We'd been together in a group on a road trip to a student government conference. Michelle did the polite thing; as I sat down, she introduced me to the guy she was with. That was her first mistake.

Across from her sat a fellow with a scruffy goatee and long, stringy hair hanging from beneath a beret. He looked like a beatnik. "Rob," Michelle said, "I'd like you to meet Matt." He looked up from his food with a gleam in his eye and nodded in my direction. Then he stared me down. "Rob and I have known each other all our lives. We grew up together," he lied, quite convincingly.

Now, I'd never laid eyes on this guy before, but he'd just lobbed the ball into my court. I returned his serve.

"Yeah, Matt and I went to kindergarten together," I replied, inventing our shared history on the fly. "Remember how, on the first day, Molly Pellerin threw up on your shoe?"

"Oh, yeah, I'd forgotten all about that," Matt laughed. "I wonder whatever happened to her."

Now the ball's in his court. After taking a bite of his sandwich, Matt continued. "Remember that time in Cub Scouts when we caught the tent on fire? I thought they'd kill us on the spot."

"Yeah, that was pretty funny," I admitted. "I still have a scar from that night."

So far Michelle suspected nothing. I watched her from the corner of my eye. The ball was in my court again. *Don't be too eager*, I thought. *Reel her in slowly.* (Pardon the mixed metaphor.)

Eventually, waving my fork, I continued. "Matt, what about that time when they took us on that trail ride and your foot got caught in the stirrup and that horse ran, dragging you all along the ground. Everyone was hollerin' and you hit your head. It was hysterical!"

*Your turn, Matt.*

We were reeling her in, all right. When you get your fish close to the boat, you have to be smooth—no sudden moves. Matt and I kept reminiscing about more and more outlandish things that had never occurred. He was good at this game. I could see that.

"Yeah, and I'll tell you what, when I woke up from that coma they told me I'd been singing country songs the whole time," he said. "And I don't even like country. Weird, huh?"

"Did that really happen?" Michelle asked, getting suspicious. "You coulda been killed!"

"Oh, it was nothing, really," Matt assured her.

Lunch was nearly over. *So how do we end this thing?* Matt leaned over Michelle's tray to say, "You think that was dangerous? Hey, Rob, remember the time that our parachutes didn't open. Talk about scary!"

Michelle bolted up and pounded on the table. "Oh, you two liars! You deserve each other," she cried, storming off.

And so there we sat, two idiots grinning at each other, my new friend Matt and me.

So who was this guy?

We discovered that, even though we'd both chosen a college about three hundred miles away, we'd actually grown up in towns about twenty minutes apart. We were both freshmen. And we were both studying sociology. While I had no specific career plans, Matt was going to be a Presbyterian minister.

One long weekend, we'd each planned to go home to visit our families. I drove this huge gleaming hunk of chrome and fins, a 1958 Oldsmobile Rocket 88. Matt and I lumbered down the interstate, swapping growing-up stories. For an accomplished liar, he proved to be an even better truth-teller. We asked each other all kinds of personal questions and listened to the joys and sorrows of the other one. I'd always been pretty reserved, except for one weekend retreat in high school. I'd been lonely for that kind of heart-to-heart truth-telling ever since. Matt was going to be a minister, so we talked a lot about what we'd each been taught about God. I told him that, back on campus, I was going each week to a little Catholic Mass just for college students, but they all wanted to keep their spiritual lives private. They'd come together for a while for the Mass ceremony, go to communion, and leave alone or with whomever they'd come with. It was lonely-making for me, I told Matt.

"Why don't you come to my prayer group?" Matt asked. It met on Tuesday nights in different dorm rooms. It was students only, no adults. They'd get together and sing and talk about what they wanted prayers for, and then they'd pray out loud for each other. Not just the formal prayers people memorized, but prayers they made up on the spot. It was very

Evangelical Protestant–sounding to my cradle–Catholic ears. It sounded both scary and attractive. But mostly scary.

Back at school, Matt and I began to hang out some together. The Tuesday night prayer group kept coming up. He'd invite; I'd decline. Eventually he challenged me: "You want to come, but you won't because you're afraid. Come with me, and we'll sit near the door. If you don't want to stay, we'll leave." For some reason, this hit home. I've never liked the way I feel when I make fear–based decisions, and that's what I was doing. So I relented and dragged my little Catholic behind to a Protestant prayer meeting.

It was pretty harmless. This tiny room was jammed with students. I learned their system. They'd number off and divide into groups of five or six and head off in different directions to whomever's room was available. Since I was a newcomer and Matt's guest, he made sure I could be with him.

Once settled into a small group, I learned more of their method. Seated on the floor in the center of a dorm room, each person would be given about three minutes to announce to the group what they'd like prayers for, no more than three things. Maybe they'd ask prayers for success on an upcoming exam or a grandparent's surgery. Maybe somebody's roommate was going through a hard time. Whatever it was, they'd explain it all, summarize it, and then be still. Someone in the group would say, "I'll take that." That meant they'd agreed to pray that person's prayers a little bit later. But before that, it was someone else's turn to disclose their three prayer requests. Someone else would say, "I'll take that." Eventually, everyone's prayer concerns were taken by someone else. They'd dim the lights, then start to pray aloud, one at a time. Everyone took a turn praying someone else's prayers, but not their own.

It wasn't as scary as I'd thought it would be. It was kind of sweet, listening in on other people's prayers. It reminded me of when my mom had taught me to pray at bedtime so long ago. I was comfortable almost instantly.

That fellowship became the spiritual center of my college life. I brought my questions about life and meaning and purpose and how God fit into it all back to that group every Tuesday night. Matt's friends became my friends.

Matt and I were sometimes prayer partners on our own time. We each had our own set of friends and activities, but we'd get together now and then. When we did, we could "go deep" with each other if we wanted to. I remember thinking of my heart–of–hearts as darkest Africa, some thick tropical jungle. Somehow this adventurous person had carefully hacked a trail through the thicket to the center of my soul. He'd created a pathway, not just for his own use, but for mine. I didn't have to be so private and cautious and frightened all the time. Having Matt as a friend opened me to loving and being loved. I used to say to Jesus, "Would you follow the trail Matt has made in me? I'd like us to be friends."

My name sometimes has academic letters behind it to show how well educated I am. Sometimes it has a job title, like Director, or Pastor, or now Author. Often it has the letters OP for Order of Preachers, my religious family.

My sister belongs to a church named "Saints Martha, Mary and Lazarus, Friends of Jesus." When I first heard that I thought, "That's what I want behind my name, not any of those other titles. Just call me Nathan, Friend of Jesus."

Near the end of his life, Jesus called his followers together. In John's Gospel his words have the form of a tender monologue. In one place he says, "You're used to calling me teacher (rabbi) and Lord, but I like it most when you call me friend." I believe that the creator and sustainer of the universe is my friend. It was my first heart–friend, Matt, who opened me to being a friend to others who entered my heart later in my life.

Being a Christian is one specific way of loving and serving God. "Christian" and "Christ" derive from the word "chrism." The ancient Hebrews used expensive scented chrism in crowning royalty. When a person was elevated to a royal status, he or she was not crowned but anointed with precious oil poured lavishly upon the head. The Hebrews also had a cleansing ceremony, baptism. Jesus received baptism in the Jordan River from John the Baptist. He heard a heavenly voice say, "You are my child, my beloved. I'm crazy about you." Or words to that effect. I believe my creator and Jesus, his Son, are crazy about me. They're crazy about you, too. When we baptize a person, right after pouring the water, he or she is then anointed on the head with sacred chrism. This is a sign of extravagant love.

Near the end of his life, Jesus was at a dinner party. A low–status woman embarrassed everyone by breaking open a jar of expensive chrism and pouring it over Jesus. Now he became Jesus the Christ, the anointed one. So he was baptized with water by a famous prophet and anointed with chrism by a simple soul who loved him dearly. He knew he would soon be killed; he said, "She has anointed me for my burial." He knew a violent death awaited him: he was threatened that he would be killed if he didn't stop associating with those the religious leaders thought were riff–raff. Instead, he loved the riff–raff and became one of them. He's always doing that, even now. I wanted to follow Jesus, but I wasn't sure how just then.

Those college years went by quickly. As we moved into our final semester before graduating, talk began to turn to what we might do next. For years, Matt had seemed so sure about his plans to attend seminary. As decision–time neared, he wasn't nearly so sure. He'd been dating our friend, Betsy, for a couple of years. Everyone assumed they'd marry one day. She kept asking me when he was going to propose. She had her own plans to make, and all this uncertainty wasn't helping.

Afterlife, *Interrupted*

It was at this time that I began to have a persistent dream about going into the ministry, too. I even had the results of a computerized vocational test that said I should be a priest. I stuck it in a drawer next to the paperclips and the stapler. I went on what I thought was a casual interview for a job recommended by one of my professors. The person in charge soon began introducing me to my new coworkers and telling me about the dress code, the vacation policy, and my start date. The job would pay so poorly, I remember thinking as I leaned against my car in the parking lot, that I might as well be a priest.

Many people in our prayer group were thinking of ministerial careers. Some of the mainline Protestant denominations were beginning to open ordination to women. Mine was the only church that didn't have married clergy. I was afraid that if I said yes to studying for Catholic priesthood, I'd end up all alone. So my prayers sounded something like this: "Oh, God, I love you. Take me, I'm yours. Just don't make me be a priest. Amen." Even I got sick of hearing that.

By now, some of my prayer-group friends who'd been raised in southern churches with an anti-Catholic streak were praying for my discernment of my call.

That job interview happened on a Friday afternoon. They wanted my answer by Monday. That weekend the Spirit put on a full-court press. There's this Bible passage. In it, Jesus says, "Come to me, all you that are weary and are carrying heavy burdens, and I will give you rest. Take my yoke upon you, and learn from me; for I am gentle and humble in heart, and you will find rest for your souls. For my yoke is easy, and my burden is light" (Mt 11: 28–30). I was feeling heavily burdened all right, having to make a decision, and quickly, about the rest of my life.

Over that weekend I heard that Scripture verse on my car radio and saw it on a highway billboard. I was singing in the university-sponsored Protestant service on Sunday when that verse was the theme of the preaching and the music. That was all I needed to hear. I called my parents that afternoon and announced my plans to study for the ministry. They were supportive emotionally and financially, even when I said I wasn't sure whether it would be in the Catholic Church. I was sure about Jesus and the "Follow me" part. "Follow me where?" was the next question.

The ink wasn't dry on our diplomas when Matt and I packed his Volkswagen Rabbit full of camping gear and headed west into the desert. We talked, sang, and prayed our way across West Texas and New Mexico. We were as open-hearted as two young people could be. What were we supposed to do with our lives? We didn't know, but we trusted that we'd find out. In Bible stories, God spoke to lots of people when they went into the desert to listen to His voice. Why not us?

We drove what became a rolling sweat lodge. Matt thought using the air-conditioner would be too wimpy for our vision quest. And, besides, it was bad for the planet; it made the car burn more gas. As we drove north from Phoenix we climbed to cooler elevations, but it was still hot. Past Flagstaff all the signs pointed to the Grand Canyon, our destination.

Have you ever been to the Grand Canyon? We arrived there in the late afternoon—on Friday of the Memorial Day weekend. Who knew you had to make a reservation to see a hole in the ground that can be seen from the surface of the moon? It's enormous. How could it possibly be full?

Well, somehow it was. We were allowed to pay a fee to look at the Grand Canyon for a little while but were forbidden to stay there. And don't even think about sleeping in your car, which was what we were already thinking of doing. Undaunted, Matt and I gaped at the magnificence of this natural wonder of the world. You can't see it at all when you approach it by car. You just arrive, and suddenly—ohmyGod, there it is! Like everyone else we stood, stared, and took tiny photos of this enormous, luminous sight. For some, it probably inspired a prayer. It certainly did for us.

It was more than an hour before sunset when Matt and I sat on the ground beneath some pine trees. It was time to say our prayers. We'd been prayer partners for three years by this time. We knew each other's habits. We'd pray aloud at first, closing our eyes and being grateful for daily–bread things like health, family and friends, and safe travel. Then we'd grow quiet for a while. Somewhere in the Bible, in one of the Psalms, it says, "Be still and know that I am God." That's what we did at God's Grand Canyon.

I noticed I was getting stiller–than–usual. I'd never been this still inside. There was a deep place inside me—a soul canyon. I gracefully floated down deep. I was being filled. Or emptied.

Then something stirred.

I felt an energy welling up from the deep. It was warm and loving; it made me joyful and frightened. It wanted me to let It in. Someone was at the door of my soul wanting to come in. Whatever this was, it was new to me. But we had come all this way to invite an encounter. We wanted God to talk to us. Then this idea began to form inside me—but it wasn't my idea, and the voice inside my head didn't feel quite like my voice:

*Would you let me speak to your friend?*

It was becoming clear: God wanted to borrow my voice to speak to Matt. If I allowed it, I–statements would move through me to my friend. As I came to understand the request, the knocking–at–my–door feeling intensified. I knew that if I said "yes," the voice of the Creator of the Universe would speak to my friend.

Unless it was the devil. Or some crazy egocentric part of my subconscious. If I said "yes" would I be blaspheming? Or inviting in some dark spirit? Wouldn't I at least look bizarre?

In the moment there was no time to waste. There was a growing urgency. Quietly, I told God my dilemma. I said that I was inclined to say "yes," but that, in case this was a bad idea, I would give Him to the count of ten to give me a sign to go no further. I was hoping to get that stop sign as I began my countdown. *Three. Two. One.* As I reached zero, the force amplified to an even more intense level. In my mind, I said, "Okay, God, if it's You, go ahead!"

There was no speech yet, just an even higher frequency of eagerness and anticipation. I was being asked to do one last thing, but what was it? Then this question floated across the screen of my imagination: What's the first thing God would want to say to my friend? Given the chance, what is the main message our Creator would like each of us to hear?

Yes, that's what I thought, too.

So I opened my eyes and for the first time in our three-year friendship said, "Matt, I love you." And as soon as I did a flood of Spirit-words started flowing through me, past my vocal cords and lips. I was full of joy and energy. While I tried to push my consciousness to one side to give God more room, Matt's Creator reminisced with him about what fun it had been to create him. I had been an art student, and I recognized the joy and pride of the Divine Artist admiring His work. God creates co-creators. God told Matt how happy He was with what Matt was creating with his life.

Once or twice, as the flow of words poured through me, I thought of the channel of a waterway. St. Francis prayed, "Make me a channel of your peace." When a word or phrase sounded too much like me, I tried to think of myself as a pipe or a wire that the water or power would flow through. (Later, God let me know that if He'd wanted me to be a pipe or a wire, He would have *made* me a pipe or a wire.)

Matt's message from God was long and detailed and intimate. Then, at one point, God called him "Milton." *That's strange*, I thought. But I was too busy facilitating this speech to stop to question anything. Soon the experience felt like it was cresting and would end soon, as heart-to-heart talks always do.

I didn't realize I'd sort of slumped over and that Matt had propped my head against his knee to keep it out of the dirt. I sat up. Was I going to have to explain all this to Matt? I thought, "God, would You move into him like You moved into me?" I felt sure that if I touched him, like the sick woman in the gospel story who just wanted to touch the fringe of Jesus's cloak, Matt would be full of this love. The image of some tent-revival faith healer came to mind, but I didn't want to do anything that flashy.

I touched the knee of Matt's jeans.

Matt instantly slumped over. We switched roles. I held his head out of the dust while something went on inside him. He didn't speak. Later I learned that this is called "resting in the Spirit." The experience is beyond words. It might have lasted ten minutes.

The sky was turning to dusk. We needed to stop soon, or we'd be walking on the edge of the Grand Canyon in the dark. Matt sat up, wide-eyed and smiling. We stood to shake off the stiffness of sitting on the ground for an hour.

"We've got to get back to the car," I said. "But before we do, tell me, what was the 'Milton' part? Why did God call you Milton, Matt?"

"Oh, that was fifth grade. We were on the playground at school, and guys started teasing me that I had a stupid name, Milton. They called me 'Milton Bradley.' I went home after school and thought of cool–sounding new names. At dinner I made an announcement to my family, 'From now on, my name is Matt.'"

I felt a rush of joy. I never knew that! He'd been "Matt" to me as long as I'd known him. But he was baptized "Milton." And that's what God called his son. I couldn't have known that. That knowledge wasn't in me, but it moved through me. I was glad I had said "yes" to letting God borrow my voice.

Years later, at my first profession of religious vows, I became Nathan. Matt and I both ended up with the names of apostles, which means, "ones sent on a mission." Neither of us heard a voice in the desert that told us what to do, but I did return from that trip knowing I belonged completely to God and that God could borrow my voice anytime He wanted to.

I did enter a Catholic seminary later that fall. They let me in provisionally. I hadn't signed up with a diocese or a religious order, which was the normal way of doing this. My parents paid for one more year of tuition while I got a minor in philosophy. If I stayed in the Catholic seminary system, that would be a prerequisite to studying theology.

Within a few months I was checking out Catholic orders. There were so many! I didn't want to live my whole life in a single monastery. And I didn't want to be a foreign missionary. I learned that the Jesuits make everybody get a PhD. Count me out. The Franciscans were a little too poetic for my temperament—too much Brother Sun and Sister Moon for me. I ruled out any group with Pain and Suffering and Blood in their name. It seemed to me that life was painful enough without focusing on it all the time. And I made one more rule: "If I've never heard of you, I'm not joining you."

One day, on a coffee table, I saw a magazine about the charismatic renewal, those people Mawmaw had told me about that prayed in tongues and asked for gifts of healing. There was a Dominican priest on the cover in his medieval robes. He had a rosary on his belt. He looked as cutting edge as he could be, but dressed in centuries of spiritual tradition. I knew Dominicans were well educated. That was important to me. I also learned that their founder, St. Dominic, was nicknamed "The Joyful Friar." Once I asked a priest how I would know where I should go. "Follow your joy," he said. So, that's what I did. I decided to become a joyful friar.

In the interview with the Dominican recruiter, he told me they were the Order of Preachers. Did I want to preach? he asked. I lied and said yes. I had done some public speaking and had some success at it, but it also terrified me. But I figured if Dominicans were good teachers, they'd teach me what I needed to know.

That first experience of helping Ray made me realize how much there was to learn. My prayer partner and I had each given our lives over to God's service. The early chapters of the Gospels—Matthew, Mark, Luke, and John—all tell the stories of people's first encounters with Jesus. They were called away from their ordinary work and lives and invited to "Follow me." And they did, dropping their nets and going on a wild, life–changing ride.

My prayer partner and I had done that earlier in our lives and had taken up work that we each felt was our calling. We were both extraordinarily busy with many commitments. At the time of Ray's visit, I was director of one of the largest Catholic campus ministries in the country and very involved with similar work at the national level. Our ministry was in the midst of a major capital campaign that ultimately led to the demolition of old facilities and the construction of new ones. And I had a network of family and friends and a home life with my Dominican brothers.

But we couldn't just tell poor Ray to take a number and wait his turn. We kept him in prayer and rearranged our schedules to work with him. The progress of his wife's cancer gave this some urgency. We both felt like apprentices or interns in this work. Around universities you see plenty of examples of graduate students and young teaching assistants getting their first taste of responsibilities they're growing into. We trusted that the Holy Spirit would give us the help we'd need at the time we'd need it. This is indeed what has happened, no matter which prayer partner I'm working with.

Meeting these stuck souls has been a part of my life for eighteen years now. Every week or so I'll have what I call a "contact dream." I use different verbs to describe different kinds of dreams. I *have a dream* about my own concerns. Those dreams involve characters in my world. Because I'm a priest, I sometimes *have* dreams of church services. Because I love baseball I *have* baseball dreams.

I *receive* dreams in which I see or hear a story as a viewer or listener. When someone moves into my unconscious, like Ray, and shows me his traumatic death, I *receive* that dream. I've done decades of pastoral counseling; that involves receiving the story of a troubled person. I call the folks who show me their stories my "night visitors." My night visitors are troubled persons sharing their stories with me.

I've learned to be prepared for my night visitors. No more startled stumbling about in the dark looking for paper and a pen. I began keeping paper in the nightstand. Eventually I got a notebook to help me stay better organized in recording the dreams. Sometimes I can tell I'm receiving the story of a night visitor while I'm not yet fully awake. I try to focus on the details. Once awake, I'll sit up and reach for my dream journal and scribble down the details as quickly as I can. Many of these seem to occur between 2:00 and 4:00 a.m. I don't know why; I've heard it said that 3:00 a.m. is the "hour of the spirit." Sometimes I'll have two visitors in the same night. When I'm extraordinarily busy in my daytime ministry, the Spirit seems to give me a break and wait until I'm less busy to send the next visitor.

These dreams differ from my own but are displayed on the screen of my unconscious, or subconscious, just like my other dreams are. As I'll explain in greater detail in the next chapter, I pray for guidance from Spirit on the best way to help these stuck souls cross over, as if my prayer partner and I are some kind of cosmic crossing guards.

People often ask, "Did you ever know these people?" No, I didn't. But that's not uncommon in the life of a priest, especially one who has lived a lot of places, like I have. Many of the weddings and funerals I've done began with a phone call from someone I didn't know. A lot of pastoral counseling is like that, too.

My night visitors aren't particularly religious. They're particularly just about everything. They have very particular stories, including the story of why they chose to interrupt the flow of their own death journey. You'll find a wide variety of humanity in just the few persons whose stories I'll share here.

As I mentioned, the little subset of the universe I serve in this way shares one very unhappy experience in common: they all died sudden, violent, traumatic deaths. They chose almost immediately not to go quietly with guides or loved ones who offered to help them. They didn't follow the path we often hear about in recorded Near–Death Experiences (NDEs). They didn't enjoy new companions, move through a cosmic tunnel or merge with a loving, attractive light. And, just for the record, they didn't go to some torturous hell, as many people might believe. They just opted out of the process, at least at the moment of death. They interrupted it.

You know how our homes and offices are designed to be protected from trauma by shutting down in a lightning storm? Our electrical systems have a breaker box. The switches automatically trip to prevent a power surge that would fry all the appliances and set the house afire. I think the Interrupted Death Experience of my visitors is like that. These people have suffered a huge shock and have gone from alive to dead almost instantly. They seem to switch off until the violent storm passes.

Most people who die sudden, traumatic deaths don't need the services of someone like me. They just transition from one mode of existence to the next as we all did when we left the womb and were born. But some opt out. As Ray had his reasons, so do all the folks in the stories that follow here. Some essentially said, "Everybody out!" or "Leave me alone!" We hope the dead rest in peace, don't we? Some seem to need more rest than others, and maybe some solitude for a time.

What percentage of those who die suddenly and traumatically choose to pause their passages and isolate for a while? I think it's very low. I'd say fewer than five percent. If you've suffered the loss of a loved one to sudden, traumatic death, please don't assume, because of anything I've written here, that the one you love has isolated; they probably haven't. I do believe that the stories I'll share here may give us plenty to think about in anticipation of our own deaths.

So I've vicariously been through lots of shootings and stabbings, falls and crashes, drownings and strangulations. You'd think I'd wake up screaming, wouldn't you? But I don't. Once in a while I wake up with my heart pounding, but I believe the Holy Spirit buffers these stories to protect me from their trauma.

Any storyteller has to choose a point of view when telling a story. I'm doing that now as I write. When my night visitors share their car crash stories, sometimes I'm seeing the scene from above, like the blimp hovering over a football game. Other times I'm on the sidewalk or in the backseat of the car. The worst times are when I'm the driver watching the oncoming vehicle crossing the center line and hitting me head on. Even then, remember, it's buffered. I'm safe. All these traumatized people are different and tell their stories in their own ways. What they have in common is that they're asking for help.

Is it true? Do we really live after we die? For most of human history this was thought to be an exclusively religious or possibly philosophical question. In recent times many people who do not hold any religious or philosophical views have come to believe in life after death through a Near–Death Experience or contact with a deceased loved one. A personal, tangible experience with the afterlife changes traditional thinking.

Cultural anthropology and archeology can tell us what people in other times and places really thought of death and the afterlife through the records and monuments they left behind. Now hospice workers may be the cultural anthropologists of our day. They are around death on a daily basis and have inspirational stories to tell about how people are facing and passing through death. We're also seeing the study of death and the afterlife move more into the mainstream of current thought. Studies of parapsychological phenomenon have become more respectable, and Consciousness Studies is now a popular field, even at major universities. These subjects, once marginalized, now bring science into conversation with the spiritual and philosophical.

I come at this topic as a well–educated man trained in critical thinking. Decades ago I joined a Catholic religious order with a now eight–hundred–year–old intellectual tradition because I wanted to be able to listen, learn, experience, and think, and only then to speak.

Any college student can tell you that to earn a degree you're going to have to take some required courses you don't want to take. For me, the path to Catholic priesthood was sometimes a forced slog through a philosophical bog. So I studied epistemology. Do you even know what that word means? I didn't. Epistemology is the study of the theory of knowing. The course was ten weeks long; for ten weeks we studied how we can know a thing.

I don't remember most of it, but I did learn that: our intellect can know a thing in one of two ways: 1) through the experiences of one or more of our five senses, or 2) through receiving the testimony of another's experience of one or more of their five senses. We can say, "I know it because I saw it with my own eyes! I heard, touched, tasted and smelled it." Or we can receive the testimony of a trusted other when they say the same. That's how our justice system works. In a courtroom the judge and jury, who were not present at the scene of the crime and did not see, hear, touch, taste, or smell the evidence, listen to the testimony of others who did. They then come to a reasonable conclusion about what occurred. Just think of all the things you wouldn't know if you never believed the testimony of anyone else.

But can't the material senses only perceive material things? Can our senses operate when we are unconscious, as when in a coma or while asleep? The testimony of those who have had NDEs affirm that they continued to have sensory experiences, even very elaborate ones, while unconscious.

And is there anything that is not material to know? Materialism as an understanding of the world says this: "If it isn't matter, it doesn't matter. There is no such thing as a non–material world. Period." But this isn't a scientific statement; it's a statement of belief, an unproven one.

Can I prove to you that dead, immaterial people find their way into my unconscious as I'm dreaming, and show me their tragic, sudden deaths? With assistance of others seen and unseen, do these persons really speak with me and through me in ways that help them move through their current "stuckness" and complete their transition into the afterlife that awaits them? Can I prove to you that this is true beyond a shadow of a doubt?

I can testify. I can try to testify clearly, lucidly, and in detail. And, in these pages, I will. Can I prove to you that what I have said is true? That, ladies and gentlemen of the jury, is up to you.

Are the events I'll describe in these case studies verifiable? Can they be proven through archived news accounts or death records? I don't know. In some cases, I've been asked to conceal names and dates that would make that impossible out of respect for loved ones still here. The kind of sleuthing it would take to do that kind of proving is not my calling. I've always got a next stuck soul to help, and so my focus is forward, not backward.

Are these folks in purgatory? That word means cleansing–place. In my religious tradition, purgatory is something like a period of recovery from our unfinished business during our time on earth. And my visitors all have unfinished business. I have helped some folks who stayed near the scene of their traumatic deaths, dirtied, bloodied, or disfigured. Sometimes getting washed up or dressing in clean clothes is part of their process. Everyone's different. The small part my helpers and I play is really just to get folks unstuck and on their way. We rarely deal in sin and grace, crime and punishment, salvation or damnation any more than a paramedic would. Our work is just to get someone out of the ditch and in the company of someone they love and trust who can help them move on to whatever is next. We leave the rest to God.

One last word about this: a Christian might ask, "Why don't you ask Jesus to come and save them?" I believe that God is love. For my frightened, traumatized visitors, it just seems to work best to invite Love. I ask them to think of someone who has loved them really well, who died before they did. I believe the person who has loved you best is the best embodiment of God's love for you.

## Chapter Three

# Rani, Swept Out to Sea by the Big Tsunami

After helping Ray move along, I began experiencing these trauma–themed dreams about three or four times a month. Sometimes they were preceded by some of my own dream–content; other times they were self-contained. They felt like short videos. I learned that sometimes the narrator would pull someone from the Contacts List in my psyche and insert her into the dreamscape as a way of communicating a name. For example, I might receive a dream about driving off a cliff, something very far removed from any experience I've ever had and nothing I'd ever dreamed of before. It all feels very foreign and "other" except that Melanie Carnright, a former classmate, is behind the wheel. I haven't seen her in years. She hasn't driven off a cliff and has no business being in this dream. I discovered that her appearance was a way that the night visitor could tell me that her name was Melanie.

From my work with my night visitors, I've learned that, even when we think we want to be utterly alone, God and the universe doesn't seem to allow that, at least not for long, because it's not good for us. The isolated folks my prayer partners and I help are given their space but are surrounded by nonintrusive love. They might be in the equivalent of an intensive care unit or a private room, but they are observed and gracefully assisted as they heal. Sometimes they need to form a new thought or release some old, unhelpful certitude. Often they get trapped in some negative thought loop of blaming themselves or others for their sudden death. Other times they just need an afterlife nap to recharge their batteries. Eventually they arrive at a moment of near–awakening. Someone overseeing their care has determined they are ready to try to move on. That's when they show up in my dreams.

How do I know they're vetted? Because, for all they've been through, by the time they find their way to me all they need is a little nudge. They don't put up a fight; they don't resist what we suggest, at least not very much. Most don't need more than thirty to forty minutes of time with my prayer partners and me. They're ready to move; they just need a little help.

I've also learned that, though I am part of a larger unseen team, I have a specific role to play. I've stopped asking my visitors, "How did you find me?" We're together. That's all that matters.

For these folks, meeting my prayer partner and me is an important first step. They've been isolated, by their own choosing, since their sudden death. The "somebody" who brought them into my sphere is their guardian angel. I was taught to know and love the angels at a young age. They come with us when we begin in the womb and accompany us through our earthly life. I think of them as secret service persons who love and serve us. We arrive here mortal; we'll certainly die of something one day. Their service might involve saving us from mortal danger, but, ultimately, they will accompany us through death into the next phase of our eternally unfolding life.

When I've asked about the surroundings my visitors inhabit, I've learned that they've put no effort into decorating. Most appear in my dreams to be in some grayish, nondescript place of isolation. But on the edge of it stands their guardian. The guardians keep respectfully quiet, but they will not abandon their God-appointed posts.

The guardians accompany even those who want to be left alone. They are not material beings, though they can assume material form for a time if the need arises. Gender is not native to them, though they realize it is to us. They can assume a more masculine or feminine way of presenting themselves if that is helpful. Our bodies are energy fields; so are those of the angels. They're just different kinds of energy. They know each other without using language, though they will use human language when necessary. Above all, they are love. Like us, they came from love. I've gotten used to seeing them put the frightened one in their care at ease by "going first" when borrowing my voice. I call it a "mic-test." Instead of saying, "Is this thing on?" or "Can you hear me in the back of the room?", the guardians will borrow the voice just to show the one in their care how easy the process is. They don't have data to transmit; they just say hello and thank us for our willingness to help the one they love. Then they yield the floor to the stuck soul who has a story to tell.

In this chapter I want to tell you the story of my new afterlife friend, Rani. But before I do, I want to describe for you the kind of protected prayer my partners and I use.

My faith tradition teaches that God the Creator created only good things and good persons. Evil in the world is some misapplication of a good. All human persons and all angelic persons are good by their very nature because they share in God's nature. But some persons, both human and angelic, are currently making choices that are harmful to others. I don't believe everyone in the spirit world has my best interests at heart, any more than I think every human person on earth does. I don't pick up hitchhikers on earth because it isn't safe. I don't pick up spirit–world hitchhikers, either. Angelic persons who are behaving badly are usually called either devils or demons. They are not just cartoon figures or cinematic devices in horror movies. They are real. I've had enough dealings with them to know that beyond a doubt. They are powerful and can cause a great deal of trouble. So when moving into spirit communication my tradition teaches us to be very specific about how to begin.

Before we begin a session, my prayer partner and I call out to and place ourselves under the loving, protective authority of God. I do that in the names of the Trinitarian God of Christianity. I cross myself and pray, "In the name of the Father, the Son (Jesus), and the Holy Spirit." This creates a safe sacred space. I then call on my friend St. Michael the Archangel to stand guard over us; he is the patron of police. I ask for the help of my own guardian angel, whom I know as Phillip James of the line of Michael. I call him P.J. or Peej. I invite Holy Mary and St. Dominic and St. Benedict and a host of others. When we do this work, wherever we are, we make sure we're surrounded by lots of loving, powerful friends in high places.

Where my prayer partners and I meet varies. It needs to be some place quiet where we won't be interrupted. It can be indoors or out. Sometimes we'll use a Blessed Sacrament chapel where we're in the sacramental presence of God. I never do this work when pressed for time or overtired. Our night visitors deserve the best of our time and attention. Sometimes there can be a gap of days or weeks between when the visitor shows me their dream–story and when I can schedule time with a prayer partner. Most of the visitors are outside of time and no longer experience it as we do, so it's not like they've been kept on indefinite hold. We just do the best we can to accommodate them promptly. Once my partner and I are together, we may help several night visitors in succession.

My prayer partners come in different shapes and sizes. They must be people of prayer and discernment who are confident of God's love for them. They must be good, compassionate listeners. They must love people and respect their privacy. They must be good at putting others at ease and unafraid of doing this work. They must be peaceable and courageous lovers of God.

After securing the space with the protective prayer I described, I'll read the person's story to my prayer partner from my dream journal to get the basic information across. Then I'll read the dream story a second time to allow it to sink into both of us more deeply. Those familiar with the prayer form *Lectio Divina*, sacred reading, will recognize the process. The left brain or the mind gets its data on the first read through; the right brain or the heart listens deeper on the second.

Some of my prayer partners have the prophetic gift of offering their voice for one of our visitors to use. When that's the case, and we invite the visitor to speak, we have to wait to see which of us he or she will choose to speak through.

Our voices are somewhat fixed; the sound produced by pushing air through a specific set of vocal cords won't vary a great deal no matter who's doing the talking. With that said, the pacing of speech can be slow and drawly or machine–gun–fire staccato. It can be full of emotion. I'm not much of a crier, but sometimes the person borrowing the voice needs to cry. I just have to give them permission. Think of an instrument, say, a saxophone. It will never sound like a harp, but different people using that instrument can produce very different sounds with it.

I've learned that only vocabulary in my stored memory is available for the voice–borrower. Sometimes they'll use a word or phrase that's part of my habit of speech that's completely new to them. Incidentally, while I'm talking about instruments, I once asked an angel–friend about the emotionally loaded words "channeling" and "mediumship." Both of those can have negative, even very negative connotations among church folk. I asked her if she could recommend a better way to describe this phenomenon, one that might help me avoid unwanted church–trouble. She said, "Try saying 'instrumental communication.' You have allowed yourself, in prayer, to be God's instrument so someone God loves can be heard and understood."

That's enough of that for now. Later, I'll fill you in on more of what this process looks and feels like. For now, I'd like to share with you the story of a beautiful, young South Asian woman.

Normally, I will begin a new person's story by recounting the notes I took immediately upon receiving what they showed me in a dream. I haven't been able to find my notes on this one so am recreating this scene from memory. I wasn't watching the events; I was experiencing them.

*I was a young girl enjoying a morning at the beach near a resort hotel. I knew I was in Sri Lanka, the island nation south of India. All at once, an enormous wave swelled up and swamped everyone and everything in sight. I was carried out into the sea, bobbing among trees and debris of every kind. The air was filled with roaring sounds and the screams of those being swept away.*

I awoke and wrote the dream down right away. It felt like the event in my dream was the massive tsunami caused by the big Indonesian 9.0 earthquake on December 26, 2004. This process is intuitive; a feeling of context can be more than a point of data. Anyway, I felt like this small story was part of the very big tsunami story. More than 250,000 people died in that Indian Ocean tragedy. I remembered that prayers for the victims and aid for the survivors came from all over the world. At the time it happened, I read everything I could find about it, especially first–person accounts of those who narrowly escaped death. It touched me personally because I've lived and vacationed along California's Pacific coast and have seen signs indicating tsunami evacuation routes away from the beaches toward higher ground. My sister Cathryn had traveled to resorts in Thailand because of her work in the scuba diving industry. She was familiar with some of the destroyed resorts.

I don't recall how long after that tragic event the dream occurred. This request for help was different from many of my other cases. For reasons unknown to me, most of my night visitors who needed afterlife assistance up until this time were from the American southeast. I haven't spent much time in Georgia, Florida, or the Carolinas, but when this work first found me, it seemed like my clientele were all southerners. Most of the rest had been Americans. It made me wonder if the Spirit had assigned me a territory for this unusual work.

I secured the space with my prayers of protection and then, as usual, read the girl's story to my prayer partner twice so that it could sink into both of us more deeply. We asked for the young girl in the dream to come forward, and she did so right away. This time, the young girl chose to speak through my partner. That made things a little simpler for me. I could just listen and offer a suggestion or two that might help the person move along.

The young girl was Indian, she told us. She had been with her parents on holiday. They were staying on an upper floor of a resort hotel in Sri Lanka. She was an only child, twelve years old. Her parents forbade her going to the beach by herself, but on this beautiful, sunny morning, her parents were sleeping in. She couldn't wait any longer; the beach beckoned. Breaking the rules and disobeying her parents, she went, unaccompanied, to the beach outside her hotel.

That's when all hell broke loose. Without warning, the massive wave swept over her and everything else, pulling her out to sea. For a brief time, she bobbed about in the turbulent water, which had become a sea of debris. She soon drowned.

When she came to us, the poor girl seemed overwhelmed. She had just suffered death by disobedience. Had she honored her parents' wishes, she would have been safe with them in their hotel suite. Instead, they would never see their only child again. She died disgracing herself and her parents. Whatever good might have awaited her in the afterlife, she felt herself undeserving. She did not go into the light or down the path with those who came for her. She stayed behind, ashamed of dying a disrespectful daughter.

The girl was very intelligent and well spoken, with an Indian–English accent. She didn't feel like a twelve–year–old. But she had labeled herself as Disobedient, with a capital "D." She wore the shame like a scarlet letter. That was the sticking point. After establishing a little trust, I asked her to tell me about her most appalling rebellious acts during her lifetime, intentionally exaggerating her own main accusation about herself to help her see that she was not, in fact, a grossly disobedient disgrace.

Nathan: If I'd known you growing up, would I have despised you for being so ungrateful to your parents?

Girl: *No, no, the times I disobeyed my parents were relatively few and mild. It's just that I really wanted to go down to the beach and my parents were still sleeping. So I snuck downstairs without their permission.*

If there would be consequences, she decided, she would deal with them later. Of course, there was no later.

Girl: *I was so unlucky to break my parents' rules at the worst possible moment.*

Nathan: Do you want to continue to punish yourself for this indefinitely? Don't you want to move on to explore whatever else the afterlife might have in store for you?

This young woman felt older than her years, her imagination inclined toward the future. It really wasn't natural to her to accept constraints, even self–imposed ones. She had to make peace with the idea that she died an accidental, tragic death that day, along with so many other people. Had she really disgraced her family and her lineage in some irredeemable way? We discovered that they let her know otherwise. I'll try to describe her experience as she related it to us much later.

Girl: *When I did as you advised and asked for someone from my family to come for me, I didn't get just one. I got all of them. I could see my ancestors in a group, wearing Indian clothing. I didn't know them all, but they knew me. Have you ever been bowling? Can you imagine the way the bowling pins are arranged with only one in the front, then two, then three, forming a wedge–shape? My ancestors were grouped like that, stretching backward through the ages toward infinity. No one said anything. They didn't need to. They made me know they were one. And I was one of them. We were all one. We all belong to the One. I took my place among them.*

She moved along and, as has been the case for almost twenty years, within a few days the Spirit brought me other stuck souls to help.

Now, fast–forward to the present, when I was in the process of putting together this book about these experiences. While choosing which stories to tell, I wanted to convey the breadth and variety of the circumstances that culminate in someone being stuck and experiencing an interrupted death. I'm convinced that most persons who die sudden, traumatic deaths pass smoothly into the next life. I'm sure the vast majority of those tsunami victims did.

Afterlife, *Interrupted*

How do I know? Because I've helped other stuck souls who died in the same multi–fatality event. While thousands died in the terrible waves and moved on into the afterlife, this dear young girl interrupted the process. I wanted to understand why.

Our absorption in worldwide media gives us ever–new stories of tragedy. Some unify us in a compassionate response, as did the big tsunami of 2004. I wanted to include at least one such story here but had the same ethical dilemma that I'd had with Ray. Was it appropriate for me to share these very personal stories, which have some similarity to a confidential counseling session, with the reading public? I mulled this question for a long time. As with Ray, I asked a few trusted friends for their opinions and got a variety of responses. One friend simply asked, "Why don't you ask *them*?"

Well, I wasn't sure if they'd respond, for starters. And because I try to let those who have died "rest in peace," I didn't want to disturb anyone. Yet, I did feel like this was an important enough reason to inquire.

Just as I'd done with Ray, I went into prayer with the Holy Spirit and said something like this:

*Holy Spirit, you've given me this uncommon gift for speaking with some of those who have died, and I've tried to be helpful and to use it prudently. I believe I'm in the flow of your love and am following your lead to write about these stories. Would it be okay with you if I ask each person whose story I'm planning to tell if I may have their permission to speak about them?*

The Spirit was quiet, as the Spirit frequently is, but I knew my motives were pure. I was essentially saying, "*Spirit, if you don't want this to happen, keep us all muted. Otherwise, please help us out.*"

I got together with a prayer partner and arranged a time and place to make the effort. Our plan was to go down our list in the order we'd chosen to tell the stories. We went into our protected prayer and asked for the Sri Lankan girl.

Sometimes, when my prayer partners and I try to contact a particular night visitor, we might wait for a matter of minutes with great intuitive openness to see if the one we're attempting to help becomes present. There can then be something analogous to getting a good phone connection or radio signal. Sometimes a conversation can begin lightly, but one or both must make the effort to dial into each other more deeply in order for more personal information to be conveyed.

The Sri Lankan girl needed no prompting. She agreed to allow me to record our conversation. What follows is a transcript. She is speaking through me to my prayer partner. As always, I'm fully conscious, helping as best I can.

Would you like to listen in? Remember, we had helped her move along years earlier. We're only asking to speak with her now to ask permission to tell her story in this book.

Nathan: *We're asking for the presence of the girl who died in Sri Lanka.*
Prayer Partner: "What is your life like now?"

There was no delay. She jumped right in, borrowing my voice.

Nathan: She's right here and she's moving into first-person speech.
Girl: *This is she. I have grown up surprisingly fast. At least, it's a surprise to me. My death is now several years ago in time. I was the only daughter, only child. I was twelve, but I wanted to be twenty. That was part of the problem that morning. I was being treated like a child, who wanted to be competent to decide when she could go to the beach. I felt my parents were of a generation that was too strict, or they remembered the way their parents raised them. They were doing the same, and I was pushing back and saying, "These are modern times. You know that I'm responsible." Some of it's probably what twelve-year-old's and parents argue about always and everywhere.*
*I think in my current way of being, I've been given my wish to be older, or maybe it was my mind didn't match my body when I was here. My parents are very well educated, and they poured a lot of educational resources into me, and I think I felt I was older than my peers. I had more experiences and more interests and, I don't know, a larger imagination. I wasn't interested in toys and children's things. Sometimes I felt school held me back more than it pushed me forward. Now I feel like I am a young adult.*
Prayer Partner: Yes. You see yourself now as a young adult, is that what I heard you just say?
Girl: *Yes. I would like to write a book, too.*
Partner: What would the book be about?
Girl: *I don't know yet. I just love the idea of having something important enough to say to merit writing a book and a book worthy of people purchasing it and spending time with it. I read many books. I would like to write a book, and I'd like to help a bit with the writing of this one, at least the part that concerns me.*
Partner: What would you like us to say about you?
Girl: *Your purpose is you've collected stories of people who died unexpectedly and suddenly and who have reasons for not following the program of following someone into the tunnel of light or the next dimension, and you're right. I didn't for reasons that I think you already know. For all that I've just said, I still, in truth, was a twelve-year—old subject to my parents' control. I did understand that the rule was I was not to go to the beach alone. That's perfectly reasonable for a twelve-year-old girl on vacation where there are no other relatives or friends around. I wouldn't allow a twelve- year-old of my own to do what I did.*

*I'm seeing all of it from a different, more mature point of view. Still, it was the wrong thing to do, and I understand why I felt bad and disobedient. For many Asian families, honoring the elders, even one's own parents, is an important value. I felt I had brought disgrace, being disobedient, causing my parents to lose their only child, to alter the course of their life, where now they have no child and have no grandchildren. I was trying to do something secretive; of course, the secret was completely transparent in the end, even though they didn't know where I was. They had to put it together pretty quickly that I must have been swept out to sea. It was a terrible day.*

Partner: Are your parents still living?

Girl: *Yes.*

Partner: Do you visit them and observe them?

Girl: *I look in on them.*

Partner: How are they doing?

Girl: *It's difficult to say. My parents were more head than heart even in their marriage. I don't know if it was precisely arranged in the style of many Indian marriages, but it was not the Western style of courtship and romance. It was always more about the utility or the functionality of the Indian. I think they continue in that mode. They look ahead to professional goals and financial goals. They continue to act as a team.*

Partner: Is there anything that you would like to communicate to them if you could?

Girl: *I'll see you again. When you're a child and adults say life is short or childhood is fleeting, none of it sounds very convincing. When you're a child, there are many things that you can't do because you must wait until you're older. It doesn't feel like childhood is moving quickly at all. You only want it to be over so that you can do the more attractive things. I'll see you again. I look in, and I don't think either of us really desire more than that. They're not ones to pine and go to seers or anything like that. They have photos of me and little artifacts, baby things, and so on. They're small. I think it would be impolite to call them shrines, but little collections of photos and other remembrances of times together that they have in their quarters and at work.*

*I hope that the memory of me can bring a smile and not just sadness and loss. I know that they're not angry with me. It was a thought on the day of the big wave that they would be angry with me, but I know that that's not really so.*

*I know that there are many others who you want to talk to. I don't want to stay on the line any longer other than to say I'm happy to be helping with the book. Maybe I'll write one of my own, one day. For now, tell them it doesn't matter what religion you are or what you think about it. You will live after you die. Even if you die in a way that seems colossally tragic, you step out of that. You'll walk out of that like one might walk out of dirty clothes and go on.*

Partner: We are so grateful that you came to visit and talk with us. We send you many blessings for happiness in this afterlife.

Girl: *Rani, R-A-N-I.*

Partner: That's her name?

Nathan: Rani. I can feel her leaving now.

Partner: Rani? Thank you, Rani.

Nathan: Glory be to the Father, and to the Son, and to the Holy Spirit, as it was in the beginning, is now, and will be forever. Amen.

As I read back over this, I'm grateful to know this beautiful person. We only learned her first name very late in the process. Does she sound disrespectful to you? She does sound mature. It also makes sense to me that she would very quickly evolve to some sense of age that wasn't frustrating or limiting, like being twelve–going–on–twenty. I knew many bright, young Asian students during my years at Stanford University. Her assessment of her parents' lives sounded familiar to me and has a ring of truth. These very traditional Asian parents are suddenly raising children in a world vastly different from the one they knew as children.

And did you hear her message to you?

*For now, tell them it doesn't matter what religion you are or what you think about it. You will live after you die. Even if you die in a way that seems colossally tragic, you step out of that. You'll walk out of that like one might walk out of dirty clothes and go on.*

Rani is a loving soul. She is made of the stuff of God, who is Love. Everyone is.

Rani, I'm happy to receive any help you can offer in the writing of this book. You don't have to limit yourself to just the chapter about you. Please feel free to help with all the others, too. I hope you'll get started on the book that's in your heart to write. I look forward to reading it one day.

## Chapter Four

# Buddy, Who Turned Out to Be the Conductor

The stories I've told you so far have involved helping only one soul at a time. The fire that caused Ray's death killed only Ray. While the tsunami that killed Rani killed many thousands, it was only Rani that we were asked to help.

Sometimes, though, my prayer partners and I are asked to help a cluster of folks who died in a similar way. Rather than each occupying some private afterlife cell, they've chosen to be with—or at least ended up among—others who met with a similar fate. The folks in the following story all died in car–train collisions, although these accidents occurred over decades. All of these people shared the Interrupted Death Experience. They didn't get escorted by afterlife greeters, pass through a tunnel, or move into an attractive light. In fact, the folks you're about to meet ended up in a far more mundane place.

Here's the dream as I recorded it in the journal on my nightstand. I received this dream in the early morning hours of February 17, 2015.

> *I was in a car stopped at a railroad crossing with no gate or warning signal. Instead of a succession of boxcars, flatcars, and tank cars, I watched a string of cars trying to cross the train tracks being hit by trains. It didn't make sequential sense. It made me wonder if these accidents had happened at different times. First there were older cars, then newer ones. There was a sedan from the late fifties or early sixties. Children were crashing through the rear windshield. One was a nine–year–old girl wearing a blue dress with white trim. There were two boys in that wreck. One car had an adult man named Briscoe. He was not given first aid. I came to help him. He was a Catholic and wanted a blessing. I offered a prayer for him, and he started crying. There might have been six or seven different crashes,*

*trains hitting cars. There was a hospital very nearby. There were two quarters on the ground. I awoke.*

Three months later, on June 2, 2015, I visited my sister Mimi at her home in suburban Houston. We sat in the shade in her backyard. It's a squirrel playground.

Mimi is an intuitive and a woman of faith. She has also studied many different healing modalities. She shares the prophetic gift I have; she can make her voice available for one who needs to speak. Mimi is wise and kind. She and her husband, Billy, have six children and three grandchildren. For many years, Mimi taught special needs elementary school children. She is a compassionate listener.

That sunny morning, Mimi and I went into prayer to try to help these folks. Facing each other, we did our protective prayer, inviting many of our saint and angel friends to gather around us. I read the dream story aloud a couple of times slowly; then we invited someone in the story to emerge to tell us how we could help.

It took a little while. We asked each other, "Is anyone with you?" Mimi confirmed that she was beginning to feel the presence of a group of people. "They feel *stamped*," she said. They all had some kind of mark on their bodies, she reported; she could feel their frustration.

Then Mimi's body shifted forward in her chair. She faced me, stared me down, and a young man's voice tumbled out of her.

> Young man: *These people want to make me the conductor. I'm not a conductor.*
> Nathan: Oh. Well, welcome. I'm Nathan. We're in Houston, and you're talking through my sister, Mimi.
> Young man: *I'm not the conductor. I never said I was the conductor.*

Besides being a little angry, the young man seemed like a reluctant spokesperson for a group of people. He said the place where they were included a railroad track blocked by a huge boulder. This was their "quarters": that's what the symbol of quarters on the ground in the dream meant. He told us he'd been a passenger in a car driven by another young guy. It wasn't easy to get this young man to talk; his manner was all business, and I could sense he wasn't feeling friendly.

> Young man: *All I did was have a good time.* (He meant drinking.) *We were just out for a good time, and I couldn't get back in my body and I ended up in this place. And I'm not the conductor, but these people keep wanting me to be the conductor.*
> Nathan: Tell me a little about yourself. What did you do for work?
> Young man: *I didn't have a real job. I just did whatever. I was handy. I did this and that.*

Nathan: Well, maybe that's why these people want you to be the conductor. Maybe they can see that you're good at figuring things out and solving problems. It's good when people can help each other out of a fix. What's your name?

Young man: *Just call me Buddy.*

Nathan: Okay, Buddy. Let's see if we can figure out a way for you to help these people.

Buddy: *Well, there's this boulder on the tracks, and it's too big to move.*

Nathan: Yeah, but people have been moving heavy boulders for as long as there've been people and heavy boulders. How have they done it? Maybe if you had a simple tool like a fulcrum, and you had enough people put their weight against it—

Buddy: *Or maybe if we had some heavy equipment, like something on a construction site. But we don't have anything like that here.*

Nathan: Well, have you asked?

Buddy: *No.*

Nathan: Well, it couldn't hurt to ask, could it? Would you mind if I ask for you, if I just ask out loud? You're good at doing this and that. Do you think you'd know how to work heavy construction equipment?

Buddy: *Not without the key. I'd need the key.*

Nathan: Good idea! Okay, then what if we ask for the key and maybe for someone with experience operating heavy machinery who could help you use it?

Buddy: *All right.*

Nathan: Now I'm going to ask out loud, and I'm going to ask God, because that's what I do. God, could we please have a piece of heavy machinery with the keys in it and an operator who will help Buddy use it?

It wasn't long before Buddy seemed to perk up.

Buddy: *Well, I'll be, would you look at that!*

Nathan: What're you seeing? I don't know what you're seeing.

Buddy: *It's some kind of construction machinery. Like a front–end loader.*

Nathan: Is it yellow? Lots of times they're yellow.

Buddy: *Yep, it's yellow, and there's a fellow in the cab waving at me to climb aboard.*

Buddy told me that he climbed behind the controls. The helper sat behind him and watched over his shoulders as Buddy maneuvered the equipment and began to move the boulder.

Buddy: *Look! It's turning into nothing. It's just dissolving into light! There's a light on the other side of it and it's coming toward us.*

Nathan: You mean like an oncoming train? Oh, crap, you folks all got hit by trains. Does it seem dangerous?

Buddy: *No. It's bright, though, and it's like a bubble and there's people in it.*

Nathan: Does it feel scary?

Buddy: *No.*

Nathan: Then try asking for somebody you know and trust. Somebody you feel safe with.

Buddy: *Look, there's Paa-Paw!*

Nathan: Does he look old?

Buddy: *No, but it's my Paa-Paw. I know it's him. He's waving for us to follow him.*

Nathan: You mean everybody, you and all the people around you?

Buddy: *Yeah, it looks like it. I'm telling them all to form a line and hold hands, and we'll all go together. It's a really long line of people.*

Nathan: We used to do that when I was a kid, Buddy. All the kids would hold hands in a long line and run around pretending to be a train. It sounds like you're the conductor they thought you were, Buddy. Sometimes trains are really long.

Buddy: *Yeah, well, we're going now.*

And off they went.

There's a line in *The Wizard of Oz* I've always liked. Dorothy's house has just crash-landed in Munchkinland. Glinda the Good Witch of the North is borne inside a huge, colorful bubble on a breeze and lands beside Dorothy. Suddenly, a crowd of munchkins emerge singing, dancing, and parading all around. The Wicked Witch of the West explodes onto the scene, threatens Dorothy over her ruby slippers, then disappears in a sulfurous cloud. Glinda advises Dorothy to "begin at the beginning" and "follow the yellow brick road" to find the Wizard of Oz, then floats away. Bewildered, Dorothy can only observe, *"My, people come and go so quickly here!"*

That's how I felt that day in Mimi's backyard. When I help these stuck souls, I usually try to spend a little time making friendly conversation in an effort to put my traumatized visitor at ease. Buddy would have none of it. He wasn't looking for a new pal. He wasn't looking to be the spokesperson for a bunch of stuck souls, either. He just seemed like the kind of guy who knows that something needs doing and, with a little nudge, does it whether he wants to or not. In the end, Buddy's no-nonsense approach got the job done. Buddy, his Paa-Paw, the heavy equipment operator, and all the formerly stuck souls came and went quickly.

Mimi's kind of no-nonsense, too. Our work was done. She went inside and made us some lunch.

Buddy hadn't wanted me to know his real name and was frankly a little cranky. I didn't think I'd ever talk with him again. But then when we decided to include his story in this book, we thought it was important to ask his permission to use it. This time he wasn't in such a hurry. But he still didn't tell me his real name! In the conversation that follows, he's borrowing my voice and talking to my prayer partner:

Partner: Are you there, Buddy?

Buddy: *This is Buddy.*

Partner: It's good to hear your voice.

Buddy: *I was messing with him* [me, Nathan] *when we were in Texas in his sister's backyard. I spoke through his sister, and I wouldn't tell him who I was. I just said, "Call me Buddy." I was still kind of angry, and I came out of his sister's mouth angry about not being the conductor. He remembers looking at her and seeing her face look so funny with a man's voice coming out of it and leaning forward in her chair, getting so angry that I'm not the conductor. People keep wanting me to be the conductor. I didn't really want them to know my name. I was just being a jerk.*

Partner: You called yourself Buddy?

Buddy: *I just said, "Call me Buddy." People do that, people that don't know you very well want to call you something familiar, so, Buddy. I don't feel the need to change that for your book. I think Buddy works just fine.*

Partner: That's fine.

Buddy: *It's more true to the moment, don't you think?*

Partner: Yes.

Buddy: *It's the way I felt at the time.*

Partner: How do you feel now?

Buddy: *One thing, I understand you're writing a book and you're choosing stories that show different ways that this could work, that not everybody that dies in a crash or some sudden violent thing gets stuck, but I did, and so did a bunch of other people. One of the ways that it can work— I think you know people that just made their own little cave somewhere, went off on their own and found some little bit of afterlife real estate and put themselves there and closed the door.*

*I didn't do that. I don't think I even—I don't remember choosing. It just sort of happened. It's not like I said please send me somewhere where there's a boulder or a railroad track. I just felt stuck, and I felt like I couldn't get back in my body and was mad about that. A railroad track: who knew that that was going to be such a big part of my life story? You don't know you're going to get hit by a train. How many train tracks did I cross in my whole life? How many train whistles did I ever hear? How many stories did I hear about trains even as a kid or movies that had trains in them or something? Then trains and train tracks became this story of my life, so I ended up in this place with this huge train track running through it and other people who had been killed in car–train crashes.*

*I didn't really want to talk to them, but after a while, there's not time to pass exactly, but there's something sort of like it. You're hanging out, so you may as well talk to one another a little bit, even though I really didn't want to be with people and it wasn't, well, it was only a little bit of chatter, nothing that amounted to anything, just like acknowledging somebody on a bus stop. What I'm trying to say is there was not the kind of conversation that got any of us to move on like this. It was just idle chit–chat among people going nowhere the way that you might be sitting talking to somebody at a bus bench because there's nothing to do except to wait until you move.*

Partner: In the place where you were stuck at the train tracks, did you have people around and occasionally communicate with them?

Buddy: *Yeah, but at a low-grade level, where there wasn't really any substance to the conversation. It's just a little bit of hanging out: "How's the weather?" Nothing that made you care about any of these people. Really, they're just people that happened to be hanging around in the same place you're hanging out. Must have been plenty of places where people are just waiting in line somewhere. All they really want to do is get done whatever it is they're there for. But we weren't even there for anything. We were just there because we got hit by a train. Pretty pathetic bunch of people.*

*Then there began to be this drift that somehow I was supposed to be the conductor, and I was supposed to somehow solve the problem. Who the hell am I to solve the problem? All I did to qualify to get here is get hit by a train. I wasn't even completely sober at the time. I've got no expertise how to get a boulder off a train track and how to get unstuck in the afterlife. All of it, I didn't get it. Like people presume that somehow I was going to be the one to get them out of there. I didn't want to be in charge.*

*When he came—I guess I came first or somebody did. The part about him seeing different crashes in the same dream and what not—I don't know. I still don't know how this works. I haven't asked, either, about all the people that were in that scene, how come I was the one that ended up talking to him and working with him and having my Paa-Paw come on a train and praying for this guy to bring a piece of heavy equipment and the key? How come I ended up being the one doing the talking? I'm not much of a leader.*

*That day, somehow I was. I don't know why, but I know it was good. We all got unstuck, and I haven't seen any of those people since because, like I was saying, we didn't have anything in common to start with except being hit by a train. We lived at different times.*

Partner: So you haven't seen them? What are you doing now, and who are the people around you that you have something in common with?

Buddy: *My Paa-Paw came. He showed me some—Let's see. What did we do next?*

Partner: It doesn't have to be right then, but just what life is like for you now.

Buddy: *I was just thinking he knew that I was tired, that that was a mix of—kind of like you've been on a long trip and you get where you're going. You get all the way to where you're staying and maybe you're with friends and everybody's excited to see you, but they know that you've had a long journey, and you have adrenaline about getting to where you are supposed to be and being with people who are eager to receive you and at the same time being tired. I think he helped me just say hello to people. Like the way that you might go off to your room and go to bed, rest a bit, wake up in the morning with a clear head, and then make a plan for who you're going to be with and what you're going to do.*

*There wasn't any plan at the beginning. I was just with different people. I wasn't sick, but it was the way that you might, like, if somebody was at the hospital or maybe right after the birth of the baby or something, everybody wants to see the baby, but you can't all just jam into the room. You have to take your turn and not stay too long. It was sort of like that. I was the new arrival and everybody wanted to see me, but everybody knew better than to come at once or stay too long, give me a chance to ease into things and get used to it all.*

*It had been a long time since I had died, but I didn't finish passing, so I hadn't really passed. They still needed to treat me like I was a new arrival because I was. For a while, I was that. Then after that, it was like the way that you might, I don't know, decide what are you going to do for lunch or what you're going to do in the afternoon. They gave me a morning in the new place just to rest a bit and get acclimated and then make some general— hardly even plans—but just seeing people, mostly people I already knew, people that had been a part of my life, grandparents and a kid that died when I was in high school. I don't know, just people, but they started me on people I already knew. I guess that just made sense. It's a little easier to say, "Oh, my God, look. Hadn't thought of you in a long time," or whatever.*

Partner: Then, after a while, did you make some choices about the things you might want to do next?

Buddy: *I'm still at the front end of that just because I wanted to go slow. If you'd known me, I was never a ball of fire. I was the kind of guy that just meandered a bit and stayed in the background. I was nobody's idea of a leader. It takes gumption just to live your life like that. I was kind of a passenger in my own life. I would just let it make its way and occasionally I would steer it this way or that, but most of the time I just let my life drift, maybe like a canoe. You don't really have to paddle, not if you're in a river.*

*Once in a while, you might need to steer it here or there so you don't end up sideways.*

*I haven't done an awful lot. There's nothing that I have to say that needs to go in a book about what I've done next other than just kind of meet up with people, relax, enjoy people's company. I'm not being punished for anything, just that I haven't seen any kind of throne room or streets of gold and ...*

Partner: No choirs of angels.

Buddy: *None of that, just people I once knew and once in a while somebody introduces you to somebody that you didn't know, but maybe you'd heard of or whatever. Nothing that needs to go in a book, just hanging out, but different. Before it was hanging out, but not talking to people or at least not talking with people in a way that was personal. Now I'm talking more personal to people.*

Partner: Are you content now, Buddy?

Buddy: *That's a good word for it. I don't think I ever used that to describe myself, but I think it would work.*

Partner: It was good of you to touch base with us.

Buddy: *Yeah, I'm gonna let you go because there's other people you folks want to talk to, and I don't really have anything to tell you I haven't already said.*

Partner: Thanks a lot.

Buddy: *Good luck on your book.*

Partner: Thank you. We appreciate it. Take care.

Nathan: *Glory be to the Father, and to the Son, and to the Holy Spirit, as it was in the beginning, is now, and will be forever. Amen.*

So, there you have it, in Buddy's own words. He said he was no one's idea of a leader, but when leadership was needed, he was just the man for the job.

Buddy, it was good to meet you and to work with you a little bit. Thanks for stepping up and helping all those folks. I looked up the origin of the word "conductor." Studying word origins is a hobby of mine. A conductor is "one who leads together." Now that you know you can be a conductor and that other people see that gift in you, who knows what you'll do with it next? You said several times that you don't have anything to say that needs to go in a book. I'm willing to bet that a lot of people who read your story will disagree.

You might be wondering: Was Buddy chosen as the conductor because leadership was, for him, an untapped quality that God wanted him to see in himself? Well, you're asking me to know the mind of God here, right? Just like Buddy would say, *I'M NOT THE CONDUCTOR. I NEVER SAID I AM THE CONDUCTOR!* Who am I to say I know the mind of God? But then again, I do have a MASTER OF DIVINITY degree and the diploma to prove it. So what's God thinking here?

Afterlife, *Interrupted*

I don't know, but here's what I think. Jesus, God–walking–around, was often called *Rabbi*, which means "Teacher." Gifted teachers can see potential in beloved students before they see it in themselves. And, sometimes, young students haven't yet had the life experiences that call for their hidden gifts to be manifested.

All that I know of Buddy (and remember, I don't even know his real name) is what he told me. I've shared that all here. So play along with me as we guess about what's going on here.

I think Buddy lived a short life. My guess is that he was in his early twenties, out drinking with a friend who might have been driving drunk. We know Buddy drifted through his life; he told us that. He did the bare minimum of steering or choosing to do anything. He hadn't chosen a career path. He did odd jobs. That old chestnut, "jack of all trades and master of none," might describe Buddy. I think he would agree. Mastering anything involves buckling down and applying oneself to the task at hand. Buddy might never have really done that before his death. It may be that the day he showed up in my sister's backyard was his first real job where he demonstrated any real mastery. He was chosen out of a large group. I think God–the–Teacher loved Buddy and knew that his moment had arrived.

Buddy could define the problem. At first he complained of being resourceless. I was going old school and low tech suggesting a fulcrum, which is nothing but a sturdy stick against which people throw their weight. Buddy was the one who was the bigger thinker. "Too bad we don't have a piece of heavy machinery," he said. I was feeling self–satisfied when I suggested asking for one. "But I'd need the key," Buddy added, one–upping me. I one–upped him right back by suggesting that we ask for a heavy–equipment operator to help run the thing, though, as it turned out, Buddy didn't need any help. He knew just what to do.

Now, in the very early days of his afterlife, Buddy has seen himself as a leader. My guess is he'll go on to lead in other ways as his afterlife unfolds. Maybe he'll continue to go with the flow as he often did. But he knows now that he can steer his and other peoples' lives in a positive direction when that's what's needed.

Buddy also told us that he's an afterlife newbie. He's seen a few loved ones and rested a bit. He told us he was no ball of fire here on earth. I think he'll progress at a leisurely pace that suits him. But I think he'll continue to be challenged to discover latent gifts and will enjoy the process. Buddy seems self–effacing to me in a way that suggests he'd been made to feel that he is No Big Deal. I believe Buddy is on his way to learning that he is, in fact, a Very Big Deal. God and the universe are full of energy. Energy doesn't flow unless it can move through conductive material. Our buddy, Buddy, still new at this afterlife business, knows a new and important truth: He's a Conductor!

## Chapter Five

# Cheryl Lynn, Training for the Afterlife Olympics

I like to begin these chapters with the text of the dream in which my night visitor showed me his or her traumatic death. For years I wrote the dream stories down on whatever random pieces of paper I had at hand. Eventually I started using a bound composition notebook.

I have good notes of the session during which we helped Cheryl Lynn get unstuck, but I haven't been able to find my notes of the dream itself. Here's what I remember of the dream:

*I was a young woman sitting in the front passenger seat of a vehicle. I looked across at the driver, a young man. We were both in our early twenties. Suddenly the car was spinning out of control. It left the roadway and flipped over. I awoke.*

A prayer partner and I helped the young woman on October 29, 2014.

After doing our protective prayer, my partner and I invited the presence of the young woman who showed me how she died in a car crash. When she came through, she did so with low energy. For me, she felt like the bass line of a song written in four–part harmony. Have you ever done any choral singing? I'm a deep bass. That means I can sing very low notes. It also means I can't reach high notes that aren't at all high for other people. We basses usually don't get to sing anything cheerful or carry the melody. We just kind of croak or drone on in the background of the song. This young woman's energy felt low and dull like that and not at all positive.

Once we connected, my partner and I met the young woman called Cheryl Lynn. She was led to us by her guardian. The guardians aren't allowed to drag in the one in their care, because in this realm, freedom of choice is all–important. But it felt like Cheryl Lynn was putting forth the bare minimum energy required to be with us. This made it more difficult for me to facilitate her speech with my partner.

We learned that Cheryl Lynn had been weary for a very long time. She had gotten used to immobility, yet now she was being invited to move in a big way. It's true she was tired and soul–weary, but she was nevertheless ready for a change, whether she realized that enthusiastically or not. She'd come forward to learn about moving on. We learned that she felt trapped in her current after–death state, as she once did during her life on earth.

My partner tried to break the ice with Cheryl Lynn. "What kind of work did you do?" is always a good place to start. It turns out that Cheryl Lynn was once a water aerobics instructor, active and athletic.

As she began to describe herself, I could feel her energy rise. Once she got started, we learned she was very well spoken.

> Cheryl Lynn: *I was in college. I was studying communications. I wasn't sure yet what I might do with it, but I knew I liked people and bringing people together. I liked the classes and the other students in the department. I was living with my boyfriend and enjoying my life.*
> Partner: But then something happened, right? You were in a car accident and died?
> Cheryl Lynn: *No, just the driver did.*
> Partner: Your boyfriend died?
> Cheryl Lynn: *The one driving wasn't my boyfriend. I don't want to talk about him.*
> Partner: Okay. But you're saying you survived the accident?
> Cheryl Lynn: *Part of me did. I was paralyzed. My boyfriend left me. He couldn't handle having a paralyzed girlfriend. Everything changed. My life became one long physical therapy appointment. I had to learn how to do everything all over again. Physical therapy people are always cheerleading and telling you you're doing great and getting so much stronger and all of that. But I never did walk again.*
> Partner: Oh. Father Nathan assumed that you had died in the car crash you showed him, because, when he has these dreams, it's usually people showing him how they died.
> Cheryl Lynn: *Well, I'm different then, okay? I guess you know I'm dead and you want to know how I died?*
> Partner: We just want to help you in whatever way we can.
> Cheryl Lynn: *Sorry. I get that. And I'm the one that came to you guys. All right. Here's that cheery story. So I do years and years of physical therapy to try to get back whatever my broken body could be re–taught to do. Some of it worked. I did get better; I could see that. But I still needed a wheelchair. There was a lot I couldn't do even on my best day. I hated that I couldn't move freely.*

Afterlife, *Interrupted*

*One day, when I was 34, I was being transported by a van service for people in wheelchairs. I did the Dial–a–Ride thing all the time. On this particular day, something went wrong. I don't know what. Was it that the lift operator made a mistake? Or did the machine malfunction? Who cares? I ended up flipping over backwards and landing on the pavement on my head. I was Humpty–Dumped right onto the street. There was no putting me back together again. Not this time.*

Partner: Oh, I'm so sorry.

Cheryl Lynn: *I'm young and healthy and athletic, and I'm living my life and I get paralyzed in a car crash. Then I do years and years of physical therapy to try to get back a bit of what I lost. Then, to top it off, I die getting dumped out the back of a van. None of this crap was my fault.*

Partner: That would make anyone angry.

Cheryl Lynn: *You think so?*

Partner: Yes, but you wouldn't be with us now unless someone thought you might be ready to move along. We help people who feel stuck get unstuck. Do you think that would describe you?

Cheryl Lynn: *Oh, God, not afterlife physical therapy.*

Partner: Well, no, not exactly. What we do doesn't hurt, and it usually doesn't take very long.

Cheryl Lynn: *How does it work?*

Partner: Different ways, but the main thing is, we know that the people we serve have been through a lot and died sudden, usually violent, deaths. All we do is help them think of someone they trust that they'd like to be with. You'll need someone to take you to the right place, don't you think?

Cheryl Lynn: *I guess. So I'm supposed to try to think of somebody who has died that I would trust to come and get me unstuck, is that it?*

Partner: Pretty much. Does anyone come to mind?

Cheryl Lynn: *It can be anyone?*

Partner: Right. We can't force anyone, naturally. We just ask. Then they show up, that's all.

Cheryl Lynn: *Oh. Then I think I know the right person to ask: Estelle.*

Partner: So, tell us about Estelle.

Cheryl Lynn: *Estelle was, or I guess is, this physical therapist. She worked a lot with me. She loved her work and was great at it. Her job was to take paralyzed people like me and get them to move more freely. She never saw wheelchairs and crutches. She saw people trying to stretch themselves to be as independent as they could.*

*Other therapists would do drills and exercises straight out of the book. They'd be all clinical and professional and write everything in their charts. Estelle was different.*

*She'd come dancing into the room like she was in a play. Then she'd get you to do what she was doing. She'd have us close our eyes and imagine our bodies doing all the things that she was doing. She made the whole thing feel like art. Her sessions always seemed to pass quickly.*

Partner: She sounds like an artist.

Cheryl Lynn: *Or like an athletic artist. Like an Olympic athlete who'd trained her mind and body to be in sync. She treated us like that.*

Partner: But to help us right here and now, you know she needs to have died, right?

Cheryl Lynn: *Yeah, I got that part. One day she showed up with news for us: she had cancer. A bad one. She promised she wouldn't leave us. She'd plow through it the way we were all plowing through our own disabilities. She'd always start a new session by giving us a bit of her own medical update. Even if the news wasn't good, she'd tell us the truth. Then she'd turn the page. We'd get to work on our session. Over time we could see that she was getting weaker. But she set such a good example. She always pushed us by doing the best that she was able. She inspired us to do the same.*

*Eventually, she couldn't come into work anymore. Estelle died. If anyone were going to come here and help me get moving, Estelle would be the one. That's all she ever did for me. She helped me get moving.*

Partner: All right, then. Is it okay if we ask for her to come and be with you?

Cheryl Lynn: *Sure.*

What happened next was beautiful. I couldn't see it for myself, naturally, while I was lending Cheryl Lynn my voice. But I could feel her grow lighter and more cheerful inside me. Estelle appeared to Cheryl Lynn, who promptly laughed at her old friend, who emerged as her twenty–four–year–old self. Cheryl Lynn told us that she looked radiant.

Cheryl Lynn: *Oh, my God, you always did love to make an entrance!*

Estelle had been older at the time of her death from cancer. Did she choose to manifest as a graceful twenty–four–year–old because that was Cheryl Lynn's age when she was first injured? Were they now going to be twenty–four–year–old afterlife companions dancing into whatever came next? That's what it felt like. There was nothing left to say; I could feel Cheryl Lynn's presence receding. I imagined them nodding and smiling in our direction as Estelle led Cheryl Lynn on to wherever her dreams might take her.

As you know by now, I was never planning to see or speak with any of my night visitors after helping them get unstuck. I would pray for them as a group sometimes, hoping I'd see them all in The Great Roundup. But then as this book project presented itself, and we chose to include Cheryl Lynn's story, we felt it was important to at least try to contact the people involved and ask their permission.

One day in early February of 2018, we did that. It was just before the Winter Olympics. Obviously, Cheryl Lynn had been paying attention to events here.

My prayer partner and I went into our protective prayer and asked to speak with Cheryl Lynn.

Partner: Cheryl, are you with us? Cheryl Lynn? Feeling that you're here, Cheryl Lynn.

Nathan: She's showing me the Winter Olympics.

Partner: Is that something you're interested in, the Winter Olympics?

Cheryl Lynn [borrowing Nathan's voice]: *I just know they're coming soon. I think they're in Korea, and I like watching that.*

Partner: Yeah?

Cheryl Lynn: *Well, for one thing—of course, they show an awful lot of those figure skater girls that are like sparrows that are fifteen years old and weigh eighty pounds and some guy can pick them up and spin all over the ice with them. I liked watching the ones that were more muscular, the women that did the downhill, the ski jumping. I especially liked those ones that go down that ramp thing and fly through the air. Sometimes it's just to see how far they can go. Other times, they do tricks like divers do, twirls and stuff. If I hadn't been injured the way I was, I would have been a really athletic woman, and I tried to be, even within the wheelchair world. I tried to do wheelchair basketball and different contests and things for people that had a handicap of some kind, but now I don't have that anymore. I'm not in a wheelchair and I'm not broken, and I don't have to do rehab. I think I'm probably a lot more—it still makes sense to say—physically active.*

Partner: Are you?

Cheryl Lynn: *Whatever people think about what it might be like to be outside your body—I don't know about the religion part of it, about some ultimate religion body or something. I think Christians have some idea about a glorified shining body. That's not really what I'm talking about. It's just that you've got something that's like a body. It might not be the same. It certainly isn't the same as it was on Earth, but everybody's still got something like that, and you can still be more or less active than normal. I think because I couldn't be very active for so long that I probably am still making up for lost time, and I'm probably more physically active than a lot of other people around me.*

Partner: What kinds of things do you like to do?

Cheryl Lynn: *I don't know. Just movement. I couldn't move without other people moving me a lot of the time and even at the dang accident at the end, I couldn't get in and out of the car. I had to wait for somebody to do that when they were ready. There's a lot of waiting involved when you can't move yourself. You can call a Dial-A-Ride and then you wait for it and it's late. Getting to appointments, doing much of anything was always a pain in the ass. Now I don't know how long it's been since I went from the way I was to the way I am now, but I think I've spent most of the time doing handstands or cartwheels, like a little girl on the lawn doing flips or rolls or whatever just because I can. I feel like a lot of the time I'm just moving because I can move.*

Partner: Must feel very freeing.

Cheryl Lynn: *It does. I don't have to work or earn a living. It's not like anybody's going to judge me and say, "Stop that nonsense and buckle down," or "Get over here and do your share," or anything like that. I think I'm just a happy person doing what she feels like doing. I think if other people have to know about it, I think the thing I like about here is there isn't anybody picking on anybody else or making fun or judging unnecessarily. People just do what they want to do. That's all.*

Partner: It sounds like you're in a good place, Cheryl Lynn.

Cheryl Lynn: *I'm not mad at the world. I think that's the subtitle of what you were going to call me. I think that's perfectly fair, but you can let people know, if you want, that I mostly remember that it's not time anymore. It's not like I've been doing cartwheels or handstands for months on end. It's just always now, and I think for right now however I can get that across, I feel like I'm an Olympic athlete who just trains all the time, that loves to train because they want to get better, and they enjoy being in the gym or doing whatever it is they do. I admire these people who have to get up way early and lace on their skates or their skis or whatever. I'm just very, very busy being physical because I can.*

Partner: We're happy for you, Cheryl Lynn. Thank you so much for coming back to talk with us.

Cheryl Lynn: *Sure. Say anything you want in that book. I thought when I was first injured that that might be one of the ways I'd go once I realized there were now things I couldn't do. I thought, "Maybe I'll become a real reader. I'll become a real student, a bookworm and all that." I tried it, but it didn't take. It wasn't my way, even though I had to do a lot more sitting than I wanted to. But sitting and reading a book? No, I wasn't much of a reader, so it's funny that I'd be helping with and being a part of a book. I'm going to go now. This poor man's tired [She's referring to me, Nathan.]. I'm going to go so that you can get on with what you're doing. I know you're working your way down a list.*

Partner: We really appreciate your coming and speaking with us. Many blessings.

       Afterlife, *Interrupted*

Enjoy your now.

Cheryl Lynn: *I'll see you later.*

Partner: Bye-bye.

Nathan: Glory be to the Father, and to the Son, and to the Holy Spirit, as it was in the beginning, is now, and will be forever. Amen.

So, do we have corporeal experiences in the afterlife? The short answer is yes.

But I still want to default to my motto: *I don't know, but here's what I think.* In my Catholic Christian tradition, we have the gospel stories of Jesus risen from the dead. There are a bunch of different ones. In one Jesus kindly but firmly tells a huggy friend, "Don't touch me. I haven't yet ascended to my Father." Later he walks through walls to be with his frightened friends. They recognize him on sight. He shows them the nail marks in his hands and feet as a form of ID. In one story, when Jesus appears, they're afraid he's a ghost. To prove he's not, he asks, "Have you got anything to eat?" And he eats right in front of them. In another story, his disciples are night-fishing and haven't caught anything. Some know-it-all, stranger-guy cooking breakfast on a beach yells, "Throw your nets on the other side of the boat. You'll catch something." Their nets almost tear from the weight of all the fish. Jesus's followers recognize him, not because of his face, but because of the superabundance that surrounds him.

I think the physics of the afterlife doesn't require people's bodies to take only one fixed form. People can manifest themselves as they please. In this story, Estelle shows Cheryl Lynn a version of her younger self that Cheryl Lynn had never seen. I believe the people I've been asked to help are on their way to greater wholeness. They don't have to trudge around like zombies in *Night of the Living Dead*. Having died and being dead aren't the same thing. My visitors have all died, and all in traumatic ways, but none of them is now dead. Remember Rani, who died at age twelve and now manifests as twenty? Cheryl Lynn did wheel a damaged body around for ten years before her death at age thirty-four. Now she tumbles on the lawn like a little girl. She didn't say she was in a little-girl body. I just think she's young at heart. I think she was back in the twenty-four-year-old healthy version of her body, but feeling even younger than that. Why? She told us. No one's around scolding, telling her to stop that tumbling nonsense and act her age. She's more like thirty-four, or maybe twenty-four, going on ten.

Cheryl Lynn spoke of some "religion body" Christians believe in and said she really didn't know about that, but that she was just enjoying her "now."

Will we one day have a "glorified body" that won't change? I don't know. But I love what I've seen through the little eternity peephole I've been given and am sharing with you.

One last word on this body–business. In this lifetime and our current bodies, haven't we all had moments when we wished we looked different? I didn't like looking too young to buy a beer at thirty–two years old, when my dad and I were at an Oakland A's game and I had to pass my driver's license through a bunch of strangers' hands just to buy a beer. My dad thought that was hilarious. That day I wanted to look older than I did. And who hasn't wanted to look or feel younger? I sometimes see a photo of my gray–haired self and wonder, who's the old man? I have seen many occasions where afterlife folk have chosen to look unlike they did at their passing. That's pretty common.

Here's another question Cheryl Lynn's story raises. Did her anger at the unfairness of it all contribute to her having been "stuck?" I'd say yes to that. Feeling angry that life has treated us unfairly is common enough. Here's my advice: Feel that anger for a little while if you must. Just don't indulge that for too long. Fixating on the past takes us out of the graced flow of the present. Time may not heal all wounds, but it can heal a lot of them. Also, while we're focused on the unfairness of our own suffering, we may completely overlook the suffering of those around us. We might have been part of someone else's healing had we even noticed their pain.

Finally, when she came to us and we suggested there was something she could do to get moving again, Cheryl Lynn groaned, "Oh, God, not afterlife physical therapy." She was exhausted, sick and tired of being sick and tired. Thankfully, we didn't need to put her through some arduous process. She only needed to do one simple thing: think of the one person best able to get her moving again. She knew in an instant who that person would be. And then we all met Estelle. What would it take for you to be the next Estelle for someone in your life?

## Chapter Six
# Don and First Responder Ralph

I received this dream during the night of April 17, 2017.

*I am a young man in the rear seat of a four–door sedan driving slowly through a freeway construction zone. Ahead a large cement beam was suspended from a crane above the traffic. It looked dangerous. Suddenly, the beam fell to the ground. It seemed not to crush anyone. But it hit some construction materials stacked near the roadway and began a domino–effect succession of collapses moving toward our car. I opened the door and tried to run to safety. I awoke.*

This was the night after Easter. Holy Week and Easter are very busy times around a Catholic church. There are major services three nights in a row, all of which require elaborate preparation. There are a lot of decorating and complex music practices, and, where I was serving, early morning and late night prayer services. Many people complete a year of preparation for baptism, confirmation, and first communion and are received joyfully into the Catholic Church. It's glorious and exhausting.

I hadn't had a night visitor in weeks. The Spirit seems to know when I'm already over–busy and need my sleep. Anyway, in the early hours of Easter Monday, this dream happened. Two weeks later, my prayer partner Laura and I met to see how we could help.

I trust the Spirit to send me new companions when I need them. Laura Dunham is a wise elder who has been given many spiritual gifts, which she has worked hard to develop.

Laura and I went into our protective prayer and waited for the young man to make himself known. He was hard to understand at first. I think it was because he was so angry that the energy he was sending off was garbled. Have you ever gotten so angry about something that you could hardly think straight, let alone express yourself to somebody else in a way that made sense? When we're trying to contact a night visitor, my prayer partners and I usually try just to introduce ourselves and ask for the name of the person we were helping. Even that was hard; I simply couldn't hear what the young man was saying.

Nathan: Are you saying German? It's a "G" name, right? Or a "D"?

I tried concentrating harder, like when you have a poor phone connection. I'm not going to complain to this person, "SPEAK UP!" or "YOU'RE BREAKING UP!" Remember, these folks have been through a fatal trauma, and, for all we know, could still be reliving it. You just have to be gentle and patient.

Later, he told us he was called different things: Germaine D., G. Don, or just Don. I wondered if he was African-American, because the only similar name I knew was Michael Jackson's brother Jermaine.

Often I record these sessions on my phone, for my private use, so I don't have to try to recall them from memory. I didn't do that this time, so I'm just going to tell you the basics.

Don, which was the name he settled on, was mad as hell. He could see the accident unfold. It should never have happened! The construction company should have never put him or anyone else in that kind of danger, just driving down a highway! Boy, was he angry!

Don had been out to lunch with three co-workers. (The ones in the front seats may have been named Fred and Peter.) They were on their way back to work. It seemed like we were in a large, expanding Southern city, perhaps Charlotte or Atlanta, where the freeway construction struggles to keep up with the population growth. As you know by now, Don saw construction material falling in his direction. He was crushed.

We're all greeted upon our deaths, however our deaths have occurred. When we first leave the womb and arrive here, there are people ready to receive us. The same applies when we leave here and emerge into the afterlife. Don wanted no part of being greeted. As you'll hear later in his own words, he told his greeters to get the F— out of his face. He wasn't ready for company of any kind, helpful or not. He'd just being crushed to death on a F—in' freeway!

Don didn't exactly find a quiet place off to the side somewhere where he could rest in peace. Instead, he stayed in a trauma–loop. Anyone who has suffered post–traumatic stress or has loved someone who has will recognize the problem. Don couldn't stop playing the scene back over in his imagination incessantly. He couldn't hear anything but his own internal anger.

But he did show up in my dream. That said to me that he was readier to move than ever, even if he didn't think so. The ones who find their way to me have been led in my direction because the ones caring for them in this first afterlife realm have found them ready to move. I think of this as like being moved from the emergency room to intensive care and eventually on to a private room in a hospital. You might be unconscious or sedated while all these changes are happening to you, but those caring for you are monitoring your improvement.

Laura, the prayer partner who helped me with Don, asked him if he'd seen the movie *Groundhog Day*. As she told him, "The central character was caught in a loop he couldn't get out of until he became aware of why this kept happening and changed his way of thinking to begin a new phase of his life." I don't think Don had seen the movie. But, to his credit, he got the point. His trauma–loop place was miserable. He was ready to try something else.

Laura and I wanted Don to think of a loved one whom he might invite to come for him. So we inquired about his family. Was Don married? "No." He was twenty–seven years old. He had little nieces and nephews, but no wife and kids of his own. That's when he got animated.

Trying to make sense through his red–hot anger, Don explained that his face was obliterated. He could hardly believe what a bloody mess he was. He didn't want anyone he'd ever known to have to see him this way! Remember, he's describing *his* imagination of himself. This was his reality. Then, like the *Groundhog Day* Guy, he changed his way of thinking.

"I don't want anybody I know to see me this way," he told us. "But what if it was somebody I didn't know and who'd never seen me who came for me? Like somebody who sees blood and guts every day. Those first responder people, EMTs, firefighters, police officers, they're used to these kinds of horrible messes. Maybe somebody like that could come for me."

That was all it took. We said a short prayer that sounded like a cellphone call to the 911 operator: "Could we please have an afterlife First Responder to come to Don's aid?"

I've gotten used to seeing marvelous things beyond my imagination. This was one for the ages. The one who emerged to answer the 911 call wasn't some whole, composed, peaceful afterlife soul. It was *another* stuck soul, coming to help someone who was as stuck as he was!

The person who emerged was EMT Ralph. Ralph arrived and just spent a few minutes with us before he got busy helping Don.

Before his death, we learned, Ralph lived in Omaha. He drove an ambulance that he called "a hospital on wheels." Ralph was responding to an emergency call when his ambulance was slammed broadside. He said he was T–boned. The inattentive driver behind the wheel was a young person wearing earbuds and listening to music; he never heard the siren. No amount of public service announcements about the dangers of distracted driving gets through to these people!

At one point, Ralph mentioned the Twin Towers and the 9/11 attacks that killed so many first responders. That told us that he'd been alive in 2001. The use of earbuds to listen to a playlist is relatively recent; that made us think that Ralph hadn't died so very long ago. But here's the best part: when we asked him how he'd learned that we needed a first responder to come to help Don, here's what he told us. "I'd been asleep, but my pager went off." Ralph, resting in peace after his own sudden, violent, traumatic death, awoke to his afterlife to take care of another guy who had died on the highway! His beeper woke him up!

Don listened to Ralph's story without comment. He told us he was ready to leave with Ralph.

"Ralph," we asked, "how will you know where to take Don?"

At that moment, Ralph told us, an ascending moving sidewalk, like an escalator, appeared. Some people at the top were gesturing for Ralph and Don to step aboard. They thanked us over their shoulders as the entire group moved away.

Remember, I've been helping these stuck souls for many years. This story fills me with joy. Heaven's creativity shouldn't surprise me. But this time it did.

As usual, Laura and I decided to check in with Don to make sure we had his permission to include his story in this book. This time I recorded our exchange.

When I felt Don's energy come into my body, the difference was striking. Whereas before, all I could feel was Don's incessant rage over the circumstances of his death, the "new" Don felt happy and peaceful.

Laura: Tell us what you'd like us to say in the book, Don.

Don: *I'm grateful to you because you helped get me, I think you say, "unstuck." That's as good a word as I can think of. For me, part of it was just anger in every direction and about everything and everybody. I just didn't think—I thought I was going to have a long life. I had all kinds of ideas about how I was going to spend it. Then it just all was over in a flash. My face was a gory mess. I do have a vague recall of somebody or a voice or a presence or something that was coming to try to help. Whoever it was said something like, "Let's not stay here. You come with us. We'll show you." Whatever. I just remember being so angry at the whole thing. I was angry at whoever came for me whoever it was. I just said, "Can you get the F— out of my face? I'm dead on a highway."*

Laura: You mean at first, or when Ralph came?

Don: *No, at first.*

Laura: At first?

Don: *I was just angry at everything. I don't think I could have a thought that wasn't angry. I don't think I could even—I couldn't get to a conclusion of a thought. I'd start thinking about a thing and be angry about the thing and didn't finish thinking anything. Then when the idea would be presented that somebody you love could come for you, I didn't want anybody I love to see me like this. It was a combination of my physical face gore, but part of it was just seeing me so angry. I didn't trust myself to be good company for anybody. Then somebody kept after me about getting more and more ready every day to rejoin the world and whatever. I guess that led to being in Father Nathan's dream and showing him how I died. I haven't thought of some of that for a while.*

*I sort of melted a little at the time, but one of the most resistant parts of me was about my face being all gory and nasty, kind of the way that people sometimes decide whether to have an open casket or a closed casket, or some people feel like you've got to come in and see the dead body for some sort of closure and whatever. I just—one of the last things that changed or melted in me was my face. That's why when I was getting close to being able to say, my last hold-out thing was, "Okay, okay, I'll go, but I'm not going with anybody except somebody that's used to seeing gory faces." They were okay with that, found me somebody, who turned out to be that—is it Joe?*

Laura: Ralph.

Don: *Ralph.*

Laura: Ralph came for you.

Don: *He was a nice guy. We didn't hang out anymore than you would hang out with an ambulance driver. Whatever, he did his job and helped me out, and I thanked him from my heart and went on with it.*

Laura: After that time and now, what is life for you like there?

Don: *It's like freshman year. I'm thinking freshman year at college. Yes, you did sign up, show up, meet new people, new routines, some stuff interesting, some of it more than others. Sometimes there'll be things that other people are usually excited about that you're mildly excited about. Other times it flips, and you get to be doing stuff that you never thought you'd do so well and crazy fun, but still not quite knowing. I'm enjoying my new circumstance, but not really sure where all this is heading. I don't feel like I need to be. Nobody's pushing me or telling me to hurry up and catch up with the group or anything like that. I'm content. I'm not angry about having died suddenly or young anymore.*

Laura: It's a real shift?

Don: *I'm done being angry, and I know exactly where that leads. I've already been there. No need to go back.*

Laura: Is there something that you're doing now that has been especially fun?

Don: *I feel like—you know how people look back at like, I don't know, senior year at high school or college years and say, "These are the best years of your life"? It's usually not people who are that age that are saying that. It's people that are older looking back, saying, "These are the best years of your life." I feel like I'm getting to live that period without the awkward insecurity of it. I'm not embarrassed about what I said or how I look or will anybody like me. I'm not insecure, but I get to have, I don't know, the advantages of life opening up before you and all kind of possibilities and no financial worries, like the good things of being a late adolescent young adult without the insecurity part with the self-consciousness. I was self-conscious about my face after the accident. Now that's all just gone away. I'm just this—sometimes I might even take on the form of a body that's like twenty.*

Laura: Do you just get to choose what you look like?

Don: *I can if I want. That's kind of cool because you can, I don't know, if you want, you can even primp. You can wear whatever you want. None of it costs money, so if you feel like it, you can—I did that sometimes. I can remember getting dressed for some Valentine's Dance or prom or something. You can get decked out and get your picture taken and all. Sometimes I do stuff like that just because it feels good to look good after so long of being a bloody mess. Sometimes I just like to look good. Weren't you guys talking a little while ago about time travel?*

Laura: Yes.

Don: *That's in the back in here. I'm in his head right now. There's an echo of that or a shadow of it or something. I've dabbled a little bit in that. Partly, I've been around some other guys who aren't afraid of being called anything by wanting to wear nice clothes. Sometimes guys can rag on each other and be cruel about just about anything. Nobody does that stuff here, which is really nice, but I've done a little bit of messing around with what would it have been like to get dressed up if you lived in this time or that time or that place. I don't know why I did that. It's just something to do and it occurred to me to do it.*

Laura: You were able to do that?

Don: *Yeah. The thing I like about it is for so long I've felt horrible about the way I looked, and now I can look like a Yankee Doodle Dandy if I want. I can have a powdered wig, or I can have a ruffled collar, or I can look like, I don't know, like a gangster in the Roaring Twenties, or I can look like whatever I want and play around almost like I was in a play with looking good in lots of different ways. I suppose I'll get tired of it after a while, but, for right now, it's just been a little aside, just a little amusement.*

Laura: Sounds like fun.

Don: *If you write anything about me, it's like I'm doing freshman year without the downside. Not having to prove yourself to anybody, not having to get drunk on the weekend to prove how manly you are or anything. You just hang out, learn things.*

Laura: It sounds like things are going well for you.

Don: *They're going great. Thanks for helping me get from here to there and there to here.*

Afterlife, *Interrupted*

Laura: You take care.

Don: *All right. I'll send the next one in.*

Laura: Thanks so much.

Nathan: Glory be to the Father, and to the Son, and to the Holy Spirit, as it was in the beginning, is now, and will be forever. Amen.

This story has stayed with me. Every time I tried to write about it, however, I felt I was forcing the narrative. So I went with my gut—which is sometimes the prompting of the Holy Spirit—and thought I'd try to talk with Don one last time before completing this chapter.

I was with my sister, Cathryn, who can facilitate speech and who is gifted in many other ways. She's very compassionate around dying persons and very connected to the holy ones in her own prayer life. Cathryn allowed Don to borrow her voice to facilitate the following conversation during a visit I had with her and her husband, Gui, in the Bahamas.

Nathan: All right. So, we pray in the name of the Father, the Son, and the Holy Spirit. I'm here with Cathryn and Gui in the Bahamas, and we're going to be inviting Don and possibly Ralph, the first responder. That's the chapter that I'm trying to write. I want to come back to the source, if the Holy Spirit allows it. I especially would like to speak with Don, because I didn't record the original conversation, and I didn't make any notes. I don't want to get his story wrong. Now that I'm trying to write the chapter, I'm kind of grasping a bit. So, it occurred to me maybe, Don, if you're available and would like to offer any kind of direction, maybe you could have some say. But let me first finish my prayers. I call on St. Michael the Archangel to protect us and guard us. I call upon Phillip James of the line of Michael, my own guardian, St. Dominic, Holy Mary, St. Thomas Aquinas, St. Benedict.

Cathryn: St. Rose of Lima.

Nathan: St. Rose of Lima. And all the holy ones. Especially any who would care about this particular conversation. Feel free to join us, and please keep us safe so that we can speak and understand each other clearly. Holy Spirit, help us to be in the flow of your grace and let us be of your service. Amen.

So, I don't know if I can call you friend, but I'd like to, Germaine Don. I know you prefer to be called Don. You're going to be in the book, and you've already spoken with us. At least with Laura and me, but now we'd like a little help. So, if you're available and would like to help, would you make yourself known? Either on this side of the room or over there. Cathryn could also bring you through. You could borrow either of our voices, mine or Cathryn's, my sister. [To Cathryn: Anything going on over there?]

Cathryn: There was a flutter.

Nathan: Don, if it's all the same to you, it would be easier for me if you came through Cathryn and then I could ask you a few questions. I wouldn't have to juggle you and me both in my head. Did we just interrupt you from doing something?

Don: *I haven't dressed up like a girl.*

Nathan: That's the first thing you want us to know? Well, there's a lot of times when you go back in history, and guys wear stuff that only girls would wear now. Sounds like you've done some of that already. The frilly collar, the powdered wig. You can do whatever you want.

Don: *Yes, sir. I have. The business of different times. I'm liking that. I heard you.*

Nathan: I'm remembering what you said to us not too long ago. Your face got so disfigured. It just felt good to look good again. You remembered how good it felt to get all dressed up for a big date and look your best, like for a prom.

Don: *Yes, sir. That is a good way to pass the time.*

Nathan: You even said that you wouldn't be doing that for all eternity. You're just kind of having a little fun with it for a while.

Don: *Yeah.*

Nathan: You keep touching Cathryn's face. You're still getting used to having an intact face, it looks like.

Don: *Just getting a sense of what that might be like. I don't want to hurt her or anything, but it's kind of nice.*

Nathan: She's a nice–looking woman. What are you now, Cathryn, 54? I'm trying to remember. I'm 62 and she's 54.

Don: *She has a sweet face.*

Nathan: Yeah. She's a sweet soul.

Don: *I'm going to leave that alone. But I was hearing you talking about inviting me. I'm going to say coax me, but it really didn't come so much from you, but just now, there was this brightness, and it's the same brightness as when I came to you the first time. It's not a light so much as it is this brightness.*

Nathan: Is it a prayer scene?

Don: *No, it's just someone saying, "You need to be awake to this now. You can't close your eyes to this. It's about awakeness. You've gotta be awake to this now. Something is happening. You have to be awake to this now." I felt at once drawn to the brightness and just ever so slightly pushed towards the brightness. That turned out to be the way that you came along, that I came to you.*

Nathan: The ever so slight push didn't feel like it was offensive to you, or bossy?

Don: *No. You know, it felt like somebody had my back.*

Nathan: Okay.

Don: *Somebody had my back, and it was gentle, not like somebody was going to shove me into traffic or anything.*

Nathan: Can you think of a time earlier in your life when you had a touch like that when maybe you were scared to do a thing, and somebody just gave you a kind of a loving nudge that wasn't forcing you but was maybe encouraging?

Don: *Yeah. You know how when you're really little and you still fit in a lap, whether it's a parent or grandparent or a grownup, you can just sort of—you're small enough to lean into them, and they can just put their arms down. I'm thinking about what it feels like to be a little child, four or five years old. Just sort of you're small enough that they've got the whole of you. They've got all of you, but it's not like they're going to hurt you with it. It's just a real feeling of safety. I felt as I went towards, closer to, the brightness, that's when I could hear. I couldn't see you talk to whoever that other lady was.*

Nathan: Laura? My friend?

Don: *Yeah. At first, I couldn't see you but I could hear you, and I knew that there were two people having a conversation. I don't think I'd heard a conversation since the accident. I think all I heard was the sound in my own head. The anger in my own head. When I went to try to have a conversation even out loud with myself, it just banged around in there. Anger.*

Nathan: An echo chamber of anger.

Don: *The echoes and angry echoes. For the first time, I felt like I was hearing something that wasn't the sound of me being angry.*

Nathan: Yeah, I get it.

Don: *So, I don't know if that gentle force from behind me was my guardian, as you say. I don't ever really—*

Nathan: That would be my guess. I'm just guessing.

Don: *I never thought about such a thing. I know I learned about angels and—*

Nathan: Did you meet your guardian?

Don: *I did. It's all in how you think. I wonder about my—and before you can finish your thought, there they are. You can't even ask for them before they're already there and before they seem to already give you a picture in your mind of the thing you want to think about. But when you have a question, the question almost gets answered before you can fully wonder it. That's been surprising. Everything happens not from a particular direction. With your guardians, they resonate out. They generate out and so I felt safe. I felt interested. Whatever it is that was going on with you and with that brightness, I felt interested. I don't think I've been very aware. And since the accident*

*I don't think I've been interested in anything until I heard you. So, I don't know if that answers your question.*

Nathan: That's helpful. What do you recall about the first time we met, Don? Sometimes, when I'm first encountering somebody after they've come to me in a dream, because I didn't know them, when I pray about them, I'm just waiting to see who shows up. It depends how well I got the dream or its level of detail. Yours at least had the detail about the crane and the highway, and there were some pictures in it. Sometimes it's just much shorter, but yours had some pictures. So, when we went to pray for you, I thought that in the dream I was a man, and I thought I was in the back passenger seat of the car. I thought that I was in congested traffic that was almost stopped on a freeway. I wondered if I was either in Charlotte or Atlanta. It felt like a southern city that was growing too fast for the roads to keep up. Were you in either one of those?

Don: *It was just outside of Savannah.*

Nathan: Savannah. All right. Okay. Well, for whatever reason, it felt like a southern city, and it felt like a place that was trying to keep up with the growth that it was undergoing, and the roads were having a little trouble doing that. I grew up around Houston and Houston's roads have been like that my whole life.

Don: *Someplace where you were earlier.*

Nathan: Today?

Don: *Today.*

Nathan: We were walking on the beach.

Don: *Savannah used to look like that a long, long, long, long time ago.*

Nathan: Oh, the pine trees?

Don: *Just like that, but now everything's concrete.*

Nathan: We're in the Bahamas today. I've never been here before, but it's not very far from the Florida and Georgia coasts. Did you ever go there? It's not very far from Savannah. To fly here from Miami was twenty minutes. So, you could get from Savannah to here in a short hop. It looks kind of like the U.S. shoreline. I once lived in South Carolina, and it reminded me a little of here. I was surprised because I thought of the Bahamas being more like Puerto Rico or somewhere else in the Caribbean, but it really looks a whole lot like the coastline of the southeastern U.S. Don, do you remember back to when you came to me the first time? All the people that I've dealt with this way have been through something traumatic and tragic, like you. So, I'm always dealing with people that are frightened because they've just been through something awful. Sometimes that little push, that little nudge that got them in my direction, they're already about as out there as they want to be. They get near me, but then they get scared. They get in my company and then they don't talk. They clam up. So, sometimes their guardian does what I call a mic–test. Did you ever see somebody go up to a microphone and say, "Is this thing on? Can you hear me?" All they're doing is testing to see if the sound is coming through. They're not really saying anything important. Sometimes the guardian will be the first to borrow the voice just to do a mic–test. They're not there to deliver a message or anything. They're just trying to model it for the one that's too scared. I can't remember if that happened with you or not. Do you remember? Or did you just start talking?

Don: *Like I said, I just remember hearing something that wasn't me being angry.*

Nathan: Yeah, I get it.

Don: *I was hearing something. It's like hearing something that came from outside of me.*

Nathan: Which felt good because you had nothing but your own thoughts.

Don: *You're right about that.*

Nathan: You being angry.

Don: *I just don't recall.*

Nathan: I read back over the notes of the last time that I talked to you, and you said in the end that there were two reasons why you didn't want anybody that you knew or loved to see you. One was because you thought your face was all a bloody mess, but the other one was that you were so angry that you didn't want anybody to see you like that either. They were both about equally ugly: your anger and your bloodied face. I thought that was well put.

Don: *Yeah. I should not say it like this, but I sort of liked the way I looked before the accident. I thought I was turned out all right.*

Nathan: Were you a man that took careful attention to what he looked like when he left the house?

Don: *You know what? I thought that was important. I was raised that good grooming is you looking the part.*

Nathan: Yeah.

Don: *You look the part.*

Nathan: I'm sort of like that, too. I don't like walking around looking crummy.

Don: *You gotta look the part. She's seeing what I look like. It's funny because she didn't mean to think it, but she thought it and then—*

Nathan: You mean, in her imagination right now, Cathryn's seeing what you look like?

Don: *Yeah. We're on the same page so to speak. She thinks she's seeing my tattoo.*

Nathan: A tattoo?

Don: *It's not a tattoo. It's a brand. It's the only shameful thing I've ever done to my body.*

Nathan: You showed it to her. She wouldn't have seen it if you hadn't wanted her to see it.

Don: *I know, but it was a college foolishness and I shouldn't have done it, and I brought shame to my family because they didn't send me to school to get branded like a slave.*

Nathan: Were you a black guy?

Don: *Yes, sir.*

Nathan: I thought so, but I wasn't sure. It was really your first name, Germaine. A white person could be named that. I just didn't know any white person with that name.

Don: *Well, this is the same thought that my mama had: why would you go and do such a thing? I hadn't felt—I'm remembering what it felt like to feel shame.*

Nathan: When did you feel the shame?

Don: *Just now. I remember when I showed myself to this woman right here and she thought to herself, "Why in the world would you have done such a thing to yourself?" I remember it's almost exactly the thing my mom said. "We didn't send you to school so that you could get branded like a slave. Why in the world would you do that? Why would you let someone do that to you?"*

Nathan: Do you have any residue with that? Do you need to forgive yourself or are you okay that you just did a stupid thing when you were in college?

Don: *No, it's fine, but I was hearing you talk about the things that I said about not being judged. That's important.*

Nathan: It is.

Don: *Because here now, nobody's shaking their head saying, "Why would you do you do such a thing?" They just see that you did such a thing, and they don't kick up anything about it. They just—*

Nathan: Do you think it could be erased if you wanted it to be?

Don: *Folks just meet you where you are. I don't even need to erase it because—*

Nathan: It doesn't matter.

Don: *It doesn't matter.*

Nathan: All right, good.

Don: *It doesn't matter, and that part of me is not real anymore.*

Nathan: I once knew some women that were pimped, and they were branded with gang tattoos. Then they did jail time and came out and were going through programs and healing and stuff. They had brands on their fingers. I didn't know that, but their pimps would tattoo the girls' fingers because you could always see them. Fingers don't get covered up by clothes. It was a way of showing that this person belonged to someone specific. They were kind of enslaved because they were under somebody's thumb. In that program, they did get their tats removed at a certain time. They had a ceremony to celebrate it, that they were getting rid of the memory of that.

Don: *This is just a memory. I don't feel those emotions anymore because there's so much more to do.*

Nathan: Well, that's good.

Don: *There's just so much more to do.*

Nathan: I think that's one of the ways that healing kind of happens in life. You don't go back and relive, spend the second half of your life reliving the first, digging through the debris. New and beautiful things happen and some of the ugliness can just sort of fade away. You know how leaves, when they fall, if you leave them alone, they just disintegrate and they just become fertilizer. New things grow. You don't have to rake them or burn them or anything. Just leave them alone and—

Don: *They just take care of themselves.*

Nathan: Yeah.

Don: *So, it's like that around here. So, I don't know if that helps you.*

Nathan: That might be all I really needed. I just wanted to kind of fill in some gaps. It's your chapter anyway, and I wanted you to have a chance to say a word or two. This book thing is beginning to be—it's moving. I've been trying all along to not just write a little book that nobody knows about. I think it's an important topic, don't you?

Don: *I do. I do. I certainly wish you all the great success.*

Nathan: Well, I'd ask you all to pray for it. Do you do that?

Don: *I do. I do. I'd be honored.*

Nathan: Well, before I go to sleep tonight, and I'm on my way to bed soon, I thought before I go to sleep there are about twelve of you that I've chosen your stories for the book, and I'm going to call a meeting if you're available.

Don: *Is that right?*

Nathan: Well, I just thought it'd be fun. I just thought, I'm going to call a meeting. I'd say to all of you, if you're not too busy—I don't know if you live in rooms, but maybe you could meet in one spot, and I'd introduce you to one another or at least have you introduce yourselves to each other. Then I'd ask you to pray for me. At least then you'd know you're praying for the same guy. Not just one person, because my sister is helping you right now, and I've got other helpers like Laura, who helped you the last time. We're our own little team, but I'd like to at least ask you all together. One of the women who is in the group died in that big tsunami. I don't know if you were still alive on earth then. There was this huge earthquake in the Indian Ocean, and it killed 250,000 people. I don't know if you were still around at that point, but, anyway, one of them is a little girl from Sri Lanka, next to India. So, you'd be meeting people from all over, but I guess you've been doing that for some time now.

Don: *Fair amount. Fair amount. Yes, sir.*

Nathan: So, anyway. That's all I gotta say. I'm going to invite you all together in prayer and ask for whatever help you guys can give to advance this project from your vantage point. You kind of have the view from the Goodyear Blimp. You can see things I can't see, and maybe there're ways that you can give a nudge like the nudge you got. Maybe there's a point at which your prayer nudges somebody to help us.

Don: *Wouldn't that be something?*

Nathan: Wouldn't it be fun? One of the people I was talking to was this other guy from Georgia. He was a lawyer. He was an old country judge lawyer. He drove his car into a river and died. He was almost senile and his daughter tried to get the car keys, but he wouldn't give them away. Poor guy. He thought he was driving onto a bridge, but it was a boat launch. He drove his car into a boat launch and drowned. So, the poor guy fretted about that for a long while before he got moving. He's done what you did. He kind of stayed stuck for a little while, and then he got over it and went on with it. But he was a churchman, and he's a real sweet soul. You'll meet him. His name, I think, is Shelby [See Chapter Seven]. He reminds me of Colonel Sanders. One thing you and Shelby would have in common is how well dressed you are.

Don: *Well, there you go.*

Nathan: One of the things that bugged him is he drove and landed his car in the bottom of this nasty sluggish river, and so his body ended up with all this river muck and silt. He knew the first responder who had to pull him out and take his clothes off. He was just so appalled to be seen that way. He was naked and so covered with nastiness. Anyway, he had to kind of get over that, the way you had to kind of get over your face.

Don: *We just need to clean ourselves back up again.*

Nathan: Well, you just do it, I guess, one step at a time. I'm not going to keep you any longer, Don, because you've already helped us. Just get ready to be called to a meeting.

Don: *Okay.*

Nathan: All right?

Don left Cathryn.

Cathryn: He's saying, "Tell him that I said thank you."

Nathan: Okay. God bless you. Thanks for being here. Glory be to the Father, and to the Son, and to the Holy Spirit, as it was in the beginning, is now, and will be forever. Amen.

Being caught in a trauma-loop, like the kind that happened with Don, can happen before or after death. Sometimes the person who relives a traumatic experience over and over again has little or no control over these negative thoughts and emotions. Sometimes the scene's violent elements seem so vivid, it doesn't even feel like a past event. A horrific moment becomes the incessant Now. Some post–traumatic–stress sufferers dread bedtime because painful thoughts they can chase away in the daytime assault them in sleep and become recurring nightmares. It takes skilled help to move past this.

Please remember, most who die traumatic deaths pass swiftly into the afterlife. Only a few get stuck. I work with the stuck ones, but even then, only after they've had some opportunity for healing. When those overseeing their afterlife care deem them ready, they show up in my world.

With that said, I've experienced more than one kind of trauma–looping. The first is simply reliving the physical event. I've dealt with war veterans still alive on this plane who have torturous recall of killing an opponent in war, or of being unable to save a mortally wounded comrade. Sometimes these traumatic scenes involve innocent children. These are heartbreaking and very life disturbing. There are many clinicians and healing practitioners who try to intervene to help such folks find relief. I do some of this work with "healing of memories," as I understand it in the Catholic Christian tradition. The Catholic sacraments of healing, reconciliation, and anointing of the sick can be beneficial here. Even then, these may be most advantageous when offered alongside other psychological and psychiatric remedies.

I've met some who have died violently and, in their stuckness, relive that moment, or some aspect of it, long after the event. Sometimes it is the looping recall of the physical event that caused their death. Other times there is a painful looping response to the event. It might be anger, even rage, at someone who intended their death or whose perceived incompetence prompted it. Sometimes they're unable to forgive themselves and perceive a need to punish themselves for a careless or foolish act that preceded and brought about their death. Yet other times people have some preconceived idea about how their embodied life ought to end, only to be shocked and angered at the abrupt way in which it actually did. Some insist that their death must "make sense." Many life events don't make sense; they merely happen. For some, their "senseless" death leaves them stuck. At some point, they come to realize that, if they wish to move on, that particular thought may have to be surrendered.

Whether on this side of the grave or the other, looping thoughts about a past traumatic event are still past events. Dwelling on them, involuntarily or voluntarily, robs the person of the appreciation of other possible presents and futures. Even in the first part of the afterlife, where I meet my night visitors, it's still necessary to awaken to the present moment and live it as best one can. That will require help. But I've found, for my little population, that the help will be there. A simple willingness to take a first step out of that loop is met with generous help that sets people on a new and no–longer–looping path.

I made a passing comment about time travel in this chapter. My prayer partner and I had been talking about it shortly before engaging Don. When he entered my consciousness to borrow my voice, he was aware of the remnants of that conversation. I've had that happen before. It reminds me of how cooking smells can linger in a kitchen or dining room. Simply entering the space can make one aware of something that was here recently, but no longer.

I was taught in first grade that heaven would be that place where God would provide everything you'd need to be completely happy. If that's true, and I think it is, for me, I'd like to travel back in time. I don't want others to simply tell me about scenes from their lives. I'd like them to show me those scenes. I'd like to go back and see the beginnings of things. I'd like to see aspects of my parents' childhoods—they were thirty-five when I was born. Much of what shaped them happened long before I was ever around.

I've always loved history and biography. I like seeing the long story arc of who people were and how they became who they are now. To do healing of memories and much pastoral counseling, it's necessary to revisit the past. I think it would be cool, not just to mentally attempt to reconstruct the past, but to go walking around in it. This has formed the plot of many books and movies. I haven't experienced that with my night visitors, but the universe is so vast and creative. Maybe we really can revisit the past.

Will I be disappointed if heaven doesn't include time travel? Just so you know, I can be a little perfectionistic at times. A spiritual director once said to me, "Nathan, when you get to heaven, you're going to want to improve it." I remember those words from decades ago because they rang so true. Still, I'm sure God has done a fine job creating heaven without my help. But if it doesn't include time travel, maybe I'll suggest it.

It does seem that people are able to choose their age and physical appearance in the afterlife, as Don and Cheryl Lynn in the previous chapter did. In fact, I think it's commonplace. For those whose bodies were damaged or broken here, they can be whole again hereafter. Many night visitors are greeted by older relatives, especially grandparents. They don't have to show up appearing as they did upon their deaths. Sometimes they choose to appear as they did decades earlier in their wedding pictures. I knew of one person who felt she'd missed out on her own childhood because of domestic violence. She manifested as the child she hadn't fully gotten to be. In an upcoming chapter, you'll meet Eric. When young Eric asked for Einstein to come for him, he didn't get the old genius with the shocking white hair. He got the cool, tweedy young professor who could be Eric's mentor. I think that's one of the first things that happens for most folks as they breathe their last and leave the physical body. They have to have some kind of form. Taking on some healthier earlier version of their appearance is pretty common.

About a year after my dad's death at the age of seventy-six, we got to have a little visit. He'd been told by St. Dominic that he has working too hard and needed to relax. This rang true. Dad grew up hungry during the Depression and worked from dawn to dusk. He would fill his leisure time with arduous activities. He took that habit with him into the next life. But they called him on it and insisted that he relax. He said to me, "Son, I don't have the first idea how to do that." They insisted, though, and wouldn't take no for an answer. Eventually he recalled that at nineteen he'd gone out to sea as a merchant seaman. He said something like this: "At first I thought I just needed a job, a cot, food and shelter. But it was more than that. I hadn't met your mother yet and didn't have all you [five] kids. It was just me out in the world having an adventure. Right now, I'm just traveling around looking for things to show your mother when she passes. So I've decided to be nineteen for now. I'm my skinny-me."

Remember how twelve-year-old Rani wanted to be treated as though she were older at the time of her death? Now she presents herself as the twenty-year-old she didn't live long enough to be here. Don might be doing the opposite. He died at twenty-seven, but describes his present way of being as similar to freshman orientation in college. He may have circled back a few years to experience himself as a younger adult no long afraid of the negative judgment of others. He made several comments about not being thought manly enough in his life; now he seemed to be enjoying the freedom of being himself without unnecessary critique. I've certainly seen that again and again. Freedom from unnecessary and unkind judgment is one of the most common experiences I've seen reported.

One of the earliest things I was taught that is found all through the Bible is this: "Judge not, lest you be judged." I've always known better, but judging others is just so commonplace. It really is in the air we breathe. I'm older now, and have been judgmental of others in lots of different ways. I still can be, even now. It's just not as fun or as interesting as it once was.

I've been a pastor for much of my adult life. That word means "shepherd." It's your job to gather the herd and keep them together. But once they're together they can be so unkind to each other, or to those they think ought not be allowed into the flock. They can judge each other over everything under the sun. Pastoring or parenting more than one child, I suppose, involves a fair amount of refereeing. Once, some unnamed guy approached Jesus and used the occasion to gripe about his brother. He wanted Jesus to settle some petty sibling dispute. Imagine that! You have a one-on-one opportunity for private conversation with Jesus, and you reduce it to that! Jesus said to him, "Who has made me your judge?" I've heard so many of my night visitors relish the joy and freedom of living their new lives free of the unkind thoughts, words and actions of others that I know it has changed me.

One more thing: my night visitors' lives were abruptly interrupted. They are therefore obviously incomplete in their current state, but they are so delightful to get to know. They are not much different from everyone I'll meet today. They've just died, that's all. They still have stories to tell and decisions to make like everybody else.

My night visitors' joy at living in a judgment-free environment has made me want to live out the words of The Lord's Prayer I've prayed thousands of times. If I really want "*thy kingdom*" to come "*on earth as it is in heaven*," I can try to stop judging people and just be more patient with them. Maybe once in a while I have to object to something someone says or does, but I don't need to make a habit of it.

## Chapter Seven
# Shelby, The Retired Country Lawyer

I received this dream very early, when these experiences were still new to me. I failed to write it down at the time, but it has stayed with me vividly over the years. Here is my recreation of it:

*I was in the driver's seat of a large, heavy sedan, maybe from the late seventies. It might have been a Lincoln or a Cadillac. We used to call these "land yachts." I was driving on familiar streets in the downtown of a small Southern town, possibly in Georgia. A river meandered through the central business district. I made a left turn onto a small side street. All at once, I was driving down a staircase and into a river! Its current turned the car sharply to the left; it began to sink. I continued to turn the steering wheel, but the car slowly sank below the water line. I awoke.*

In the early days of my ministry to the night visitors, many of those who sought my help were from the southeastern United States. This one seemed to fit that pattern. Behind the wheel of this vehicle I felt like "Mister Magoo," the comically near-sighted cartoon character from my childhood who was forever courting disaster by stubbornly refusing to acknowledge his poor vision. In the opening credits, Mr. Magoo drives his Model T onto train tracks, through haystacks and pigpens, into fire hydrants, onto rollercoasters, and into high voltage wires, miraculously without loss of life or limb. Whenever he drove his Model T through the streets of his hometown, mothers pushing baby carriages would scurry out of his way as he careened onto the sidewalk. Again, Mr. Magoo never seemed to come to harm, nor did anyone in his path.

Obviously, for the guy in my dream things didn't turn out so well. When my prayer partner and I first went into prayer to help him get unstuck, we learned that he'd died as a result of driving under the effects of dementia. What appeared in the dream as a staircase was in fact the ridges in the cement of a boat launch. This poor fellow's "land yacht" didn't float.

Separation of this man's consciousness from his body brought an immediate end to his dementia but ushered in the painful realization of what he had just done. We learned that he'd been widowed after a long marriage. His daughter was trying to get him to surrender the car keys because of his increasing mental lapses. He'd have none of it.

He became a stuck soul because of embarrassment and loss of reputation. Instead of being remembered for a lifetime of service to his community, this man believed he'd died an old fool. Surely, he was harder on himself than anyone who knew and loved him would be. Nevertheless, he isolated himself. When he came to us, we tried to help him come to peace with what had happened and look to a brighter future.

You'd think that, in these encounters, we'd learn the person's name right away. That's often true. This time it wasn't. If I had ever learned his name, I couldn't recall it. I'd refer to him as either "The Old Southern Lawyer" or "Colonel Sanders," because his grooming and upright bearing reminded me of the fried chicken icon. Even as many more night visitors passed through my life and the lives of my prayer partners, this man stayed in my heart. If you've ever loved someone with dementia, perhaps you can understand. My dad suffered that long, slow decline before his death. Watching a dignified person suffer the indignities of such a passage can break your heart.

Still, the most beautiful part of this ministry is seeing human resilience on display. My old lawyer friend's death came in the worst possible way. But it wasn't the end of his story. I knew I wanted to include it in this book, but I'd need more than just his permission. I'd need him to remind me how he'd gotten unstuck. I couldn't even remember who came for him. Sometimes I have my own mental blank spots—I won't call them "senior moments" because I had some of those long before I qualified for any senior discounts.

As has been the case in most of the conversations where we sought permission to tell a person's story, Laura and I got much more than we asked for. We said our protective prayers and asked if we could speak with our lawyer friend. I'd like you to meet my afterlife friend, Shelby. You'll see that he's very well spoken.

Nathan: The Old Southern Lawyer, my old friend. I started calling you Colonel Sanders because you looked so distinguished. Not sure of your name. Is it Shelby?
Laura: We thought we'd heard Shelby the last time we talked a while ago. You know who you are, so if you're here, we'd love to hear from you again.
Nathan: Yours is one of my favorite stories of more than two hundred fifty of these. I hope we get to be friends.
Shelby: *I'm Shelby. Yes, when I left here, I was an old man, who mostly looked back,*

Afterlife, *Interrupted*

*enjoyed the company of old friends, hung out at a café near the courthouse, had very little to do. Thought a great deal of himself and his reputation and who was not sufficiently aware of the fact that he was losing his skills and his mind, which was his demise. I'm sure it wouldn't surprise you to learn that I am not old anymore. Does anyone want to enter the afterlife and be old? At least I didn't want that. I had enough of moving slowly and thinking slowly and having mostly past-tense conversations.*

*After I went through the—after you helped me move along, I did of course have to get over the—would you call it shame? Something like that about the way I died, ashamed of doing as I did, driving my own car into a river. You tell the story well of me being fastidious in my appearance and being disgusted with the river muck covering me inside and out, having to be removed from my clothes by people who knew me and see my wrinkled old body covered in river muck. That bothered me a great deal and that the conversation at my funeral was, "He was such a fine old man, who came to such a foolish end." That really bothered me. Maybe the dumbest thing of all was saying no to a very intelligent daughter, who was only trying to love her father by suggesting it was time to surrender the car keys, and then having a fatal accident, only to prove her right.*

Laura: How are things for you now?

Shelby: *Much better than that.*

Laura: Are there things you're enjoying in this new life?

Shelby: *Late in my life, I felt like one of my greatest treasures was my reputation, that I had plaudits and credits, and it was not fraudulent. I really did set out to lead a distinguished life, and I did so, but still a great deal of it put too much importance on what others thought of me. I kind of knew that in the back of my mind. Nobody would tell me so. It would be too rude. But as I've moved into the next way here, it's likely I'll have to leave behind a lot of that. The image comes to mind of when it comes time to leave a house, move to a new place. It becomes obvious that something that was once a treasured possession is now excess baggage. It's funny because I didn't even do this. I still lived in the house that my wife and I built, but I know that situation where people have to fit everything into the back of the truck or whatever, and you're standing there. I had to do it when I closed my office. There were all the trinkets accumulated in a life as a lawyer that now went into a box, a series of boxes. They couldn't all be displayed. It would have looked ridiculous. There were a few things that came into my home office, and then the rest of them went into the basement. It's sort of like that. You leave behind so many things because they'd be ridiculous here. The most ridiculous for me was this exalted notion that I have of the importance of reputation.*

Laura: That was a big one, wasn't it?

Shelby: *It was for me. Somehow that became outsized in my imagination. In fact, I'm well reputed here, and so is everyone else. None of us needs to wear our medals. We all look beautiful. That's without the fussiness that I approached the beginning of the day with, my boudoir. I had my fussy routines and my—even when it came time to buy my toiletries, they all had to be just the right brand and all that. That's all gone away. I don't need to be adorned.*

Laura: So everyone where you are is valued and loved for who they are?

Shelby: *And there's a delight in—I'm seeing something inside him—you were nearly present to this. Last evening before dinner, the television was on, and Father Nathan saw this story. There was a report of a young Down Syndrome teen on a basketball team in Nebraska, I think. He perfected standing with his back to a basketball backboard, heaving the ball over his head from half-court and sinking the ball. He did that, there was a video of him doing that, at a high school game, and it went onto the Internet and became a sensation and caught the attention of the Harlem Globetrotters. They got one of these Globetrotter players to come to this small school in Nebraska. I'm sorry to be laboring. I'm trying to pull it all out from inside him* [Shelby's referring to his efforts to pull something from my, Nathan's, memory.]. *It was a school assembly with cameras going, television cameras. The Globetrotter man said, "Do it again," and the young man did it again. Of course, the place was raucous with applause and joy. The reason I tell this long story slowly is things like that happen here all the time, where you see overlooked persons or people who had no pretensions of importance have to learn that they are quite remarkable. Some of them who might be characterologically* [Shelby's word, but I like it] *disposed to self-abasement have to unlearn that the way I had to unlearn my concern about reputation. Some who have always sought the shadows, more out of humiliation than humility, you watch them do their learning. They have to step into the light and let the rest of us see them shine. It might be that because this was what held me back, this is what I needed to learn, so I've been exposed more to this than other ideas of living, I guess. I think I have had to spend—I don't know that I chose it. I think someone simply guided me in this way that this was an initial lesson I needed to learn so that I could go on to other things.*

Laura: It sounds as though you have learned that.

Shelby: *I think so.*

Please allow me, Nathan, to insert an observation here. Shelby's issue wasn't the need to repent of a sin. He had simply let something virtuous—behaving uprightly so as to be an exemplar to others—become overdone into a vice. I'm reminded of St. Therese of Lisieux. She was a cloistered nun who lived to be only twenty-four. She was a mystic who was ordered, under the vow of obedience, to keep a journal. She prayed in the cloister garden and noticed that an untended garden could get overgrown, not with weeds, but with some valued plant. Something beautiful could run riot in the garden, soaking up all the water and sunshine, crowding out all the other flowers. Before long, the garden is no longer beautiful because one plant dominates over everything around it. She taught that virtues must be cultivated, even pruned, to keep within their proper place in the garden.

I think that became Shelby's issue. Propriety, uprightness and, most of all reputation, became far too important to him. The death that seemed so disgraceful and embarrassing to him threw him completely out of gear. Upon his death, the poor man was mortified. He just wanted to crawl in a hole and die—but he was already dead. How does one do that in the afterlife? Shelby found a way. Thankfully, he was eventually persuaded to seek a way out.

Laura: Are there other things in sight for you, things that you would like to explore?
Shelby: *Those are two questions. I'm going to be the lawyer who separates out the language. The first part again please.*
Laura: Are there...
Shelby: *Are there new things?*
Laura: …new things on the horizon for you?
Shelby: *I have to say that I didn't even see the horizon in this one. I didn't choose this precisely. I was guided toward it, so I might be guided to something else, but I wouldn't be able to tell you yet what it is. That's a possibility. Another would be the second part of your question, which presumed that I was the free agent picking the new thing. And that's a possibility, too. If I were, that's not right now. That's not my present moment. I'm not standing about choosing my next engagement. I simply seem to be in this place where watching people come into the light, being part of—I feel like I've kind of already done what I needed to do, but I'm here to support or applaud, encourage others.*

*I think you're onto something. It might be that I'm near the end of this and near the beginning of the next thing, but I don't know the next thing yet. In earthly life, for example, there might have been moments when you knew that you were about to conclude one thing and to begin another. But then there were also moments when you didn't know that the next thing that was about to happen was you were going to meet your spouse. That wasn't part of any plan, at least not one that you were aware of. Something just emerged that began to send everything in another direction.*

*I'm not sure which it will be. Will it be that somebody leads me to a next thing? Will I pick a next thing, or will a next thing simply emerge that will later be proven important? I just know that, somehow, I'm on the cusp of a next thing.*
Laura: Yes. It sounds as though you're just fine with that.
Shelby: *I am. One thing I'm enjoying very much is the sense of ease with which life can*

*just be enjoyed in the moment. In my old age, I got a taste of that because I did have the leisure to hang around the courthouse, but, mostly, it was backward thinking. It was retrospective. Even though we might have talked a little bit about events of the day, by the time you got to the age that I was, the events of the day really feel like the events of somebody else's day. The city council is talking about building a bridge that'll be built five years from now. You reach a point where even whatever it is that people are planning, you feel like you're really not fully on board for it because it's probably going to take longer than you're going to be here anyway. That's just all gone away. I'm part of whatever I want to be.*

Laura: Yes.

Shelby: *I'm talking a great deal.*

Laura: You're a lawyer.

Shelby: *Yeah, well, people did pay me to speak, but they also paid me to listen. I don't know what will be next. I just know that something is about to be next. Let me help you with the book somehow. What can I do to help you with the book?*

Laura: If you are able to share with Father Nathan any thoughts about how you came to him in the beginning. You were one of the earlier ones for him. At that time, he wasn't keeping a lot of notes. Writing a book about these experiences wasn't even a thought at the time. He remembers the initial dream very vividly. Some of the rest has grown fuzzier over time.

Shelby: *He can't remember who came for me. Remember?*

Laura: Oh, yes. Who did come for you?

Shelby: *You would think I would have that at the ready because I brought it up, but—*

Laura: It doesn't have to be a name.

Shelby: *Let me—*

Laura: A category of person.

Shelby: *I don't know why, but there're some tumblers at the vault that need to fall into place. Hang on. Let me go quiet for a bit. I don't think it's in his memory to begin with, or it might be and he just doesn't know where it is.*

It's Nathan again with another aside. Allowing someone to speak through me involves some kind of connectivity on both of our parts. There are times when it isn't strong enough, and we have to pause to do something that feels mechanical. It can be like getting a stronger signal by walking outside with your cellphone. Sometimes it's like carefully tuning the radio dial. In this case, Shelby thought of aligning the tumblers of a locked vault in order to open it.

Afterlife, *Interrupted*

Shelby: *I have it. It was a colleague.*

Laura: A colleague?

Shelby: *Yes. It was—*

Laura: Someone from your hometown?

Shelby: *He was from my church.*

Laura: Oh, from the church.

Shelby: *He had passed a few years earlier. It's funny. The reason he was in my imagination is because I'd thought of him as upstanding and respectable and all the things that I'd thought were so important, having a fine reputation and for whatever reason that made me most comfortable for him to come for me. Walt was his name.*

Laura: Walt?

Shelby: *Walt. He just seemed like, if anybody belonged in heaven, it would be Walt. He just led an exemplary life. If it worked that way that God let in the ones that kept the rules and were exemplary—he wasn't a kind of persnickety rule keeper, but he was just a guy that led an upright kind of life. For whatever reason, somebody knew that that would make me very comfortable. It was very proper or right that Walt would be the emissary that would come and say, "Let me take you from here." He was only a few years older than I was, but I always admired him.*

Laura: If we could return for a moment to your previous question, which was how might you help with this book in progress, is there anything that you can suggest to Nathan about how to speak of it to different audiences to find just the right publisher that could bring it forward?

Shelby: *I don't know what we can do. He has asked us. One of your prior persons, I think the one you were speaking to right before me. Was it the young man Eric? [See Chapter Fourteen.]*

Laura: Yes, Eric.

Shelby: *Eric mentioned that we've all been collectively addressed as a group to pray for Father Nathan according to whatever that means to us and to try to affect an outcome, like as members of a legal team. Let's all get together; the outcome we want is for this person to be found innocent or guilty depending upon where we are in the process. Father Nathan wants us to scan about and figure out whatever we can or can't do to somehow be influencers. Can you help somebody from here? Can you help somebody pick this one and not that one? Can you let this emerge to float to the top of someone's consciousness or awareness? Have a beam of light land on this manuscript in the pile? In my career there were a lot of exigencies where, had it not been for this one detail being discovered, the case would have gone a different way. I think that's what he's asking. If you can see anything, if there's anything that you can do that's in right order that sets a chain of events in motion such that this book gets written, published by the right publisher, and gets to a large audience, could you help with that?*

Laura: Yes, that's the basic question.

Shelby: *He's asked us. I am still exploring how that might work, but I was a man who prayed, so I'm praying the way I know how, which is just to be in God's hands and say, "God, please bless this man and his attempt to serve you." I know from experience that this is a holy work. I want to help him be unconcerned about accusations that perhaps it's not holy, because it is. I think I have an affinity for one piece of the large picture in holding him in prayer around the question of will he be sanctioned or punished from the church world? I was on church boards sometimes and saw how petty believing people can be. I have something of a résumé in that area, and I would like to spare him any pain that he can be spared.*

Laura: That was very helpful. We're very grateful for your support, however it turns out.

Shelby: *I think you should show me to the door so that the next person can have their say.*

Laura: Thank you so much for coming back.

Shelby: *It's delightful to be with you. You're both people that I would like to know better and deeper.*

Laura: I hope we will have that opportunity.

Shelby: *Let's make it a point.*

Laura: God bless you.

Shelby: *Right back at you. That just flew out. I've never said that. That's his phrase.*

Laura: Thank you.

(Shelby departs.)

Nathan: Glory be to the Father, and to the Son, and to the Holy Spirit, as it was in the beginning, is now, and will be forever. Amen.

He's fun. His mind works in very categorical ways.

Laura: Yeah, I could see that very much.

Nathan: He's speaking and thinking into the next category. He's clear that something new is coming to him.

Laura: Yes, clarity was important to him.

Can you see why I love Shelby? He wants to have my back. He didn't viciously slam church people; he just knew they can be harsh sometimes. "Petty," he called it. He and I also follow Jesus, the crucified one. Jesus warned us many times in the gospel stories that following Him could cause us big trouble. Jesus was betrayed by a friend. Many of Jesus's closest followers died violent deaths for associating themselves with him. I don't think that's likely in my case, but this book could get me into church trouble. But not if Shelby has anything to say about it. I've got afterlife legal counsel. By the way, a Greek New Testament word for Holy Spirit is Paraclete, which means "defense attorney."

I want to share with you portions of a letter I wrote my provincial superior as I was preparing this book. When I took my vows, those included a vow of obedience. I want to be obedient to my superiors; I also want to be obedient to God's call for me. I've sought my church's support for this book and at least a bit of protection from those who might accuse me of doing something unholy. In it I reference lyrics from a song:

> *Because of you*
> *I never stray too far from the sidewalk.*
> *Because of you*
> *I learned to play on the safe side so I don't get hurt.*

Is there a song that always gets your attention? It doesn't matter where I am or what I'm doing. If I hear Kelly Clarkson's "Because of You," I listen hard. I focus. I turn up the volume. The power of it vibrates through me and almost hits the bull's-eye, the place too near the center of my heart. The place where I am afraid.

> How can I move forward? *Don't stray too far from the sidewalk.*
> How can I go about my work? *Play on the safe side so I don't get hurt.*
> How can I trust not only me, but everyone around me? *I can't.*
> *If I'm afraid.*

May I share with you a story that's probably already familiar to you, at least a little? It's a story Jesus told. He is my friend. I think it's one of his best stories.

This guy is walking down a road. It's a dangerous place, the kind of scary road where it's best to keep your head down, eyes straight ahead and don't stop for anything or anyone.

There's someone ahead and off to one side in the ditch, someone whom life has beaten and bloodied and left for dead.

The guy doesn't stray at all from the sidewalk. He plays it on the safe side and keeps walking. This guy is a priest.

A second guy comes walking down the same road like characters do in stories. We know already that it's dangerous and scary. We know what playing it safe means: keep your head down, eyes straight ahead and definitely no stopping to see about the bleeding guy in the ditch. Stay on the safe side so you don't get hurt. This guy is a priest, too.

Then a third guy comes down the road. He does what we'd all do if we weren't afraid. He stops to help even if it is dangerous and scary. He turns his head toward and focuses his eyes straight into the suffering of the traumatized person right in front of him. He has healing oil and wine with him. He anoints, pours, and bandages. He gets the bleeding guy to a safe place where he can heal. Only then does the guy go on his way. This guy isn't a priest. He just behaves like one.

In Jesus' story he doesn't say the two priests who stay on the sidewalk are bad guys. His first-century listeners knew that there were rules about priests not coming into contact with blood and corpses. It would make them unclean. Then they couldn't perform their priestly rituals. They were just following the rules.

Many of Jesus' listeners liked so much of what they learned from him that they became his followers. He warned them that following him would lead them off the sidewalk and into the ditch where a lot of the world's suffering people are. He told them they'd have to "take up their cross" and follow him, even if they couldn't possibly know ahead of time what that might mean.

Sixty-two years ago, I was baptized as a follower of Jesus. Forty years ago, I did a very frightening thing: I entered a Catholic seminary. Thirty-nine years ago, I joined the Dominican Family, and thirty-three years ago, I was ordained a priest.

Over the years, I've worked in parishes and campus ministries. I've baptized babies, witnessed the vows at hundreds of weddings, anointed the sick and buried the dead. I've raised funds, balanced budgets, managed staffs and spent hours I'll never get back in meeting after late-night-meeting. I've accompanied twenty-five-years-worth of students through their college careers.

In the midst of all that, nearly twenty years ago, the Holy Spirit, quietly invited me to step off the sidewalk and into the pain of some people whom life had beaten and bloodied and left for dead. These people had, in fact, died horrible, sudden deaths. I was given a prophetic gift to allow my voice to be used to help some of these "stuck souls" to pass safely from this life to the next. Allowing these poor souls to move into me and speak through me to a prayer partner, long enough to tell their stories, and to find loving guides has been a part of my priestly ministry these past two decades. I'm well into the writing of a book about this that I hope to have published soon.

Jesus is always saying, "Peace be with you," and "Don't be afraid." Much of the time I'm peaceful. Sometimes, like the person in the song, "I am afraid."

What am I afraid of? That the work I do will be associated with the occult. That I'll be called a "medium" or "channeler" by those, especially within the church, who believe all such activity, without exception, is of the devil. That's what I'm afraid of. And that will I be beaten and bloodied and left for dead in an ecclesiastical ditch.

When I'm not afraid I'm hopeful that I will be heard and respected, and possibly understood. Being believed would be good, too, but I know the first followers given the message, "Jesus is risen from the dead," found they often weren't. I have stories to share, some in dead–and–risen folks' own words, which I hope will inspire belief and joy. I think what I have to say belongs in the heart of the New Evangelization.

If you would like to share a conversation about this, please let me know.

I'll close here with a hymn that, these days, I find myself singing to the Friend of My Heart:

> *Because of You I won't stay too long on the sidewalk.*
> *Because of You*
> *Don't have to play on the safe side so I don't get hurt.*
> *Because of You*
> *I can trust not only me, but everyone around me.*
> *Because of You*
> *I'm not afraid.*

*(At least some of the time.)*
*–Nathan, OP*

My friend Shelby knows he's in God's hands. He doesn't feel the need to steer his life in any particular direction. He's a good team player who doesn't have to call the shots. He's a compassionate guy who has been encouraging people to shine. And he's already praying for someone here on earth, trusting that he can help somehow. I'm sure there's room in his heart for you. I'll bet he'd take on your case *pro bono*.

Thanks for the prayers, Shelby. You'll be in mine, too.

## Chapter Eight

# Paul, Who Thought He Was Minus–Four Man

This dream occurred on October 12, 2015:

*I was driving an old sedan from the early fifties. It was in good shape. I'd borrowed it from my grandmother. I took a wrong turn and mistook a narrow, wooden raised bit of roadway for an old section of road. The car fell through and landed in water. There were three other passengers, one beside me and two in the back seat. Somehow the four of us were on dry land. I lingered at the scene trying to take photos for the insurance, but I didn't really have a camera. I was disoriented and confused. I explained to the others and to a man who seemed to be in charge the mistake about the wrong turn. Then I lost track of the other three passengers. Someone gave me a ride somewhere afterwards. I awoke.*

*But an hour or two later that night I dreamt a very similar scene. This time I was in a car flying off the end of a pier. But the car disappeared mid–flight, and it was just me, flying, falling into the water. I tried to fly–fall all the way to the opposite shoreline but couldn't make it. I found myself in the water, just as I had in the earlier dream, but this time I felt calm despite the confusing scene. Where was I? Why was I here? I felt guided and accompanied and knew it was important that I write this down. (I hadn't recognized this as a contact dream at first. I came fully awake from this vivid scene, feeling around me for the pen and paper on the nightstand.)*

On December 21, 2015, my friend John Sanchez agreed to help me with some of my night visitors. John was new at this, but he wasn't at all afraid. He's a kind soul who has known suffering in his own life and has turned it into compassion for the suffering of others. John is also humble; humble people make the best listeners.

I taught John my prayers of protection, and we both settled in and called for the driver of the car. It wasn't long before I felt him come into me. I discovered that the driver was a young man named Paul. As John chatted with Paul, asking him gentle questions, it became clear that Paul was a bright, down–to–earth fellow; he knew who he was. He wasn't the most talented or the most athletic at his school, he told us, just an above–average student if he applied himself. And he applied himself! He saw other kids fight the system and bend the rules. Paul saw that most of the rules made sense; breaking them just made things more complicated. Paul knew he was trustworthy. Adults knew it, too. His grandmother trusted him enough to lend him her sedan on occasion.

Here's how Paul remembered that fateful night in his grandmother's car:

Paul: *Her car was a four–door sedan. In upstate New York, where we lived, it was important to have a car that held the road good in ice and snow. It was a heavy, sturdy car. We had just graduated high school a few weeks before. It was late spring or early summer. Since I had access to my grandma's car, I was the driver on our double date. My date was more of a gal pal. The two in the back seat had romance on their minds. They wanted to go someplace dark and private. They had some beer. I didn't drink any. I saw a side road that went into some woods. It was dark and private.*

John: Had you driven on this road before?

Paul: *I'm not sure. I don't think so. It was very dark. There were no other cars. When the road surface changed from pavement to wooden boards, I thought we were on a small bridge.*

John: But it wasn't a bridge?

Paul: *I didn't know what was happening, why we were falling. We might have flipped over. I've tried to remember if there were crashing or splashing sounds or crying or screaming. I can't remember. The car sank in the water. It was a pier. I had driven my grandma's car off the end of a pier and into a lake! I don't know where the others went. I was confused. Everything was happening at once. All I could think about was the car. I needed to take pictures for the insurance or the police, but I didn't have a camera. I needed to stay there to take responsibility for what I'd just done.*

John: Didn't you know that you'd died?

Paul: *Not right at first. I just knew I was responsible.*

John: What was the next thing you remembered?

Paul: *The funerals. There were four of them, and it was awful. Our whole school and the whole town and everybody's families and relatives were crying, and it was all my fault. I'd always followed the rules. I didn't drink and I wasn't reckless, but it was all my fault. I felt like that Scarlet Letter woman that got pregnant and had to wear a red*

Afterlife, *Interrupted*

*Capital A on her chest. I turned into Minus-Four Man.*

John: Minus Four?

Paul: *Yeah, because of me, all four of us went away.*

Paul was stuck trying to solve a mystery. He was struggling with how he could have followed all the rules, only to have his life and the lives of three young friends end so abruptly, tragically, and nonsensically because of one simple mistake.

My friend John had an inspired idea. Paul had reduced his life and his identity to a simple mathematical equation. John jotted this down in his notebook:

x - 4 = y

The problem looked simple, but it was complicated. What was "x" exactly? Or "y"? "Minus–Four Man" felt responsible for the other three. They'd been young like him. He felt responsible for shortening their lives, lives that had been filled with potential. He'd attended their funerals in his spirit–form and knew the tremendous loss their family and friends endured. This problem still puzzled him. All he saw was subtraction. John decided to approach this as a soluble math problem. My algebra was rusty, but luckily he was able to figure it out.

John: Do you see the other three with you now?

Paul: *No.*

John: Don't you think they must have gone to the other side already? You're not a – 4. How can we solve this problem? Let's add three to each side. That's how we're supposed to do it, right?"

x – 4 = y
x – 4 + 3 = y + 3
x –1 = y + 3

Now he was Minus–1 Man. Paul knew there was something on the other side of the equal sign. Who would he be when he was alongside his three friends who had crossed over? We were getting closer to the solution.

I didn't know who I should suggest for him to call to help bring him over. At first, I thought his grandmother would greet him. It was her car, after all. But Paul wasn't interested. John suggested we stick to math, which we found out later was one of Paul's favorite subjects.

John: Paul, how about we solve for "x"? Why don't we add plus one to both sides to solve for it? How could you do that?

As soon as John proposed this mathematical solution, an unexpected helper arrived.

Paul: *Mr. Waumbacher showed up! My high school principal. He's a short distance away holding a purple and gold football jersey from our school. It has a big Number One on it. If I put it on, I'll become Plus One Man, and I can cross over to the other side.*

Maybe your algebra is rusty too, so let's walk through the solution. Let's add +1 to the problem.

$$x - 1 = y + 3$$
$$x - 1 + 1 = y + 3 + 1$$
$$x = y + 4$$

Paul wasn't a −4 or a −1 anymore. He was now a part of the + 4. *X* could be earth. Before, it was x − 4, the earth minus 4. *Y* could be the Kingdom of God as a whole. The others had crossed over, and they were no longer stuck in the earthly world. Let's move them over. Paul was the last one to move over. We did the same math again by adding + 1 to each side. Earth was just *x* again, and heaven was *y* with 4 new additions.

John: And so, Paul, you're not Minus–Four Man anymore?
*Paul: Nope.*
John: And you're not Minus–One Man either?
*Paul: Not anymore.*
John: So what do we call you now?
*Paul: Just call me Paul.*

Then he added with a smile in his voice: *Or Captain Infinity!*

Paul's story got me thinking about the mathematics of love and how we put ourselves into the equation of life. Paul had never thought of himself as number one at anything. He was content to be himself. He knew he was pretty good and didn't feel the need to be superior to anyone else. On his own, he would never have worn a shirt that said, "I'm Number One." But the best educators often see potential in their students and draw forth the best in them. Isn't that what Mr. Waumbacher did? Do you really have to be the valedictorian to be Number One?

I'm not talking about that self–esteem–boosting technique of giving every child in the race a Participation Trophy. People find that so annoying. Some of us run faster or slower than others. But I do think God looks at each one of us as singularly wonderful. When we see each other through the eyes of love, we see greatness everywhere we look. In the Kingdom of God could we see each other as Number One and equally beautiful?

I once saw a printed T-shirt that read:

*Another Day That I Didn't Need Algebra.*

It made me laugh because I remember the whining in my high school about being forced to study algebra. Sometimes I do use simple algebra to solve for an unknown when doing measurements for artistic or home improvement projects. But I did join in the anti-algebra whining when it came to Algebra II. And Trigonometry? Forget it. I was right about that. I've gotten through life very well with my ignorance of sines and cosines.

How in the world could algebra be the key to anyone's getting unstuck in the afterlife? I wouldn't have thought it possible until Paul showed up in my unconscious. It's funny. He even had to move into my dream world twice in the same night to make sure he got through to me. When it came time to choose which of these stories to include in this book, Paul, Who Was Minus Four Man was near the top of the list. That, of course, meant getting his permission. What happened in what I thought was going to be a short and sweet conversation follows.

I got together with my prayer partner Laura to get Paul's permission. We offered our prayers of protection and called him in.

Nathan: Paul, Minus–Four Man.

Laura: Paul, you have probably been waiting in the wings.

Paul: *Yes, here I am. I want Father Nathan to know that I have taken up, let's just say, "haunting"—I don't know what the other word for it would be—his friend John, who was the one who helped me in the crossing over at the very start.*

Laura: His friend John Sanchez?

Paul: *John Sanchez. He was in Father Nathan's study, in his big house back in California. John—it was the first time he had ever done this work, being the prayer partner. I think there were two or three of us in succession, as you've done this too, I believe. I was one on the first day he ever was given this to do. He was just so bright. He understood what my stuckness was around. I had formed this idea that it had to make sense, it had to make sense, it had to make sense. How do I make sense of this nonsense? How could I possibly have done this? How my life ended was an unsolvable problem.*

Laura: Yes, how could you have ended your life so abruptly by a simple driving mistake.

Paul: *I drove my grandmother's car off the end of a pier, killing myself and three friends! I subtracted four young lives from the world. How in the world could I have done that? How could this have come to pass? I rolled it around in my head over and over and over again like it was some, I don't know, some conundrum. Like something*

*of a Greek tragedy or some epic puzzle. I don't know enough Greek epics. I just know*
*there was one about somebody like that Atlas fellow that constantly pushes a rock up*
*a mountain like somebody that's doomed. Or is it Sisyphus? Is that who it was? Some*
*Greek mythology guy does that. I was this person that just did the same thing again*
*and again and again and again because I couldn't imagine that it could all be so futile*
*in the end. It has to make sense. My life has to make sense. Instead I'm stuck being*
*Minus-Four Man.*

*I don't know how John picked up on it that, that the problem as I framed it seemed*
*algebraic. I was really good at algebra. John picked up on that and showed a lot of keen*
*wit for a person doing this for the first time. He reframed the whole thing in terms*
*of algebra. As soon as he did, I thought, "Oh, I hadn't thought of algebra. How could*
*driving your grandmother's car off the end of a pier and causing four deaths be solved*
*in a quadratic equation?"*

Laura: The equation that was formulated made sense to you, and that enabled you to
let go of the sense.

Paul explained to us why math was the solution to his puzzle.

Paul: *When you look up a word in the dictionary, most of them mean several different*
*things. You can say stuff in plain English and still be misunderstood. But numbers are*
*different. Nine is always one more than eight and one less than ten. And that's true in*
*any language. Numbers are a more precise way to know things than words ever are.*

We wanted to know more about what Paul was doing with his time now that he'd crossed over.

Laura: You said something at the very beginning about how you were kind of
haunting John.
Paul: *I was just kidding. I didn't know the word for it. Visiting or—*
Laura: Visiting or looking in on him?
Paul: *Looking in on, caring about. It's proper, not creepy.*
Laura: Yeah, looking out for him is what you're doing.
Paul *Yes, and showing sustained interest. Listen to me. I'm talking like Father Nathan.*
*I'm inside him and I'm using vocabulary in him that's above my vocabulary, but*
*anyway, I was talking about haunting. Sustained interest. Let's just go with that. I'm*
*just trying to care about John. Maybe you know a little bit that he has some depression*
*sometimes. When a person is depressed, they can exaggerate how alone they are. I*
*try to be near him and if I can, whisper in his ear or see if there's anything I can do to*

*change anything around him that might help him to feel not so alone.*

Laura: That's lovely. Perhaps Father Nathan can pass that onto John, let him know that he has a spirit-friend.

Paul: *I wish he would, because I'm not rapping on the doors or rattling the teacups. I'm just trying to hang around him.*

Laura: Yeah, you're there for support. I'm sure he'll appreciate that.

Paul: *I'm grateful for what he did for me. I would like to accompany him as best I'm able for now, and then perhaps after his passing, we can get to know each other well.*

Laura: What about you now, Paul? What are things like for you now?

Paul: *They're relaxed. I think wise guides have decided that what would be best for me was to take the summer off. I passed right after graduation and had the summer ahead of me. It would have been a summer of maybe a light summer job. I wasn't going right off to school or didn't have grand plans. It was going to be an in-the-moment summer with probably some summer job just for income. I think what they've let me know is there's no need to make big plans right now. I think unlike some of the people that you have helped—I think some of them after their deaths went to a place where they didn't think very much. I, on the other hand, went to a place where my thoughts raced the whole time. I was just grinding at the solution that never came. I was way more active than passive, and so I think the balancing now is to be more passive than active. It's that equal sign thing again. I think I'm supposed to just relax, rest in peace, chill out. This is an idiom that wasn't around when I was. Chill out. More Father Nathan vocabulary.*

Laura: That's right.

Paul: *Even "idiom": I don't think I've ever used that word before. I could hang around in this guy's head and get pretty intelligent. There's not much to be said about that. I'm mentally relaxing because my poor mind was overworked, I think. I don't know how it works, but it seems that people just want me to be still and enjoy myself calmly for a while.*

Laura: That feels good to you?

Paul: *It does. One thing that I do is, I look at the lake that I drowned in and see it not as a killing place, but notice. It smells nice. I like to watch the sun on it. I watch the fish and the frogs and the bugs. It's like claiming this place back as a good place.*

Laura: A place of peace, maybe.

Paul: *Yeah, I don't know. I think I was angry at it for a long time. It was dark. I couldn't see it anyway. That's why I drove into it. Now I'm seeing this place for what it really is. That's taking some of the sting out of it. It's helping me not be so angry at it.*

Laura: That's interesting, seeing it as it really is, not as you were thinking of it, as a terrible place.

**Chapter Eight**

Paul: *I have inquired about the other people who died that day, and I was told that'll be for later, that I'm not ready for that. That's just fine. I wanted to apologize, and somebody said, "Well, just hold that thought for a little while longer." I'm okay with that.*

Laura: Good.

Paul: *The rest is a short story. How many ways can you say, "I'm relaxing"?*

Laura: You've given us good illustrations. Thanks so much for coming back, Paul. We appreciate it.

Paul: *All right. I'll continue to pray in my own way for the success of what you're trying to do. It's good work.*

Laura: Thank you. Thanks for helping John as well.

Paul: *Sure.*

Nathan: Glory be to the Father, and to the Son, and to the Holy spirit, as it was in the beginning, is now, and will be forever. Amen.

There are two issues raised by Paul's story that I'd like to comment upon briefly here. One is the nature of forgiveness; the other is the spiritual presence and activity in our lives of our beloved dead and our guardian angels. Both issues could be books of their own. For now, I'll offer a few thoughts.

The need to forgive is always directed at some object. When a person harms you intentionally, and you rightly blame them for causing the harm, that person becomes the object of forgiveness. When a person's incompetence causes harm, the same is true. Even when a person's innocent, accidental action causes harm, they can become the object of forgiveness. All of these examples involve an "other."

Some folks feel they can rightly blame God, whom they have been taught is all–protective, all–loving, all–just, or all–something–else, when a tragedy strikes. This can be immensely painful and disorienting. Think back to Ray, whom we met in the preface. This was his issue.

For me, God, as revealed in the universal person of Jesus the Christ, is also all–vulnerable. He is not in charge of everyone's actions. He just loves everyone. He gets crucified, and no one says they're sorry. He uses one of his dying breaths to ask that his Father forgive those who have thrust nails through his hands and feet. When we see with unitive vision like Jesus's, we see everyone as part of the One, which includes us. We identify with the other.

Paul's challenge was self–forgiveness, though with a twist. He had a strong belief, at eighteen, that life's events must make sense right now. In his mind, his and his companions' deaths must make rational, metaphysical sense. We watched him move through a solution with the help of his new friend, John, and his old friend, algebra.

I often teach that forgiveness can be unilateral, but reconciliation must be mutual. In my earlier example, Jesus forgave an offender who was unrepentant. We can all do that, or can ask God's help to do that. But we cannot be reconciled with another without the willingness and readiness of both parties. Notice that Paul invited an attempt at reconciliation with the three persons who died in the accident he caused. Wise guides told him that the time was not yet right; it would come later. For those of us living on this side of death's divide, we might forgive, but not experience reconciliation until later, even in the afterlife. Apparently, even in the afterlife, we might still have to wait for perfect reconciliation until all parties are ready.

Now, about those wise guides; often, they are angels. Angels are not humans who have died. Angels are intelligent spiritual beings of light with whom we share the universe. We've each arrived here with a guardian angel who loves us, constantly accompanies us, and is dedicated to serving us. I interact with my guardian many times a day. All of us can do that. We need only desire the relationship and begin to cultivate it.

Paul mentions that he has begun to hang out with his new friend, John. He jokingly called it "haunting" him. Our deceased loved ones can learn how to be with us from time to time, and many do. Chances are, someone you love who has crossed over, continues to look in on you. They may even be able to get you to notice them. Dreams, daydreams, thoughts, tactile experiences of warmth, or goosebumps are common ways in which that can work. There are many books available on that topic.

What can they do to help us? They can be a loving presence. Isn't that what we do in the lives of those we love? We offer practical, specific help when we can. We help carry in the groceries. We fill in for a coworker with a family emergency. But we also show up at the bedside of a loved one who is ill, not really knowing what to do.

Yes, we may fluff up a pillow, or refill a water glass—practical things. But loving presence is the real gift these things betoken. Our angels and deceased loved ones can bring powerful, loving presence. They can enrich our lives. Love always does that.

## Chapter Nine
# Sophia*, Who Forgave Herself

I received this dream during the night of December 1, 2015:

*A friend of mine was doing laundry and asked for my help. He'd started a load in hot water but wanted to add another product, a stain boost or fabric softener or something. He wasn't sure how to do it. I thought about reading the instructions, but instead opened the machine to interrupt the cycle.*

*The machine morphed into a walk-in chamber. It was dark, wet, and very hot. As I walked in I thought, "It's dangerous in here. I could be trapped."*

*Suddenly, I saw the face of a woman, white, brunette, perhaps in her late thirties, with a long face. The door clicked shut. Had someone shut it on purpose? I heard the words, "Scalded to death in (city and state names)." I awoke.*

My friend John and I went into our protective prayer, so that I could allow this woman to speak through me to John. We didn't do an audio recording of this one, and only John made notes at the time. Relying now on his notes and my memory of events, I'd like you to hear her story. As you'll see, we have changed her name, at her request.

Sophia*, we learned, was from the Philippines. She and her husband had two small children when he died suddenly.

> Sophia*: *I did what I had to do to feed my children. I took a job as a maid on a cruise ship and left my children in the care of relatives. This was not so uncommon. Many of us had to leave our children, at least for a time, to earn the money to support them. I wanted to save up enough money to put my kids through school.*

Sometimes on the cruise ship, there would be a few days between cruises when there were no guests aboard. This time was used for heavier cleaning than could be done when all the rooms were full.

A man who was also on the ship's crew cornered Sophia* in one of the bedrooms and raped her. He threatened her with the loss of her job should she report the rape. He told her no one would take her word against his. Sophia* chose to keep the incident quiet and hoped that it wouldn't happen again. But something even worse did.

> Sophia*: *His wife also worked on the cruise ship. Everyone aboard knew them. How she found out that he had raped me, I don't know. One day she created an excuse to ask me to help her with something in one of the ship's mechanical rooms near the laundry. She lured me into a small room that was dark and very steamy. Suddenly, she slammed the door shut behind me and locked me in. I was trapped; no one could hear me scream.*
> John: Did you die quickly?
> Sophia*: *Yes. My body was all red. It was horrible. I felt so ashamed and ugly. I didn't want anyone to see me or know about all that had happened to me. I wanted it all to just go away.*
> John: So did you choose not to go when, after you died, people came to help you?
> Sophia*: *I just wanted to disappear. Be lost at sea or something. I don't remember much more. I just slid off to the side somehow, until not very long ago when I was encouraged to show up in Father's dream.*
> John: I'm sorry you were raped. I can't imagine the loss of dignity like that. But when people come into Father's dreams, it usually means the ones who have been caring for them think they're ready to move along.
> Sophia*: *I just couldn't forgive myself for letting all this happen. Leaving my kids orphans. Not saying goodbye.*

Then something began to shift. John began to explain to Sophia* that many assault victims blame themselves for what happened to them. Such an intimate offense to the body can leave victims wounded from the inside out in a way that makes it hard for them to see that the violence was something done completely from without.

Somehow, Sophia* began to receive some kind of healing energy or grace. I don't know how else to describe it. Her "present" self began to see and to have compassion for her former self, the person she was at the time of her rape, and a few weeks later, at the time of her murder. Rather than blaming herself or recoiling in shame, Sophia* began to comfort her earlier, violated self. This was all new to Sophia*, and something that neither John nor I could bring about.

John: Sophia*, this is important. Do you see how much you've just changed? You've begun to be tender to yourself. Maybe it's time for someone who loves you to comfort you, too. Are you ready to see your husband?

Sophia* could see him at a distance. He was waiting to be invited closer.

Sophia*: *I feel like there's two sides to me, the regular side and the abused side. I don't want him to have to see the abused side.*

John: He's right here and I think he loves all of you. Do you think you could let him show you that? You can go slow if you need to.

Sophia*: *He's standing there smiling with his arms stretched out wide, just like he used to.*

Sophia* allowed her husband to hold her, both sides of her. All of her.

At this point, the two of them didn't need two strange guys watching them. It wasn't so much like they walked off together into the sunset. It was more like John and I discreetly left the room. Our work was done anyway.

We said our quick prayer of gratitude together: "Glory be to the Father, and to the Son, and to the Holy Spirit, as it was in the beginning, is now, and will be forever. Amen."

By now you know, when it was time to write this book, I chose to seek the permission of these night visitors to include their very personal stories. This time I did make an audio recording. My prayer partner was Laura; Sophia* is borrowing my voice. She moved in easily in order to use my voice.

Laura: Sophia*, have you been waiting to be with us?

Sophia*: *I have, and I think I will have less to say than many of the ones who came before.*

Laura: Whatever you have to say we would welcome.

Sophia*: *I wasn't very much of a talker, and if that's supposed to change, it hasn't yet. I made beds and cleaned bathrooms. I wasn't really much of a talker.*

Laura: That's fine.

Sophia*: *But you do remember that we spoke once in your home in California?*

Laura: Yes.

Sophia*: *The question that was asked was, would I allow my story to be told and was there a need to leave out any detail that would identify me as a murdered person. I told you at that time, "Go ahead. It's the truth."*

Laura: Yes, I remember.

Sophia*: *What do you think? My children are adults now. Maybe this book would never find its way to them. If it did—*

Laura: It's hard to say whether they would ever see it or how they would feel about it. It's really your call. Are you able, where you are now, to look in on your children and see how they're doing? Do you think they would be able to accept what's true?

Sophia*: *Yes, I did look in on them very early, as soon as I was helped to move on. I always wanted to be with them. Of course, after their father died so young, I had to leave them with relatives in order to earn money to feed them. That meant going on a ship and being away a lot. Even before dying, I already felt like I was a mother who peered over the hedge or through the transom to see into their lives because I couldn't be with them all the time. That feels familiar. Now they're adults and have children of their own.*

*I wondered, and still do, if they've discovered that my death wasn't accidental, but in fact, a murder. They didn't know of my being raped. That wasn't part of any—Because that had happened previous to the day of my dying, the way the police handled the death scene, I wasn't a rape victim because that had been days before, weeks before. I was a scalding victim. My body was red with burns. They wouldn't have known that I had been raped. They wouldn't know that my rapist's wife murdered me. If they were your children and your grandchildren, would you—even though the story would be in the past, would it leave a legacy that would cast a dark shadow?*

Laura: That's a very important question for you. I think only you can answer that. It's something we could pray about, but as you said when you first heard the question, go ahead and say it because it's true. Is it important that they know the truth? They'll know the truth some day when they see—

Sophia*: *It's true.*

Laura: —when they cross through death, what they wish they'd known, what they—

Sophia*: *I don't care to—Even though this husband and wife team turned out to be a rapist and a murderer, I don't want to concern myself with their outcomes. In other words, when you hear of—I've heard of people who had a loved one murdered, and they would say, "We must have justice." Sometimes once there's been a killing, people say, "Well, now she can't rest in peace because her soul is—"*

Laura: No.

Sophia*: *I want nothing of that.*

Laura: Okay.

Sophia*: *It's true. I might not have had eternal rest granted unto me right away, but that was not God's doing. It was my own. I was the one who felt like I needed to stay back or run off to the side until you folks helped me, but if there's still more peace for me to have, I don't know that there is. I think I'm at peace, but if there is more peace that I need to gain, it won't be by having these people found out and punished. I trust* *that there will be a day when—I was Catholic, if God and Jesus and the Kingdom of God are true the way I was taught, I think God wants us all to forgive each other and all be one. Jesus did that on the cross. I would participate, but I would need to be shown what to do and trust that later—It's just not time for that yet. I would hope that they had remorse and were sorry and promised never to hurt anyone in such ways ever again, but I also have good advisers around me.*

*I think I have extra ones because of being twice victimized in very violent ways. I think if you can imagine some health care setting—a lot of my relatives are nurses—if you would have encountered me in a hospital setting or in a mental hospital setting, I would have needed and perhaps gotten extra help. I think I'm getting extra help here.*

Laura: Sophie, would it—

Sophia*: *Sophia*, with an "a" at the end.*

Laura: Sophia*, would it help for our purposes if we changed your name so that there was less chance of an identification? Would that help solve the question of whether you would want your children to know or not?

Sophia*: *Call me Sophia with a—is it an asterisk? With the little mark like a flower at the end at the top?*

Laura: Yes.

Sophia*: *Let's do that, but don't lose track of my name.*

Laura: We won't.

Sophia*: *Maybe you can put in a note that because of her children and grandchildren, she didn't want her real name used.*

Laura: We can do that, yes.

Sophia*: *But the rest of the details could be...Maybe you could leave out* [the name of the port city where the ship was when she was killed.]

Laura: Leave out [the city's name.]

Sophia*: *And* [the state] *because where the boat was isn't important to this story.*

Laura: That would protect you, but still allow your story, your important story, to be told?

Sophia*: *Yes, but it would be good maybe for some purpose of your own—I know that he is trying to do work with scientists about this question of can dead people talk and can you know things and so on. Maybe it's best that there be in his own note-keeping. I don't want him to have to pretend he never knew my name.*

Laura: Yes. We'll put the disclaimer in which says that you requested that your name be changed, but that we do know your identity.

Sophia*: *I don't think I ever told you my last name ever, so there's no need there. I don't think you know the last names of a lot of us, right?*

Laura: That's right. Are you comfortable with that, then?

Sophia*: *I am, thank you.*

Laura: Okay, very good. Is there anything else you'd like us to know?

Sophia*: *No, I just want to thank you for doing this kind work. It's an unusual work. You seem to be blessed to do it.*

Laura: We feel blessed. It was very good to meet with you, and many blessings to you as you continue to heal and to enjoy some peace where you are.

Sophia*: *I'll pray, too, for pointing the project in the right ways to the right people.*

Laura: Thank you. We'll say goodbye for now.

Sophia*: *Okay.*

Nathan: Glory to the Father, to the Son, and to the Holy Spirit, as it was in the beginning, is now, and will be forever. Amen.

Sophia* is the only one of these stories where it was necessary to alter a person's identity. In the initial dream, my friend who was doing laundry has the masculine form of Sophia's* given name. That's one of the ways my visitors tell me their name.

Sophia's* stuckness seemed to be around her sense of herself after being sexually and physically assaulted. For her, the key to the lock was forgiving her earlier self. Raped, then murdered by her rapist's wife, Sophia* blamed herself. Forgiving the earlier version of herself got her unstuck. She did a life review.

I have pastored women who have been raped, but I've always worked with their mental health professionals, who are usually women. I wouldn't have chosen two men to help Sophia*, but in the end, it didn't matter. I felt the presence of the Holy Spirit at the turning point in this story. That ability she was given to see herself from a different point of view, and to feel compassion for herself was, I think, a gift of the Holy Spirit. In the Judeo–Christian scriptures, that presence of God is referred to in the biblical Hebrew and Greek with feminine pronouns. That which is called Wisdom in Hebrew, becomes in Greek "Sophia."

Even now, Sophia* is loving her adult children and grandchildren. She thinks their lives might be happier without the knowledge that she was raped, then murdered. If they ever need to know that, it can be in the afterlife. She seems to be trustful of whatever the afterlife is as it unfolds for her.

Wasn't it beautiful when she spoke of the two who raped and killed her? Sophia* heard the message that God's hope is that we'll all one day be beyond all that separates us. She knows it's not her job to fix all of this just now. She does not will any evil on those who harmed her; she's leaving that in God's hands. No wonder she is at peace and is even receptive to growing into deeper peace.

Finally, it was very sweet to see the beginning moments of the afterlife reunion of spouses who still love each other. Sophia*'s husband was ready to help heal her afterlife body, soul, and spirit. She was beginning to trust that she could give all of herself, just as she is, to her beloved.

Thanks, Sophia*, for letting us be a part of and to be sharers of your story with others. And thanks for doing whatever you can to support this book project in prayer. How did you put it? "Pointing the project in the right ways to the right people."

## Chapter Ten
# Shelley, Who Used to Tipple

In the previous chapters, I've often simply described the contact dream in which I first met a new night visitor, shared the dream with you, and invited you along into the crossing over of this stuck soul. In this case I'd like to make a comment first.

I normally like to try to establish a rapport with the one my prayer partner and I are helping. The woman in this story, whom we learned was named Shelley, had extraordinarily low energy. She was hard for me to bring through. She didn't offer her name and seemed only barely able to take part in the process. As her story unfolded, it became apparent that she'd stopped relating to people years before her death and had brought that habit with her into her afterlife. Nevertheless, we were together because she had agreed, at least a little, to take part in this process. You'll notice that her responses are all brief.

I received this dream in the first half of 2013:

*A woman was in a station wagon from the mid-sixties with lots of children in it. They were loud and rambunctious. I was in the back seat. The driver was a blonde woman, and I remember her hairdo that flipped up and was heavily sprayed, typical for the 1960's. She looked over her right shoulder while she was backing up and hit something. She said, "Oh, no." I awoke.*

My prayer partner for this one was my friend Richard Kingsley. We did our usual prayers of protection. I felt someone come in. Her guardian angel spoke first, just to do the mic–test. It's like saying, "Test! Test! Can you hear me now?" The content is not the point. The guardian just wants to show the wary soul that borrowing the voice isn't hard or scary.

I invited Shelley to borrow my voice long enough to tell us what had happened to her so that we might help her. She stepped in, but her energy felt low and sluggish.

Richard: Did Nathan get the dream part right? Were you driving a car full of noisy kids when you hit something?

Shelley: *I was backing up. The kids in the back seat were laughing and squirming, and I was trying to look over and through them to see where I was going. I hit something. But it wasn't something; it was someone. I ran over and killed a child.*

Richard: Oh. That's terrible.

Shelley: *I wish I had died. My life blew up that day. So much of it ended on the spot. But I didn't die. I wish I had.*

Richard: Well, eventually you did, or we wouldn't be talking to you now. When somebody shows up in Nathan's dreams, it's usually because they died but kind of got stuck and didn't pass peacefully or happily. They have often isolated. Is that what happened to you?

Shelley: *I guess.*

Richard: So, why don't you tell us what your life was like before that really bad day? It looked like you were a housewife with kids in school. And your hairstyle and your station wagon made Nathan think maybe this happened in the mid–1960s. Is that right?

Shelley: *Yes. My husband and I had three kids. We were just living our lives. He'd go off to work. I'd take care of the kids, the laundry, the shopping and cooking, all the normal stuff. For a long time, it worked. I looked forward to his coming home, and we'd have a cocktail and relax a little.*

Richard: Did something change?

Shelley: *He said his work got harder, and he needed to focus on it more. When he did come home, he was overtired. He came home later, often after dinner. Our marriage suffered. I started tippling while I was cooking, sampling the wine earlier in the day. I thought I was okay.*

Richard: And then the accident?

Shelley: *It was my carpool day. Everything was normal, just another day. I felt the car hit something. My life fell apart all at once.*

Richard: But you didn't die that day. What happened after that?

Shelley: *I was over the [drinking] limit. I was a drunken mom who killed one of the neighbor's kids. Everybody hated me. They arrested me on the spot. I never stepped foot in my own house again. I was found guilty and sentenced to nineteen years in prison. My husband divorced me and remarried. The new wife raised our kids. I lost everything.*

Richard: But still you hadn't died. What happened after that?

Shelley: *I just passed the time in prison. Everyone I'd known was mad at me. They probably tried to not even think about me.*

Richard: Did anyone stay in touch or come to visit you?

Shelley: *Only my mom. Which was strange because I never thought she even liked me. We'd never gotten along that well. We may have been too much alike. My sisters had done better in life. But you have to give Mom credit. She was very faithful in visiting me. She didn't act like she was ashamed of me.*

Richard: Did you serve your full sentence?

Shelley: *More or less. I got along, didn't cause trouble. That usually means you can cut a little time off your sentence.*

Richard: So you were released?

Shelley: *Yeah. I was released. But it was impossible for me to go back where I had come from. They wouldn't have me. So I moved to another town where nobody knew me. Nobody knew my story. I got a job as a hotel maid. One day I was flipping a mattress when I felt my back go out; it was ruined. I couldn't work anymore and went on permanent disability. Then my mom died. I was all alone in the world.*

Richard: So what did you do?

Shelley: *I had a little place, a second–floor apartment that looked out over an asphalt parking lot. Mostly I stared out the window and smoked. I paid a neighbor lady to grocery shop for me every week just to pick up a few things. I didn't even let her in. She'd just knock and set the bag outside the door.*

Richard: Is that where you died?

Shelley: *No. I got sick and had to go to a nursing home. Nobody knew I was there. That's where I died.*

Richard: What happened after that?

Shelley: *You mean after I died?*

Richard: Yeah.

Shelley: *I ended up here.*

Richard: And where is here?

Shelley: *I don't know. Just someplace. Or no place.*

Richard: Is anyone with you?

Shelley: *Just that one that talked first a while ago. He just sits in a corner and leaves me alone.*

Richard: Don't you suppose that if he were really leaving you alone, he wouldn't be there with you at all?

Shelley: *I don't know.*

Richard: It kind of sounds like you've found yourself in another cell, like in prison or in that sad apartment.

Shelley: *I guess.*

Richard: Well, our job is to help people go from being all alone after they die to being with at least one other person. Think about it. When you were all alone after the accident, all those years in a prison cell, who came to visit?

Shelley: *Only my mom.*

Richard: Your mom proved she wasn't afraid or ashamed to join you in a prison. Surely, she'd be willing to come and be with you in the place or the no–place you are now, don't you think?

Shelley: *I suppose so.*

Richard: Well, would it be okay with you if we asked her to come and be with you?

Shelley: *Is that all it takes?*

Richard: Usually. You'd just have to give the okay.

Shelley: *Okay, then. Okay.*

Shelley's mom did come for her, but they didn't stay there. They did move along. At the time, we never even learned the woman's name, so we just called her "The Tippler." Did she move along happily? Not so much. But she didn't protest. She allowed her mother to escort her onward. Hers was not a peaceful soul, but when we last encountered her, she wasn't agitated either. Had she "rested in peace" long enough that she was at least willing to allow her mom to come for her? She didn't go joyfully, but she did go.

Unlike so many others who move into my dreamscape, Shelley didn't show me the day she died. I think she showed me the day she felt as if her soul died. But then, souls don't really die. This one just might have been more wounded and forlorn than most.

We don't always get to see others' happy endings. I think Shelley needed some kind of healing environment. She was at least in the company of, and I think in the care of, the one person who had loved her most. That's a good start.

I prayed for and wondered about Shelley. I hoped that some day in the eternal future I would get to see her again. I hoped to see a happier, more whole version of her then.

Now, fast forward. I wrote up much of what you've just read a couple of years ago. When it came time to write this book, Shelley's story stayed on my mind. Many of these encounters have left me feeling joyful and inspired. These poor souls have left this world so violently and suddenly, but then I'm privileged to be a part of their continuing afterlife story. So many are resilient.

Shelley didn't show me her last moment on earth, as most have. She showed me the

Afterlife, *Interrupted*

moment she shut down, years before her eventual death. She showed me the day her life blew up, the day she accidentally killed a child.

I think this story illustrates that some souls are stuck before they leave this plane. When they do move, the stuck souls don't have to be enthusiastic about moving on or excited to see the person or persons who come for them. This soul had no enthusiasm left to give. But Shelley did agree, as she was able, to take part.

As we did with all the others whose stories we've shared here, my prayer partner and I went into our protected prayer to ask if we might speak briefly with Shelley to ask her permission to use her story. She did come when invited. I didn't know her name at the time. With no disrespect, I just called her "The Tippler."

The Tippler moved into me in order to borrow my voice. "She feels so different from the way I remember her," I told my prayer partner. "She feels a lot lighter somehow."

She was more talkative this time, too. Her replies weren't as blunt as before. In fact, what follows wasn't really a back–and–forth conversation. Once Shelley started talking, she was sort of on a roll.

Shelley: *I want to explain why I'm different. Once upon a time, I was a beautiful young woman with a husband, children, and a lovely home. It's true I began to drink before dinner. That began the whole descent. Death didn't change that. I was operating at such a low level. If anyone came for me then, I didn't want to go with them. In a book, that's a sad chapter. I think people would like to be able to say, "She's in a better place." They think they have only heaven, hell, and purgatory to choose from. I don't know that I ever made a choice. I just slid into death. The day I backed over the child was a tragic day, but my decline started before with my marriage and drinking punctuated by a tragic event. I'm being told that the day I showed him [Nathan] my sad little movie, I was already in an ascent. I didn't know that. That day was an important milestone for me. When I was reminded that my mother had been willing to visit me often in prison and that she'd probably be willing to visit me in my afterlife no–place, all that was required was for me to say, "That makes sense," and to go with my mother.*

*With my mother, growing up, I didn't want to have that kind of close mother–daughter relationship. But by the time she came for me, she was brighter and freer, happier, a peaceful version of herself. She led me out; we came to some place sort of like a spa. They did something good for me. They sized me up and put me in a place where people attended to me, kind of like in "My Fair Lady." I was a diamond in the rough who needed tending to. I liked that. I didn't mind being "Queen for a Day." I was pampered into a clean, peaceful, happy version of myself. Eventually I got dressed and was ready to rejoin things, so there's your happy ending. I am rested and happy and remember that I have a life not attached to that sad story. I haven't met the child—that's unfinished business—but that's not timely yet. They haven't put me in charge of my own schedule—but it's not like life in prison; they want what's best for me.*

*I never told you my name, and I know you feel bad about calling me just "The Tippler." You can call me Shelley, Who Used to Tipple. I will be interested in your book and praying for you.*

And with that, Shelley was gone.

## Chapter Eleven
# Dwight, Discovered to His Shame

I received this dream in the early hours of August 13, 2015:

*I was looking directly into the face of a young white man, perhaps in his late twenties. I saw only his face and upper torso. He was shirtless. Something sharp and pointed was pushed into his chest, near the heart. Some other sharp object, but not a knife, was pushed into the other side of his chest. He did not fight or try to defend himself. He just asked his attacker, "What are you doing to me?" I awoke.*

In prayer with my friend Richard, we invited this young man to let us help him. Whoever he was, he was afraid. His guardian emerged first and explained that the young man he guarded, for reasons of his own, had created, at his death, a place as close to nowhere as he could imagine. It had nothing visual or auditory at all, nothing to describe it, just an isolated place where no one would see him. His guardian emerged to show him that it was safe to talk to us. I began to sense that his named started with DW, maybe "Dwayne" or "Dwight." At last, the young man introduced himself.

Dwight: *Here I am. My name's Dwight.*
Richard: Nice to meet you, Dwight. We're Nathan and Richard. How can we help you?
Dwight: *I don't know for sure. Were you ever stuck? Like you drove into mud or sand and tried to gun it to get unstuck?*
Richard: Sure, like from snow?
Dwight: *Yeah, you try to get loose but end up digging yourself in a deeper hole, then maybe you try putting something under the wheel to make some traction, but you just*

can't get out. Then you have to ask for help like somebody to push or rock your car while you try to get out. I think that's why you're here, isn't it?

Richard: I guess. Where are you? How'd you get stuck?

Dwight: *It's embarrassing to talk about.*

Richard: Then skip that part. Tell us where you'd like to go.

Dwight: *I can try to tell you a little. Have you ever heard of people that like to feel or cause pain during sex?*

Richard: You mean sado-masochism?

Dwight: *Yeah, well there was this place you could go to meet up with people and it had a room in the back. I didn't know this guy—I'd just met him. I let him tie me up. And instead of cutting me a little, he pulls out this thing he brought with him. It was kind of like a curtain rod that he'd sharpened to a point like a pencil. He just pushed it into me, into my chest near my heart. Then quickly he took something else, not a knife, but something sharp and homemade and shoved it into me on the other side of my chest into my lung. All I could do was to ask, "What are you doing to me?"*

*Then stuff started happening. There were people around, muffled voices like in another room.*

Richard: You mean where you were stabbed?

Dwight: *No, I mean on this side, whatever this is. Like the soul. Like as you're dying, people wanting to greet you or whatever. No, where my body was, I don't think anyone was there, even the guy that did that to me. I think he left pretty quickly. Nobody'd want to stay very long where they'd done what he'd done.*

Richard: I guess not. So what'd you do next?

Dwight: *Not much. Now I was dead and there was a funeral, and my mom and my family and everyone at work and all the neighbors found out how I'd died. And what I'd been doing. It was awful. I didn't want to be around anybody, anywhere. My guardian guy—I didn't pay much attention to guardian angels—he came with me and stayed with me at a distance. You guys are Catholics, aren't you? I was, too. Altar boy, Catholic school. I just didn't want anybody judging me.*

Richard: Well, what do you want from us? You want to become unstuck, to go somewhere?

Dwight: *Yeah, I suppose. This worked for a while, I guess, but it doesn't change. I haven't let it change.*

Richard: And you want it to change now? Where do you want to go?

Dwight: *I think I'm supposed to let someone take me with them. I've been told I should start simple. You guys are golfers, aren't you?* [Dwight pointed at the TV in the room we were in; we'd been watching a golf tournament moments before.] *You know how when you're trying to teach someone, you start simple and help them succeed and feel good. Like sinking short putts or having them do a half-swing with a pitching wedge. Help them get something positive going. Something simple.*

Richard: So you've been talking to someone? You mean your guardian?

Dwight: *Yeah, but not just him. This might be hard for you to believe.* [There was a pause.] *Jesus, but not the judging one.*

Richard: You mean Jesus has been visiting you, and you let him?

Dwight: *Yeah, he's been coming the way you might visit somebody in a hospital or a prison. Show up. Don't stay too long.*

Richard: So tell us about that.

Dwight: *He told me he died naked and that people had stuck sharp things in him and that it was in public in a busy place with people all around, and that his mom and some other women saw him like that.*

Richard: They didn't only kill him; they shamed him, too.

Dwight: *Exactly, and there wasn't any little cloth covering him.*

Richard: And now you have to think differently and get over the shame?

Dwight: *Something like that. But I want to start simple. Not with my mom or my family or co-workers or neighbors. I don't want to meet up with anybody who knew me.*

Richard: Then whom would you want to start with? Who would you be willing to go with?

Dwight: *Something's changing. Gimme a second.*

Richard: What?

Dwight: *Here, where I am, this nowhere place I made. Something's shifting. There's an old woman. Our people were Irish and Italian. This old lady's a lioness. She's not gonna let anyone mess with her kids. I think she's like my great-great-grandmother, somebody I belong to, but who died long before I was born. She looks brown-and-gold colored, like those old, old Civil War photos, or the old ones with people sitting up straight in uncomfortable furniture staring at the camera. And she's not alone. There are others behind her, other old relatives I've never met. She's out in front, like the front pin in bowling, the one in the middle the ball's supposed to hit. Is that the ten pin?*

Richard: I don't know. I think so.

Dwight: *Whatever. She's out front, and there're lots of others in a wedge behind her. They're mostly solid, but not completely. They're letting me see stuff inside them they were ashamed of that doesn't matter anymore. They've all got stuff. They want me to know I already belong with them.*

Richard: So, are you ready to go with them?

Dwight: *Yeah, I suppose. But wait, somebody else is coming. Well, would you look at that! Check that out!*

Richard: What is it?

Dwight: *It's the President! Eisenhower! Dwight. They named me after him: Dwight William. What's he doing here? Wasn't he a general or something?*

Richard: Yes, he was.

Dwight: *Well, he's standing next to the relatives. He looks good. And he's smiling and waving at me to get over there, like it's kind of an order.*

Richard: Well, do you want to go with them?

Dwight: *Sure. It's time. Thank you for helping me get unstuck.*

Richard: You're welcome.

Dwight, who went to a lot of trouble to hide from everyone after his death, is allowing Jesus, but not the judging one, to visit him. He said it's the way you'd visit someone in a hospital or prison: show support, don't stay too long. I've visited folks in hospitals and prisons. In hospitals it's important to keep it short because the people are sick. They often have other visitors, too. Or some nurse comes in to check on something or perform some procedure that ought to be done privately. In prisons, folks don't usually want you to leave quickly. They're just going back to boring routines anyway. When prisoners get to visit, they want to spend the whole of the allowed time with their visitors. Remember, Dwight wasn't sent to a place of punishment. He was ashamed and didn't want anyone he knew to see him. I think Jesus's visit was more like one to a place of healing.

That Dwight allowed that was remarkable. I know Jesus well enough to know he wouldn't come crashing in where he was unwelcome. Somehow, he put Dwight at ease enough to enable a helpful visit. To my Christian readers, I want to ask, "Does this surprise or shock you?" Dwight died during S&M gay sex. He felt horrible shame. Why would Jesus want to visit him?

Because God is love.

Dwight called his visitor, "Jesus, but not the judging one." In our creed, we say of Jesus, "He died and was buried. He descended into hell. On the third day he rose again from the dead. He ascended to the right hand of the Father. From there he will come to judge the living and the dead." If there is a need for judgment, it's more medicinal than punitive. I think it's about learning from our mistakes.

*Disciple* means student. *Being disciplined* means either showing orderly self–mastery that can make us productive, or being held accountable for wrongdoing. My disciplinarian dad used to ask me after I'd hurt myself or someone else, "What have you learned?"

Dwight had isolated himself from everyone he knew, but he was still accompanied and cared for. I loved hearing how Jesus drew parallels between their two deaths. That's what compassion is and does.

Dwight may not be over all of the shame he experienced at his death, but it seems to me that he's letting go of it a little at a time. Because I'm a golfer, I liked the way Dwight talked about starting simply and creating a sense of successful momentum. Sink short putts, perfect half–swings. You can graduate to the more difficult things later. It wouldn't surprise me if, sometime in Dwight's eternal future, he circles back around and helps others who die in circumstances like he did, which involve carrying a load of shame into the afterlife, heal and move on.

That Dwight's ancestors, most of whom he'd never met, came for him does not surprise me. I've seen this before. They don't always come in a large group, wedge–shaped like bowling pins. (This happened with Rani too, you'll recall.) They were mostly solid, but some translucence showed remnants of what Dwight just called "stuff." *"They're letting me see stuff inside them they were ashamed of that doesn't matter anymore. They've all got stuff. They want me to know I already belong with them."*

One of my favorite depictions of Jesus is of him resurrected and glowing. Out of the wounds in his hands, feet, and sides flow rays of light. His wounds identify him, but are not ghastly. They're beautiful, even healing. Dwight called him *"Jesus, but not the judging one."* That's the Friend I've been trying to introduce to people all my life.

The last surprise was President Dwight Eisenhower showing up. Our Dwight had been named for him. Our Catholic practice is not only to name our children but to place them under the spiritual care of the saints. Now, Dwight Eisenhower wasn't Catholic, but he was a Christian. He was there for his namesake when young Dwight needed a little help. I think that's beautiful.

As you know by now, before presuming to include someone's story in this book, our practice is to return to protected prayer and seek their permission. This is how that inspiring conversation went:

Nathan: We ask for all of the saint and angel guardians we mentioned earlier
to stand guard around us and also ask for the team of all the nice folks who are
allowing us to tell their stories in the book. If you would gather around, that would
be great. We want to ask Dwight if he would like to join your merry band and let his
story be used.
Laura: We would also like to ask President Dwight Eisenhower, who accompanied
Dwight when he left to move on, if he might be willing to be with us as well.
Nathan: Do you have the recorder going?
Laura: Yes.
Nathan: It's the president. He's a large, powerful, but gentle force.
Laura: Mr. President, it's a privilege to be in your company.

Dwight David Eisenhower: *The privilege is all mine. I would never have known how to do what you're doing. I was given a lot of responsibility for a lot of things, but I was never asked to do this.*

Laura: Well, we're grateful for your help for your namesake, Dwight, and for being present now with him. We have some things we'd like to ask. If you are willing and able to stand by him during this time as well, we'd appreciate it.

DDE: *Sure. I knew that lots of people get named for somebody or other. When you do become a recognized leader, some people that you don't know that well name a kid after you. I knew that had happened, even when I was general. Sometimes, you know, in the band of brothers, you begin to forge bonds, but you couldn't name everybody in the unit necessarily, not when there's hundreds and thousands of them. But I knew that I ended up being a notable, admired figure that some people named a son after. One of the things after I passed, I ran into saints and learned about being a patron and all that. That's more of a Catholic thing, and I was not a Catholic. We were discouraged from thinking that way. But anyway, I learned that all of those kids that were named after you, and now that there's a bond there, you know, that after you've died you're not limited in the time you spend. You can be in more than one place at a time. Anyway, I began to take that up and think, okay, that's something I'd like to know more about. These people were trusting enough to want to take my name and attach it to their child; well, then maybe I ought to pay attention to that. And so I did, and one of the ones who came across was this fellow Dwight, who you've gotten to know a bit.*

Laura: Well, that's fascinating and it's lovely, too. So you're kind of patron saint of all those Dwights as they cross. And you're more than notable, certainly famous, very well–known and highly respected and admired, so it's no wonder these Dwights would look up to you. And our particular Dwight, is he there?

DDE: *Yes. I'm going to step to the side, so thank you for helping him.*

(The president steps aside. His namesake, Dwight, emerges.)

Laura: Thank you so much. Dwight, I'm Laura. You're acquainted with Nathan. It was his voice you borrowed. I'm one of his prayer partners. You remember talking with him a few years ago and President Eisenhower coming for you, so we wanted to connect with you again, if you'd be willing to speak with us.

Dwight: *Yes, and one of the things I have had to do is get beyond my secret and it being known. And I understand that you know about that already.*

Laura: Yes.

Dwight: *And thank you for not judging me.*

Laura: No judgment here, nor was there on the part of Jesus, more to the point.

Dwight: *Yes, when I spoke with [Nathan] before, I wasn't sure. I never spoke with*

Afterlife, *Interrupted*

anyone about those visits, because there were more than one. On the one hand, it was extraordinarily surprising, but in the moment it was not. Mentioning it out loud, it sounds outlandish, but it wasn't. I'd heard many stories about Jesus, but when he did show up he didn't show up in a blaze of glory or anything. He was just some kind soul there to, kind of like—Laura, you've had a surgery, haven't you?

Laura: Yes.

Dwight: And so you know how, when you're in a hospital or health care setting, there end up being lots of people who come and go in and out of your room. They're looking over you, or some part of you, and studying your chart, and having an opinion and so on. And Jesus was so like that. He wasn't like Chief of Staff or trying to look like he was medical anything. It wasn't like he needed credentials to prove he belonged there. He was just this nice guy who might have been on a chaplain staff, somebody who knew how to comfort. He wasn't there for some mechanical thing or medical thing. He came as a person who was a nice part of a team and was there just to let you know he cared.

Laura: That's really amazing and wonderful. I just want to say that Father Nathan has probably worked with more than 250 people who, like you, got into kind of a loop and got stuck when they crossed over because their deaths were so traumatic. Yours was the only one in which Jesus actually came to be with the person to help him move on. And that's really an extraordinary thing, as well as the way that he connected with you, connected how others had stuck sharp things into him, you know, talking about his crucifixion.

Dwight: He made that sound like the most normal thing, and he wasn't embarrassed to talk about nakedness. You know, I guess that when people are that cruel to other people they torture, they often want to do that to private parts. Anyway, I didn't know that. Every crucifix I ever saw had a little loincloth thing covering him up. He's the one that volunteered that, no, that's not really how it was.

Laura: You mentioned that Jesus had visited you several times, and you said more like the hospital room setting, where he would kind of float in and check on you. Would you speak to him during those times as well?

Dwight: Yes, but not for very long, because he wouldn't stay for very long. He did what a good compassionate visitor would do. He'd realize you were weak and tired. All that he wanted to do was convey a sense of presence, acceptance, and care. It didn't take too long to do that. There was always the promise that next time it'll be a little longer, or when the circumstances allow for it, we'll have a nice visit.

Laura: That's something to look forward to, isn't it?

Dwight: Yes, well now, it's interesting because my—this is difficult to speak of—I knew the gospel stories, and I was a Catholic. But then as I got more into the middle *of my teens and a little later, it was undeniable that I was homosexual and after that attracted to a particular, I don't know, the pain thing, that fetishism. I don't know why it was and still don't. I hope to get an answer to that sometime. But anyway, I kind of had to make my way and feel like I belonged in the church, even though I was as I was. And I always felt that Jesus was the thing I could hang on to. I could hear in the stories that there were plenty of people in his time that were rejected for one thing or another, and sometimes it had to do with sex. There were the prostitutes, or, anyways, there'd be people who were from the wrong group. What did they call them? The Samaritans?*

Laura: The out-groups of various kinds, yeah.

Dwight: *There were plenty of stories where there were people somebody was trying to run off. I felt like people would like to run me off; if my secrets were broadly known I'd have plenty of people wanting to ride me out of town on a rail. And, of course, that's the way it ended for me. My secret blew up, and I thought, "Before they come for me I think I'll run." I won't wait to be chased off. I tried to take a look at my family and my funeral, but it was just too much to bear. It was just too much to watch them greet me and then be shocked to learn about me.*

Laura: Yes, and I'm sure that's been part of your consciousness for a long time. But if you look at the two people who came to you in Spirit, first of all Jesus, it's just extraordinary. The one person, the human and divine son of God, who could understand in compassion and love who you really were at your heart, not the way that you died, and General Eisenhower, President Eisenhower, after whom you were named.

Dwight: *Yeah, and we've gotten to know each other a little bit.*

Laura: It just doesn't get any better than that.

Dwight: *Well, one of the things that is so nice is that even though I haven't been at this for very long—I don't know, how did I get to go to the head of the class? How did I go from the way I died and the shame I felt about it to hanging out with these two? You know how it is there, if you want to invite the president out for lunch, how in the world would you do that? But here you just ask him and that's all there is to it.*

Laura: Isn't that amazing?

Dwight: *It is. And no wonder it's eternity, because even if that's all you wanted to do, that's a whole lot of breakfasts, lunches, and dinners. If all you ever wanted to do was just meet up with famous people, you could spend a whole lot of eternity doing only that and have yourself a fine time.*

Laura: That's right. I want to come back to your relationship with General Eisenhower, President Eisenhower, in a moment. But the reason we called to you today, Dwight, you may already know. Father Nathan is writing a book on people who've had this kind of Interrupted Death Experience, like you. Their stories can bring out some extraordinary dimension of that, the compassion and love that's surrounded them on the other side, and how they managed then to move on. Yours is a very compelling story, a dark kind of environment when it happened, but you came into the light with that love and compassion of Jesus surrounding you. It's a very powerful story, and Father Nathan would like to include it in his book. There may be around you now some of the other people who are going to be featured in the book, who have given their permission to tell their stories. We're wondering if you would allow your story to be told.

Dwight: *I would, and here's why. I think one of his concerns is, depending upon the amount of detail that was given in the dream or that was revealed in conversation later, when the book comes out, if it finds a broad readership—I think that's his phrase—we might be recognized by next of kin, family, or friends. In my case, my family and friends already endured the shock of my murder. They may also have been wounded that I kept a secret from them, or were just shocked to learn more about me. I think they've already been through all the hell I could give them. I don't think reading of my story would be opening a wound or be some kind of fresh assault, or something like that. I wasn't married, and I was old enough that my parents didn't need to think of me as their little boy. The simple answer is just yes, please take my story and use it.*

Laura: It's redemptive. I think it will be for a lot of people. The lack of judgment on Christ's part, the kind of life review that you've experienced, the prominence of President Eisenhower as kind of being your patron saint, it's quite a remarkable story of redemption.

Dwight: *Well, and I had no idea. I knew that I was named Dwight; it's an unusual name. I never knew it was because of President Eisenhower. I never paid any attention to it. When he died I didn't pray for President Eisenhower or have pictures of him hanging around. I was named for him, that's all. I didn't know he paid any attention to me until that picture, when Father Nathan was present, I had all these—suddenly here's President Eisenhower.*

Laura: We're not going to focus on how you died that much. I think that in the story that Nathan wrote up—

Dwight: *He's already written it, hasn't he?*

Laura: Yes. It's well handled, and he might put some of this narrative we're having now in the book.

Dwight: *Yeah, I didn't show him anything lurid. In the dream I just gave him what I thought was necessary to know what happened.*

Laura: Well, we're grateful for your permission, and also grateful for the way you've been healing. I wonder, before we go, if there's anything more you'd like to share with us about what's been happening for you since you moved on with President Eisenhower and Jesus came to see you.

Dwight: *Well, I think when people are injured or when they have a serious illness or heart attack or something—even you've been through cancer surgery, I think—there's something that happens right away. People want to know how bad it is. Is it a Stage 1, 2, 3, or 4? Or they want statistics, percentages; they want to compare the person's state of being with others in similar circumstances and want to know what are my odds, and all that. Well, what they've taught me is that even though I've spent some time in hiding, it was really more like I was in ICU. I was treated in the afterlife as a wounded one and not as somebody who was to be sentenced or convicted or have the book thrown at them or anything. I wasn't treated as somebody who had violated sacred rules as much as that I was a wounded soul who needed medical help. And I got that, and the time that it took, nobody made me feel like, "Well, finally! You'd think after all this time you'd be better than this." It was just—I just healed to the point that I could take part, say yes, and be welcomed by the president and others. And now what I'm hearing is that I've rebounded, like my healing powers are quite strong. Didn't that happen to you, Laura, when you had cancer? Or you've certainly known about people where there was a certain prognosis or expectation or whatnot, and you flew past the standards, or whatever. Anyway, I'm much healthier and happier than I have any right to be.*

Laura: That's wonderful and inspiring. It will give many people hope, so thanks very much, Dwight.

Dwight: *If that's so, I would only be grateful and happy for that. And if anybody wanted to think about me in the future, rather than think about me as someone who died in a shameful way—well, they can think that if they like, because it's true—however, it's only one bit of truth in a much larger story and there are better and larger things to think about.*

Laura: Well, and the way in which you were treated was so remarkable and hopeful that it will really help people who are thinking about what might happen to them in the afterlife. So we will leave it there, and just are grateful for your coming today and bringing the other people who will be featured in the book, as well as President Eisenhower, with you. So, many blessings to you, Dwight, and we'll hope to connect another time.

Dwight: *Okay, thank you for your help. And I do know of this team of people who've already said yes to having their stories in the book. They are in the background today. We've already become a little bit acquainted, because for me this was a formality. I had already decided, yes, I'd be happy to have my story included. This just makes it official.*

　　　　　　Afterlife, *Interrupted*

Laura: Very good. Well, we'll say hello to all of them as well.

Dwight: *Okay.*

Laura: Many blessings to you.

Nathan: Glory be to the Father, and to the Son, and to the Holy Spirit, as it was in the beginning, is now, and will be forever. Amen.

## Chapter Twelve
# The Plane Crash

I want to share this story because I really care that people who have lost a loved one to a violent, traumatic death understand that, even in such cases, most people pass quickly into the afterlife and don't get stuck. How would I know that? Well, the story that follows involved twenty people dying at the same time in the same event. On the basis of what I've seen of it, only one person out of the twenty interrupted the process and needed this kind of help.

I received this dream early in 2006:

*I was in some tropical place. It seemed Caribbean. I was lingering over a late lunch, or at least the remains of it, with a companion. We were outdoors in a leisurely, cabana–like setting somewhere after 2:00 p.m.*

*All at once, there was a loud buzzing noise. I turned and looked up into the sky. There was a plane flying very low, but it wasn't an ordinary plane. It was like an antique plane of unusual design.*

*When I got a closer look at it, it really wasn't a plane, exactly. It was more like a flying casket. It was rectangular, with two levels: ten people on the bottom row and ten just above them, almost like you would stage a photo with people seated with another row of people over their shoulders. It looked sort of like an old biplane, but, anyway, a very unusual-looking flying thing.*

*It was noisy, and it flew very low, almost clipping the top of a palm tree. I said to my dining companion, "My God, those people are lucky. They could have all been killed." The plane flew over us, out of my field of vision, over another set of palm trees.*

*Suddenly, there was a loud bang and a plume of smoke. It was pretty clear the plane had crashed. I ran in that direction, then stopped abruptly because I found myself in an ethereal field with bodies on the ground. There appeared what seemed like a black gospel choir with people dressed in white robes with their hands outstretched, extended down as in blessing over the recently deceased people in the field. It felt as if it might've been a Pentecostal kind of Christian, maybe Afro-Caribbean, choir singing over this field of people who had just died. I awoke.*

I sat up in my bed and thought, "I'll bet that's that plane crash that was on Miami Beach." I remember seeing it on the CBS Evening News the night it occurred. Because it was on Miami Beach, lots of people had camcorders and cameras with them. (This was before we all had a phone in our pocket that could record a video.) Anyway, there were videos of this plane as it was smoking and crashing into shallow water pretty near the beach. As it turned out, it was on December 19, 2005 that this crash took place. I received the dream sometime within the following few months.

When I went into protected prayer about it with my prayer partner, a lady came forward and said her name was Sophia and that she was on the plane, and that she had her infant daughter, Bethie, in her lap on the plane. She said that she was seated near the front on the left–hand side, near where you normally walk onto a plane as a passenger. She said that it all happened very fast, but that she understood right away that they were in very serious trouble. She turned and shouted for everyone to brace for impact. The crash was not survivable; everyone aboard died.

Sophia made it clear that she wasn't here about herself, that is, she wasn't the person who needed to be helped. But there was one lady on the plane who was stuck and that was the reason that we were engaged.

This all happened thirteen years ago; I didn't record it, and I don't have written notes, so some of this is confusing even to me. I thought about not even including it in the book because of my own lack of clarity about it. However, it might not hurt for you readers to know that this process sometimes has a lack of clarity about it, and you just move through it the best you know how.

Anyway, Sophia explained that one of the women passengers needed our help. This woman was married with young children; she was traveling with a female friend, also a wife with young kids. School was out for the children; the women had left the children in the care of the two husbands and gone Christmas shopping. The woman whom we were to help had persuaded her friend to buy tickets on this odd little commuter plane that was sort of a novelty. So rather than going to the Miami airport and taking a standard airplane, they were going to Ft. Lauderdale to ride in this antique plane from the late forties.

The friend thought it was a poor idea. She thought it sounded creepy and unsafe to fly in such an old plane. Her friend countered with, "Well, surely they wouldn't put it in the air

*Afterlife, Interrupted*

if it were unsafe," and her friend relented. They got on the plane. Then, the plane crashed moments after taking off for the return trip to Bimini, Bahamas, on Miami Beach. One of the wings had fallen off on ascent.

As I mentioned earlier, most people passed swiftly, but the one lady didn't. Sophia said she looked like she was ready to talk. She came in quickly and didn't offer her name; we just launched into the story that was keeping her stuck. It was a heartbreaking one.

This poor lady had not only suffered her own sudden death, but felt responsible for ruining the lives of her husband and children. And if that weren't bad enough, she blamed herself for ending the life of her friend and ruining the lives of her friend's surviving husband and children. No wonder she couldn't rest in peace or cross over.

"It's all my fault," she said. She was blaming herself for everything. "Now my children are all going to have awful lives because they lost their mother so early, and my neighbor's kids will all have terrible lives because they'll have lost their mom, too."

She was obviously in grief, but she was also going well beyond what could be known. I had to counsel her to calm down and help her deal with the facts.

"Remember that you're in grief," I told her, "and that people who are in grief are in a lot of pain and might not be thinking as clearly as they will be sometime later when the first layer of their pain lessens."

I reminded her, "You know, all you did was buy a plane ticket. I fly a lot. At any given time, I probably have several saved reservations for future flights. If you're guilty of anything, it's buying a very unlucky plane ticket. And yes, I understand that you feel bad that your neighbor wouldn't have been on the plane were it not for your persuasion. However, you committed no sin here. You did invite your friend into that, but you had no way of knowing that you were doing anything unsafe. All you and she really did was be in the wrong place at the wrong time."

She didn't really want to be persuaded away from her feelings of guilt, but I could at least remind her of the truth as a counselor. I think that's one of the things that a counselor can do: help people check their facts so that if they get all upset over things that aren't factual, you can at least point that out to them. When I've been on the receiving end of others' counsel, I know that has helped me. Jesus once said, "Don't worry about tomorrow, today has trouble enough of its own." Life has enough real trouble; no need to borrow the unreal kind. If a traumatized person can't digest that just now, there might be a later, calmer, time when they can. Then they might get some relief so that they can focus on what's real in the midst of a scene that also involves some kind of exaggerated unreality.

"You know," I told this woman, "you have no way of knowing whether your children or your neighbor's children will end up having bad lives because they lost their mothers early. It's nothing you would wish for a child, but surely in history, there have been plenty of people who grew up to have happy, productive lives after the sudden death of their mothers at an early age."

She did listen to that. I asked her if her neighbor was angry at her, and she said, "No, I don't think she is, but it's still my fault."

"Well, you can accuse yourself of wrongdoing as long as you please, because that's your perfect right, but I don't believe you'd be talking to me unless you were open to change. I think there's a reason that we're talking, and I'm going to at least offer what I have to say and you can do with it as you like."

I said, "You're not the first mother to have died leaving small children behind, are you? Surely there's a way that you can continue to be a part of their lives and to be in some way supportive of them, even though you can't be with them in the way that you were prior to your accident and sudden death."

"Well, how would I do that?" she wondered.

"Sweetheart, you're asking the right question of the wrong person. What I'd like you to do is ask around, ask your guardian: How does one learn how to be a helpful parent of small children that your death has forced you to leave behind? It seems to me there would be some learning curve. You wouldn't want to be some sad, creepy ghost, right? You'd probably need to learn when are the right and wrong moments to hang around your family. And because there are surely other persons needing to learn those same lessons, there are probably classes, probably something like an academy. I know that here there are grief support groups for widowed spouses with small children. Why wouldn't there be afterlife ones?"

That's where I think I'll leave it. I just don't remember that much more about how our time together concluded. I remember the conversation was long, but I was mostly trying to help this poor woman separate fact from fiction. She had a very good reason for her exaggerated grief. She died in a dramatic crash, but her dramatic response to it was painful to her and not at all helpful. She was not resting in peace, nor was she moving on. I felt like my job was to help her attain some peace such that she could make a plan, or at least cooperate with others who might help her figure out what to do next. She needed to stop punishing herself for everything in sight. It was quite clear that she was most highly motivated to figure out how she could still be a loving contributor to the upbringing of her children. That was the way forward.

Because I'd received this dream relatively recently—I think I was dealing with her within six months of the accident—and the Internet was just emerging, I thought, "Maybe I'll see if I can search the Internet and find out more information about that plane crash and who died in it." I've watched a lot of television shows that involve detective groups, and they often have at least one geeky computer whiz who, with only a few keystrokes, can unravel mysteries that save the day. Oftentimes, these people have access to massive databases and with just a minimum of effort can find all kinds of information about everything.

But in 2006, I was a late arrival to the Internet party. I was by no means skilled at navigating the web, and wouldn't say that I am even now. However, I did find a *Miami Herald* article that included a passenger list. It wasn't easy. There are all these sites that you go on that immediately want you to become a member, create a password and a username, pay a fee, and all that. But this *Miami Herald* passenger list included a child named Bethany Ann Sherman; I figured this might be "Bethie," the daughter Sophia had mentioned. But I had no way of knowing which of the other passengers might be the woman Sophia wanted us to help. I'm a Catholic priest, not a detective; I couldn't afford to spend hours trying to sleuth out a solution. I decided I'd have to let that be the road not taken.

Years later, as this book was coming into form, my partner and I did go into protected prayer to ask for permission to include this story here. My prayer partner and I said our protective prayer, surrounding ourselves with the holy angels and saints. We asked if it were possible to speak with those we'd met years earlier in the story about the plane crash in Miami Beach. The first person to come in was Bethie's mom, Sophia.

Sophia: *If Bethie had grown up, I'd be known as "Bethie's Mom." Even though I died and my baby died that day, we went through the passage. The reason the dream came to Nathan was because of one woman. I didn't know her. In the short time we had, I was on the front left side of the plane and shouted to everyone to brace themselves. The plane just had a flight attendant and a pilot. The crash wasn't survivable. It was abrupt.*

*Everybody was up and out of their bodies. I was kind of like a sheep dog and continued to be the boss, telling everybody to "Come this way," but everybody had a guardian. Then I stood down, and others were in charge.*

*The name of the other woman was something like Lynn, or Linda or Lydia, the lady who needed help in the plane crash.*

And at that point the other lady came in. I'll call her Lynn, although I'm not entirely sure of her name and in fact the passenger list I found doesn't seem to have a match for this name.

Lynn: *That would be me. He [Nathan] helped me get over feeling guilty. It wasn't the first time, but it was a pattern. I often thought things were my fault; that I needed to be punished. At the time of the crash, I didn't want to go to a good place because I was a bad girl.*

*He helped me. People don't show up in his dreams unless they're on the cusp, closer to moving than they think they are. I had to stop lying to myself. In this process the truth is important. "How can I still be a part of raising my kids?" That was my question. He told me, "You're not the first person to die and leave children." It made sense that there was a school system to figure things out in an organized way. I still feel responsible for my neighbor's kids, my husband, and my kids. I can still be a force; there are ways to continue. Love doesn't die. Space and time aren't really issues. There's still a way to make the most of what you had. There's some good to be had for hovering around. It created a world of love.*

There was a shift. The woman left. Sophia, the helpful woman, returned.

Sophia: *If you need to verify this, go to a list of the victims. Linda—not confident he got it right—I'll leave it to you. It might make life easier for you. Thanks be to God, I'm over that. I have met other people whose lives ended abruptly. We've had to calm down and find another way to be, not a wife and mother of children. I dream about different versions of my life and explore those. It's like group therapy. Others had helpful experiences that were helpful to me. Right now, I've got what I needed.*

So that's how this particular story ends, at least for now.

Helpful Sophia didn't hang around. We're not buddies the same way I feel I am with some of the folks I've met doing this work. Sophia doesn't seem particularly connected to the tragic crash that caused her death. As she said, she's having new experiences and is finding other ways to be.

And the other woman? She's learned that love doesn't die. She sounds at peace, which is all I wanted for her in the first place.

## Chapter Thirteen
# Help Your Brother Johnny Castle

It was the fall of 2009. I was in my office at Stanford University, where I was the director of the Catholic Community, just minding my own business, going about my morning, when I got a phone call from my sister Cathryn. "I think I have a message for you," she told me.

At the time, Cathryn lived in Oregon on an alpaca farm. Alpacas are native to Peru. They look like llamas, only smaller. Cathryn had a love for them, but she felt that it was important to love the people of Peru, too, and not just their exported exotic animals. While learning about alpacas, she learned about the people of Peru, specifically the Quechua Indians, who live way up in the Andes Mountains above the vegetation and tree lines. The Quechua people eat mostly potatoes, whose carbohydrates, when digested, turn into sugars. That sugar had a profound effect on the dental hygiene of these people, which was quite poor, and they were vulnerable to abscesses, rotted teeth, and infected jaws. The jaw isn't very far from the heart. Bacteria from the infections would then travel to and infect the heart. People there died young of all kinds of coronary disease related to bad dental hygiene.

Cathryn visited Peru several times as part of a volunteer team that provided dental care to the Quechua people. She served as a dental assistant. While in Peru, she'd developed a prayer relationship with the Dominican saint, St. Rose of Lima. St. Rose was famous for her lifelong acts of fasting, penance, and contemplation and for her extraordinary efforts and sacrifices to help the poor. She became the first person born in the Americas to be given sainthood.

"I just was in prayer with St. Rose of Lima," Cathryn continued, "and she was very loud and insistent. She kept telling me, 'Help your brother Johnny Castle. Help your brother Johnny Castle. Help your brother Johnny Castle.' I tried explaining to her that I had brothers named Nathan, David, and Mike, but no Johnny. She changed the message to, 'Your brother.

Johnny Castle.' The message came slower than before, but just as loud. Over and over again. So I got on the Internet and searched 'Johnny Castle.' That's why I'm calling you. Like I said, I think the message from St. Rose is for you."

"Okay," I said, "What have you got?"

"Well," she said, "It turns out Johnny Castle is the name of Patrick Swayze's character in *Dirty Dancing*. It was a low-budget picture that hit it big. It really launched his career."

"Okay," I said. I had a feeling I knew where this was going.

"And you know where Patrick Swayze is now, don't you?"

"I do. He has pancreatic cancer, and I think he's dying in Stanford Hospital." Sadly, news of the actor's grave illness had been all over the media.

"Well, then, I've delivered the message," Cathryn said. "We're supposed to help our brother Johnny Castle."

"Okay. Well, I'm used to people coming in the night with their scenes of traumatic death, but we've never been approached this way. I wonder how I'm supposed to handle this."

"Tell me about it!" Cathryn laughed. "I'm not used to serving as your spiritual secretary, so I don't know what else to do, either. I'll pray for you and Johnny Castle, but I think this is all yours now. Oh, and by the way, Maximilian Kolbe was with St. Rose this morning. He said to tell you hello." Maximilian Kolbe was a Franciscan friar who volunteered to give his own life to save a stranger at the Auschwitz death camp during World War II. Cathryn and I had prayed, asking him to be with our dad, Max, when he was dying. Maximillian became our spirit-friend.

"Okay, baby sister. Consider the message delivered. I'll see what I can do."

I had the credentials to visit in Stanford Hospital as a chaplain. I'd been through all the protocols and had the little badge with my picture on it that entitled me to move freely about the hospital to visit the sick. However, you just don't go barging in where you haven't been invited. I only visited people who'd asked me to visit them. And this request was so strange. I just thought–well, I prayed about it–and I thought, "Okay, Lord. I'm your servant. I'm ready to do whatever I'm supposed to do, and it seems like you want me to help Johnny Castle."

So, I went to the Director of Chaplains at Stanford Hospital, who was a Catholic priest late in his career, a very sweet soul, an old gentleman of a priest. I just kind of laid it all out. I said, "John, this might sound as crazy as the day is long, but I have these experiences where people come in the night and show me their traumatic deaths. Then, I get with a partner and pray about it. We're usually able to help the person who is stuck to move along. This time though, my sister has called me and said 'St. Rose of Lima wants us to help Johnny Castle.' So, what I'm wondering is, is it okay for me to know what room Patrick Swayze is in, and is it possible for me to get in to see him?"

"Nathan," he said, "you couldn't have asked at a worse time. Just this week at UCLA Medical Center, some tabloid journalist crashed the hospital room of a celebrity and got pictures of their medical chart. I don't even know who it was, what celebrity, but now we're all on high alert, and we're all having to reexamine what protocols and standards we have to keep celebrities free from prying eyes when they're sick in the hospital. So, no, you may not go visit Patrick Swayze unless Patrick Swayze asks for you to visit him first."

"Okay, John, thank you," I said. "I knew I could get a straight answer from you. And if you think I'm crazy, thanks for not saying so."

So now what do I do? I was all dressed up with nowhere to go. I went down to the lobby and sat in the middle of the busiest place in the lobby of Stanford Medical Center. I looked conspicuous in my priest suit with communion in my pocket. I said a prayer to the Holy Spirit: "Okay, here I am, Lord. I've come to do your will. I'm here to help Johnny Castle. You're going to have to open some doors, especially Patrick Swayze's, because I've done all I know how to do. Amen." So, I sat there and watched people go by and anticipated that at any moment somebody was going to come rushing up to me and say, "Oh, thank God you're here. We've been waiting for you," and lead me into Patrick Swayze's sick room.

Well, I waited, I prayed, and I people-watched, and I checked my cellphone messages. Then I waited and prayed a little more. Half an hour later I said, "Okay, Lord, this is as long as I can afford to sit here. I have other things to do. I can't sit here all day waiting for some odd person to run up to me and escort me into Patrick Swayze's hospital room. I have to get back to my other work."

Some days later, I met with one of my prayer partners, because I still had a backlog of night visitors that we hadn't yet helped to cross over. I said to my prayer partner, "This is what's happened. Could we go into prayer and ask about what we're supposed to do about Johnny Castle? I'm sure the Holy Spirit won't keep us in the dark indefinitely. I just don't know what we're supposed to do next. So, we need to ask the Holy Spirit: what are we supposed to do about helping Johnny Castle?"

My prayer partner and I went into our protective prayer and surrounded ourselves with the angels and the saints, including St. Rose of Lima, who didn't speak to me this time. She's chatty with my sister, but not necessarily with me. Incidentally, I'm a Dominican, and so is St. Rose. We belong to the same religious order, as did both of my aunts. So this is kind of all in the family on the spirit level.

We went into prayer, and my prayer partner was able to facilitate speech. "There's somebody here that wants to talk to you, but it's not St. Rose," she said. "It's a woman, and it's about Johnny Castle."

Well, the person who came through was Vicky, the elder sister of Patrick Swayze. I can feel her presence now even as I'm remembering that encounter and writing about it. I didn't record these sessions years ago when this happened, so I'm having to recall this one from memory. It turned out that Vicky and I both grew up in southeast Texas. The Swayzes were from North Central Houston, I think. We learned that, as children, Patrick, Vicky, and their other siblings attended St. Rose of Lima Catholic School. Isn't that the coolest thing? You think the school or the building is merely named after some dead person, but in fact you're a child under the patronage of this saint that's still looking out for you.

We learned from Vicky that she had wanted to be become a famous musician. Vicky joined a garage band in Houston and played at local clubs right about the time her brother's success was meteoric. He went to New York, and hit it big quickly. Suddenly he became a big movie star, with all this fame and a future that seemed unlimited. All the while, Vicky was struggling in this garage band in Houston. Then, she started getting into the alcohol and drug scene that's often a part of the late-night, after-hours lifestyle in clubs. Before long, she was an addict. So from her early twenties until her death at forty-five, she never was really clean and sober. For two decades, she was always struggling with substance abuse of one kind or another.

It really bothered Vicky, after she passed, that she had spent years running through her parents' retirement savings (her father had died twelve years before her) attending and failing at rehab programs. She thought of herself as this drain on the family. They were always kind to her, but it was difficult because she was always a challenge. Even when she wasn't problematic, everybody was waiting for the other shoe to drop. She got tired of being this irresponsible ne'er-do-well member of the family who people liked having around, but who also came with this big downside. Frequently, she would end up having to be taken care of one way or another, oftentimes by being sent to yet another rehab.

Anyway, Vicky eventually died. Now her brother Patrick was in late-stage pancreatic cancer. This is the issue she presented to us: all she wanted to do was to be with her brother and help him as he passed. So our work became helping her get her head around that and learn what she would need to do.

It turns out that she hadn't really completely crossed over because of the complexity of her own journey and of the mental mess that she was in. My prayer partner and I talked to her a little bit and helped her reason to the fact that, after you die, you don't have a body with cells that crave addictive drugs. There would likely be fallout in the afterlife from having lived a lifestyle that had substance abuse in it for so long. Surely there would be behavior patterns that she would have to mature through, or challenge, or confront, or change. But she could do all of that without the burden of addiction-ridden body chemistry.

Vicky was able to take stock of herself. She was able to say that she felt like she was well enough put together that she could be of some use. She wouldn't have to think of herself as being just this drag on family energies that she had been prior to her passing. She was able

Afterlife, *Interrupted*

to see herself as someone who was ready to help her brother. I don't remember all the nuts and bolts of it, but I do remember encouraging her to ask her guardian angel for the help that she needed to learn how to be a part of Patrick's crossover team.

That's really the way that our role in this story ended. Vicky didn't need for us to guide her to the afterlife, as we did so frequently with others. She wanted to stick around here a little while longer and accompany her brother, so that when his time came, they could cross over together. She just needed some encouragement that indeed she could aspire to be a helpful afterlife presence for her brother and perhaps help him pass when his time came.

That's the story of helping our brother Johnny Castle, at least as far as it goes. The person that we were really asked to help was his sister Vicky. When we decided to put this story in the book, as with the others, we felt it was important to get Vicky's permission. Recently, with a prayer partner, I went into prayer asking to speak to Vicky Swayze. Not surprisingly, we first got St. Rose of Lima.

Would you like to listen in?

Nathan: [We began with our usual protected prayer.] We're grateful for all you always do for us. We would like your help again to keep us safe. We call on our own guardians and our patrons, Dominic and Benedict, and St. Mary Magdalene.

Laura: And all those in the realms of light who would like to be present to surround us with the light we need in order to contact Vicky Swayze.

Nathan: And I'd like to call on any who are in the family line of Vicky, Patrick, or their whole clan, any who are among the holy ones who might like to gather round, be with us, keep us safe. And we call on St. Rose of Lima, who started all this.

Nathan: St. Rose wants to go first.

Laura: Thank you for coming, St. Rose. This is quite an honor for you to come to us. I'm Laura, and you're talking through Father Nathan's voice. So please go ahead.

St. Rose: *And I understand that you are on a schedule, and you have other work to do, so I will be brief. I merely wanted to greet you as a woman of God who is working, I know, with Mary Magdalene and has had office in the church. The current project you're helping Nathan with goes to the heart of something so simple and so basic. It ought not need to be complex because it's just the Easter joyful message: Jesus is risen from the dead! And when that's well understood, He's the first–fruits, and we all take part; there's nothing simpler or more basic. It has offshoots, because that simple message tells everybody that they are as important as Jesus, that we're all sons and daughters of the Light, that we're all part of the one Father. So everything that involves fighting injustice or raising up the poor, or every other thing that the church does, I think, is rooted in this work you're doing, or at least it can be. Your work needn't be thought of as* some odd manifestation of peculiar gifts given only to a few, although it's really beyond anything you can do to prevent that perception. I think perhaps you know a little of my story, and it included gifts people thought of as astounding and amazing, and so on, and there's a certain spectacle that attends these things. Even though one might try to downplay them, people will act and think as they please, and so there's a certain amount of hubbub, of glare, associated with these experiences. But nevertheless, one must be undeterred and go about one's work, and I'm grateful for the work you're doing._

Laura: Thank you, and thank you for that explanation. I wonder if you would be willing to be quoted in Nathan's book.

St. Rose: _He's wondering right now if you have pushed the button to record._

Laura: Yes, I did.

St. Rose: _Very good. Would I mind being quoted in a book? I would not, because it's true._

Laura: Thank you so much. We appreciate that very much, and we're hoping that Vicky Swayze will come through to speak with us. Is she nearby?

St. Rose: _She's right here. So I shall move aside and let you be about your good work._

Laura: Thank you very much. God bless you.

We felt Saint Rose fade away and then felt Vicky Swayze come in.

Laura: Hello, Vicky. My name is Laura, and you'll be speaking through Nathan.

Vicky: _Yes, I remember him._

Laura: Good, good.

Vicky: _I've been here all along. I was overhearing you, and he trying to recollect, or you were questioning him and trying to get him to remember, who he was with and how it moved when he first helped me. He's had many of these, and even though my brother is famous and this story moves a different way than some of your other ones, still he's had so many, and we only talked briefly. All he did was help me in a short conversation, and we've not connected beyond that._

Laura: Well, thanks for coming to be with us today. And maybe you can help refresh Nathan's memory a little bit about what went on with your conversation. And his sister, Cathryn, you'll remember, was part of that as well. He and Cathryn will be writing a chapter of the book about this experience, and we asked all the others who are going to be featured in the book this way if they would be willing to give him their permission to be presented and quoted as accurately as we can, because we're recording this.

Vicky: _Yes, I can do that without any hesitation. I can only speak for myself, and the story involves my brother. Others might have an opinion about it because we have surviving siblings and all of that, but I don't think you need to go to that level of_ *permission if you're simply telling a story that is not an embarrassment or there's no reason for anyone to feel like, I don't know, there's been some intrusion. Even being a relative of a celebrity—I mean, I had a little bit of difficulty with it because I was envious, and then much of that was moving through addiction. My life was partly cloudy with a chance of thunderstorms. There'd be parts of a day or parts of a month that were clear and parts that were muddled. But I'm making this harder than it has to be. The simple answer is yes, you may use my story as far as I'm concerned, and whether anyone else's permission needs to be sought is beyond me.*

Laura: Well, thank you so much for that, and I hope you're doing well.

Vicky: *I am, and I think I'd like to talk a little about what opened up for me as a result of St. Rose's, Cathryn's, and Nathan's help because it's simple and not a complicated story to understand. It might even help people. There are so many—I never lived anywhere other than the U.S.—but there are so many addiction issues of one kind or another. There are so many people who care about loved ones who get drawn into the web of all the sadness and confusion and expense and hope and broken-heartedness. There's just so many people who might benefit from hearing a happy story. I died in addiction, or as a result of it, and never really did get both feet on the ground firmly before moving from here, and that's why I was in between and didn't cross over. It was so important for me to show my family that I do have my feet on the ground, so to speak, and I can be a helper without being a drag. Fortunately, there are no more finances to deal with, so I'm not costing people money anymore, and I'm not as unreliable as before. I'm not a picture of afterlife mental health—I don't know what you call it—but I'm not the mess that I was before I passed. And I really was capable of being part of a team when my brother was dying. And being able to be useful, and that's all I wanted. I wanted to be able to show up and be someone people started thinking of as competent. I wanted people to be happy to see me, because if you lived as erratically as I did, people might be genuinely happy to see me, but it always had an asterisk next to it. We're happy to see you while you are as you are, but the subtext was always "how long are you going to be this way before you're drunk or stoned or depressed or crying?" I wasn't able to stay positive and helpful long enough for people to relax in my presence and be glad I was there. They didn't know how long it would be before they had to caretake me somehow.*

Laura: But it sounds as though you've done remarkably well since your passing. And you were there for your brother?

Vicky: *Some of this is simple. Nathan has taught this to people, that it's as simple as leaving your body and leaving behind things that are just bodily. You've had cancer, haven't you?*

Laura: Yes.

Vicky: *Well, a lot of people die of that, and then in the moments after they leave their body, one of the immediate sensations is, "Oh, my God, I don't have cancer pain anymore," and "I'm not wrung out from chemo," or whatever. "I can move! I can get from the chair to the bed to the potty—and I don't even need to do that anymore." And for people like me that had cells that craved alcohol or drugs, there's an immediate release from that, and so one level of crap falls away, although plenty of other things don't. You still have to work through being trusting and confident that you can make a plan and follow it and that you can have a positive future. All of those things need to be learned again or trusted in or something. They wouldn't have let me come as far as getting into Father Nathan's work if they didn't think I was far enough along that I could handle it. Because I was asking to be put to work, and I wouldn't have been of any use, even in an afterlife way, if I started being some erratic, pain-in-the-ass relative you'd wish would just go away.*

Laura: Well, the story of how you came through Cathryn is so interesting, in that it was Johnny Castle, and their family name is Castle, so…

Vicky: *Yes, and St. Rose. We went to the school and the church, and it's not like we were—we were sort of casual about all that. I never paid that much attention to St. Rose. Who knew after all those years that she was still following us and paying attention to us because we had gone to a school with her name on it?*

Laura: Well, yes, it sounds as though she has watched over you.

Vicky: *A little, and I don't want to be too bold or overstepping, but we're kind of friends, in a bit of a way at least. It wasn't easy for me to make friends because I wasn't an easy person to be around. You know, when you're in a band and you're drinkin' and druggin' and stuff, you have these people who are friends, but then they disappear when things go bad. And so I use the word "friend" cautiously, because I may still be learning how to be one, but she and I have spent some time together very pleasantly, and there's nothing about her that's snooty even though she's a saint. One of the benefits of having a famous brother is that you've already dealt with the awe of being in the presence of famous people. So that might be one benefit of all of it, that now when I run into people that others recognize right away, I'm not necessarily stumbling over myself to feel like I'm worthy of their presence or anything. And I had that problem a lot— plenty of people I felt inferior to—but somehow a lot of that's gone away, and I can just be who I am. And part of that is because, as I think you've learned from other people, here there just aren't the unnecessary judgments that people get so used to living under or have inflicted on others.*

Laura: That's a huge blessing in itself.

Vicky: *Now about my brother: one of the nice things about him is that he was not that guy. I can't remember a time when he ever said an unkind word—well, there must have been an unkind word somewhere along the line in his life—but he was just not known for that. He pretty much took people as they were, and he didn't see downsides of people. We'd talk a little bit about the industry and contracts and projects and things like that, and sometimes he would not want to work with a certain person because they had a reputation for treating partners badly. Sometimes people in that industry feel the need to shove others out of the way to make sure their best side is facing the camera. There were times when he would, I don't know, make critical judgments about decisions, not because he just wanted to be unkind, but sometimes he would say, you know, "I'm going to stay away from that guy because I just don't like what I see." But that didn't mean he had to go on and elaborate about people's sins and so on. Anyway, he was never one for judging, and sometimes I feel like I would be inflicting that on myself and feel like, you know, I would compare myself to him when I was in a bad mood and would think, oh, you know, he's Mr. Perfect, and he's got everything and I'm this mess, and so on. But he was patient with me even during that. And he had his own struggle with alcohol at one point so he also had to learn some of the way out of that. He succeeded in getting out of that in a way I never did.*

Laura: Do you spend any time with him now?

Vicky: *Sure. In fact, it's one of the nice things about both of us having died and me finishing passing over, because for one thing you can kind of start over. We've spent a little time looking at each other's lives from a 360 point of view: what was it like to be you? And him learning what it was like to be me, and without a whole bunch of unnecessary drama, but just a kind of factual look at "this is what led to that," and then when some of it begins to be, I don't know, like in conversation sometimes you'll be—the conversation will go in the direction of problems and trouble and so on, and at some point you want to come up for air and say, "Let's talk about more pleasant things." And sometimes we do that. We have an ability to laugh and enjoy memories, although, remember, we've been gone for a time from here, and we've had plenty of other experiences since. None of them involve addiction, and none of them involve pancreatic cancer, and, you know, we've linked up with our dad and other folks and had lots of adventures. I always did like music, and I've gotten to meet other musicians. I did want some of what my brother had. I wasn't in the kind of garage band club scene very long before bad things started happening, but you kind of get to jam with people. You know my life wasn't all that long compared to other people's, and parts of it I moved through in a cloud and didn't get to fully live freely, and so some of what I've done is circling back and kind of finding places where other people do the same thing or want to do the same thing, to go back and live parts of their life they were somehow not fully present to. I've been doing some of that. It's not like Patrick and I are joined at the hip because we never really were. Even when we were children, we were living in the same household but weren't necessarily side–by–side. He was busy all the time. He was always in sports, and you know our mom taught dance. And I don't know if we were as over–scheduled as a lot of kids seem to be now, but we didn't have very much idle time, and often that pulled us in different directions.*

Laura: Well, this is fascinating, Vicky, and so uplifting and inspiring to hear your story and your good life in the afterlife. We'd love to talk with you more, but I think for today we're going to have to leave it there. Thank you so very much for sharing with us, and we'll hope to connect again another time.

Vicky: *Yes, that would be nice, and I know you have other people to talk to, so I'll be on my way. Blessings on your book—that's your phrase, isn't it?*

Laura: Yes.

Vicky: *That's not a phrase I'm used to saying, but it was in here. I think it was more yours than his.*

Laura: And blessings on your life.

Vicky: *Thank you. That's sweet of you.*

Laura: And to your brother and St. Rose.

Vicky: *Yeah, and Patrick's been kind of standing here listening all the while, but he doesn't feel the need to step up to the mic or into the spotlight. He feels he had quite a lot of that, and for right now if they wanted to know, well, what about Patrick? Well, he's quite content to say, "This is Vicky's moment. This is Vicky's story. I'm standing here." Well, I'm not going to say this, but he said, "I'm proud of her." That's as close as he's going to come to a quotable line.*

Laura: That's lovely.

Vicky: *Okay, Bye-bye.*

Laura: Bye-bye.

Nathan: Glory be to the Father, and to the Son, and to the Holy Spirit, as it was in the beginning, is now, and will be forever. Amen.

I'm happy to report that I've spoken to other night visitors who have likewise appreciated the opportunity to step away from alcohol, drugs, sex addictions, and other afflictions. Free from the burdens on their bodies, they can look at the harm they inflicted and begin to make amends. It's never too late for redemption.

## Chapter Fourteen
# Eric, Alone With His Thoughts

I've read a lot of books. Most have an acknowledgments page near the front where the author thanks a bunch of people you don't know. It's easy to skip over, like the boring part of the Academy Awards show, where the statuette–holding winner starts thanking an endless list of family, friends, and co–workers. If they go beyond a few seconds, the theme music starts to play, and they're dragged off the stage.

When I started writing this book, I thought I was the sole author. I should have known better. Writing a book, like many things we do in life, is something we do with the help of others. In my case, I want to acknowledge the assistance of many friends in the afterlife as well as quite a few on this side. They've helped me beta test many of the ideas behind this book.

For example, I thought I had the perfect title and cover image at the outset. The cover would be a close–up photo of a big universal TV remote control. If you have a DVR, one of the buttons you can hit while you're watching your show is PAUSE. Then you can take a bathroom break or fix a snack. You still want to see the rest of the show; you just need to pause it a bit. When you're ready, you hit PLAY, and you're good to go. My book's title would be *Eternity Paused: Helping Stuck Souls Hit Play*. Isn't it brilliant!

When I started to work with my night visitor stuck souls, they explained why they'd paused things between the moment of their sudden deaths and whatever might come next. I began to see my job as helping them hit play!

My title and subtitle got vetoed along the way by more than one editor. They liked the "paused" idea but weren't so crazy about the whole remote–control concept.

I'm about to introduce you to Eric. My discarded subtitle might not have worked well for the whole book, but it's a good fit for Eric. The only child of PhD parents, Eric had just finished an undergraduate degree and was taking what many call a "gap year," pausing his life on purpose to have time to ponder what he'd do next. But a freak accident took his life while he was paused. He didn't feel as stuck as the others. He just needed some time—outside of time—to think, an afterlife "pause" before he would be ready to press "play."

Like the others, Eric found his way into my unconscious in a dream. I received it one night in mid–May, 2015.

*A young man, white, in his early twenties, had fallen along a hilly hiking trail. The land gave way beneath him, and he was in an avalanche of loose dirt. He came to rest upside down, buried in the dirt. Only his legs were sticking out; he couldn't move his arms, couldn't breathe, and was barely alive. I stayed with him and shouted for help. I told the young man I was Nathan Castle and asked if he knew that name (I don't know why). I told him we were at a place that was well traveled and that someone would be along soon.*

*A group of three student doctors arrived. We got him to safety. They said he'd be fine and would need little treatment. Then they spoke among themselves about how the treatment for head injuries differed in Europe (we were in the United States). Someone was wearing a Disney sweatshirt. Medical students from Stanford and Duke arrived on the scene. They came in pairs and in large numbers. I awoke.*

This time I was with my friend Katie. She had heard my stories of helping stuck souls and offered to help if needed. Katie is a college campus minister, and was nervous about doing this for the first time. When she heard that one of the stuck ones was a young adult, she suggested we start with that one. Katie and I were able to engage in conversation with this young man and learned that his name was Eric. He was thoughtful and insightful. Katie and I did our usual prayer of protection and then introduced ourselves.

> Eric: *I'm Eric.*
> Katie: Tell us about yourself, Eric.
> Eric: *I was the only child of two very intelligent, curious parents, the kind who try to teach you to read before you're potty-trained. I think they played me classical music when I was still in the womb. They tried to have other kids, but that didn't work out. So it was just us.*
> Katie: Were you a college student?
> Eric: *I had been.*
> Katie: What did you study? Was it physics?
> Eric: *No, but I was interested in it and admired people who studied physics and chemistry. I liked to know how things worked and what they were made of. But I wanted a broader knowledge. I studied philosophy and anthropology and literature. I*

*studied psychology and economics, all kinds of things.*

Katie: Were you in school at the time of your passing?

Eric: *No. I hadn't really found the thing I wanted to pursue. I saw lots of peers who knew exactly the careers they wanted to prepare for. I just wasn't there yet. My parents didn't rush me about that. I was always reading and traveling and learning new things, but I wasn't in graduate school when the bad day happened.*

Katie: What was that day like for you, Eric?

Eric: *Well, I knew lots of people, and liked them, but I had few close friends. I think when people began to get close, I'd kind of pull away, keep it light. As an only kid I was used to being alone. My parents had a great marriage and were each other's best friends. They spent little time with other people. Our family was just this little cell. That's what I was used to. But I did like exploring new groups—showing up to advertised things and meeting new people having new adventures. I didn't usually make friends, though, except briefly and casually.*

*That day I joined some young people going on a group hike on a trail in the Appalachians. At first, I stayed with the group, but, as it turned out, everyone had come with someone they already knew and were in their own little groups and conversations. As the hike unfolded, I let people pass me until I was at the back of the line. I slowed down to let them get well ahead of me so I could be alone with my thoughts.*

*Suddenly, the ground beneath me gave way. I slid downhill. It was like an avalanche when people snow-ski off-trail. Except I was upside down in dirt with just my legs free. I couldn't move my arms. There was no air; I couldn't breathe. I knew I was in big trouble. It was over quickly.*

Katie: Didn't anyone show up to help you after that?

Eric: *Yeah, there were a bunch of people who had died while they were medical students. They helped me out, but I didn't really want to go with them. I just wanted to catch my breath, kind of regroup. I wasn't angry, just stunned. In the moment I just wanted to be alone.*

Katie: That makes sense. But when we get involved in these kinds of conversations, it's usually because folks are ready to move on and have some companionship now and might need a little help in figuring out what to do next.

Eric: *That would be me, I guess. So what do I do?*

Katie: Well, when we get to this point, sometimes they ask for a specific person they trust. Other times a relative or old friend shows up. Or people ask for whomever they want. Is there someone you'd like to meet up with?

Eric: *It doesn't have to be somebody religious? I wasn't religious.*

Katie: Sometimes it is, but lots of times it's someone you knew as a kid. You don't seem at all scared. In fact, when you were describing the bad day, you didn't even sound scared about dying. It sounded like you just sort of went with it. You wouldn't want the first face you see after dying to be someone scary, would you?

Eric: *But you said I could pick anybody?*

Katie: Well, I don't know how it all works. They'd have to be willing and available, I suppose. The main thing is you have to form the idea and ask and see what happens. Are you up for that?

Eric: *Sure.*

Katie: Okay. Who will we ask for?

Eric: *Albert Einstein.*

Katie: Well, alrighty, then. Albert Einstein! You heard the man, Dr. Einstein. Would you please make yourself available to my friend Eric here?

At this point, I quietly said a prayer. For non-religious people, I think that's best. For the record, the Creator of the Universe is wonderful at being present through the perfect person for each of us. Ever curious, Eric wanted Albert Einstein.

I don't always see as much in these situations as I feel or hear or just know. But I could tell we wouldn't be getting the elder Einstein. He'd be showing up as a much younger man, maybe as he looked at the beginning of his teaching career. And soon, there was the man himself. I could see him. He was maybe about six years older than Eric, old enough to be a mentor yet young enough to be a friend to someone unaccustomed to having friends. Albert's hair wasn't old-man white and wild like the picture of him in my mind. He was around thirty and was wearing a tweed jacket, very professorial.

We all just kind of nodded at each other. There wasn't a need for words. Eric and Albert went for a walk, the beginning of a new adventure. Eric wouldn't have to fall back and be alone with his thoughts any longer. He'd done enough of that. Now he had a traveling companion and universes to explore. Eric was about as unstuck as a guy could be.

I've been a campus minister for most of my career and have loved many college students and young adults. Eric stayed on my mind for a long time after he and Young Einstein went off together. When this book began to take shape, I thought of Eric and especially of the way he plucked Albert Einstein out of the blue. If this whole topic—night visitors in my dreams, little pastoral conversations with the dead, and helping them get unstuck with the help of their Nana—wasn't outlandish enough, now add celebrity to the mix! I wondered if anyone would believe me at all.

If you get to know Eric, especially in his own words that follow, the choice of Einstein makes perfect sense. So does the surprise of Dr. Einstein showing up as his young-professor self.

I had prayed for Eric and tried talking to him (without hearing anything back) for a couple of years when I thought it was time to ask his permission to use his story in this book. Prayer partner Laura and I had made a list of the people whose permission we wanted to seek and started down the roster. Though it wasn't my intention, I guess it was like we'd invited them all at once into a waiting room, then called for them one at a time; several of them had mentioned others who were waiting to talk with us.

Laura and I said our protective prayers as we sat outside my little casita on the campus of the University of Arizona. Don, whom you met in Chapter Six, showed up to give us an update on his afterlife and permission for us to proceed with his story in this book. When Don was finished, he offered to send in the next person. There was no need for subtle discernment. At my invitation, Eric hopped right into me and stepped right up to the microphone. He spoke to Laura, who was finishing up a book she titled *Extraordinary Time: Spiritual Reflections from a Season with Cancer, Death, and Transition*.

Laura: Hello, Eric.

Eric: *Congratulations on your book. Your book, not his book. You're working on a book, too, or you got a book deal?*

Laura: Yes, thank you so much. It's nice that you knew about that.

Eric: *I've been paying attention.*

Laura: That's sweet. How are things going for you now, Eric?

Eric: *Good. They were good for me pretty much. I know that I was in this category of people that were stuck. I don't mean to be conceited. I just think I was in it in a different way than a lot of people that you have dealt with were. I wasn't so much stuck like the poor fellow just now with the bloody face [he meant Don]. I just got covered in dirt. That's all. I didn't really care anyway, and I didn't pay that much attention to clothes and grooming. My parents weren't that way, and they didn't raise me that way.*

Laura: What are the kinds of things that you're interested in now and able to do?

Eric: *If you remember, I hadn't decided what I was going to study. I'd finished an undergraduate degree and I wasn't in grad school yet, even though my parents were PhDs, and it was pretty clear that that was the script I was going to follow. One of these days I was going to start the next part. I was playing around. Father Nathan was at Stanford. It's funny the way this works. He's let me come inside his consciousness. Like just now, all I did was mention Stanford, and it's like a light went on in a part of him that has all the Stanford storage. It's sort of like a video library.*

Laura: Like the Stanford part of Father Nathan's memories?

Eric: *There were a lot of people at Stanford that did–they did these blended, blurred-together degrees, where they would finish four years of an undergraduate degree, but then they would do a co-term, which meant staying on for one more year and getting a master's degree. Or they would start a blended professional program, where they went directly from a BA into a PhD. I was trying to decide what I was going to do, but I was pretty sure that it wasn't going to be more than a year off. I didn't think my parents would tolerate more than that. I don't think I would've tolerated it myself to spend much more than a year figuring out what was the course ahead. Then I was going to look for some sort of accelerated course once I settled on it.*

Laura: What kind of degree program did you want to follow?

Eric: *I just knew that—it's not that I hadn't thought of it, but I knew that I didn't want this clunky process of doing four years of something unrelated to what the next two-year thing was that then led to a PhD and yet a third thing, or whatever. I wanted something that was more seamless than that.*

Laura: I see.

Eric: *I had some ideas of what I might do, but I knew it was too early. I knew that I was going to be in for a lot of school and a lot of other people's rules, a lot of other people's schedules. I knew that I wanted a year where I wasn't on the clock on somebody else's time. That's the year that I ended up in that little rockslide thing I was in.*

Laura: So it was like a gap year? During the time that you were in that place of stillness—let's not call it "stuck", and let's say "in stillness"— and you were alone with your thoughts, had you formulated any ideas of what you had wanted to do with your life or that are translated into what you're able to do now?

Eric: *I wanted something that involved broad thinking. Partly that involved—I was interested in quantum physics and unified theory. It wasn't that I necessarily wanted to be a physicist. I didn't really like all the math involved that much, and I didn't want to be a mathematician or theoretical physicist. I wasn't looking for a job in some industry of the future, some sort of building time machines or God-knows-what people do when they go into these tech firms. I didn't want to do that. That's why I wasn't in a program yet. I knew I wanted to be in something that was really mentally stretching. I didn't know how it would have an application. I didn't want to be a philosopher. I wasn't particularly religious, so I wasn't going to be in religion, but I liked the way that people in religion and philosophy had respect for mystery and wonder. I liked the way that that overlapped with some of the new physics.*

*That's why I liked Einstein, because he was both. He did have the chops in math and all that that I admired but didn't want to emulate, but I also knew that he—I'd read some stuff that he'd written about God and what he thought about God, and how none of this would be possible without supreme intelligence and whatnot. I just hadn't made up my mind what I was going to do.*

Afterlife, *Interrupted*

*But after I died and when it was time to move and I needed a guide to help me out, I heard an aside that most people choose a family member, grandmother, or someone they trust and that sometimes they—what was the other one? Sometimes they take the luck of the draw, like maybe it would be somebody that they hadn't quite thought of that was a good fit, like their scout leader, or their piano teacher, or God-knows-who.*
Laura: Yes.
Eric: *Then the last option was: who would you like to be with on a desert island? Something really more aspirational and inspirational and cool and exciting even though when he [Nathan] rattled off the list, he added that one as sort of an asterisk. I jumped on it and said, "Did you just say anybody, it could be anybody?" That's when I thought, "Then, damn, if it can be anybody, I want Einstein." It was the coolest thing because he didn't come as old Einstein, the big shock of crazy white hair and big oval walrus mustache and kindly sparkly eyes with magic in many ways. You know the story. Instead he showed up as this tweedy young guy, young academic, cool. Possibly mentor figure, older brother, really, really smart older brother.*

*I got what I asked for. I said, "Well, I didn't even think to ask for that." I just said Einstein, and then he's the one that decided, "Well, okay." You do get to—I learned that right away that you do get to be—there's different kinds of you. There always are. All of us are always much more than meets the eye, and we have lots of different roles and different temperaments and different ways that we express ourselves to different people. That's the kind of thing I wanted to talk about or think about. Sometimes I was interested in the psychology of the human person. I didn't want to study psychology or be a psychologist or a therapist, but I was interested in how people craft a life, how they create new realities. It was just all so interdisciplinary. I couldn't figure out what to apply for. As it turned out, I didn't need to anyway. That part of my life ended before it could start.*
Laura: Yes, but now you're able to craft the kind of life that you would like to have, aren't you?
Eric: *What it turned out is I really wanted to be an explorer all along, but how do you get a degree in that and how do you get somebody to pay you to do it? Now I'm free from the shackles of—I just remember hearing my parents complain all the time about how laborious it was to get the PhDs, and all the drama within the departments and the dissertations and rejections and sniping and hating your thesis topic. You're sick to death of it, and all like that.*

*I discovered that now I can be at the university, and I can learn all kind of stuff and I don't have to tell somebody that I—I don't have to register. I don't have to sign up. Today, you were just trying to fit this book project into a form, right? Into a formal written book proposal just to send to people you don't know to explain yourselves to people that don't know you? I don't have to do any of that anymore. I can just–I just go out, and I just explore.*

*Father Nathan called me "Eric alone with his thoughts" because a lot of times I was alone with my thoughts, not just because I wanted so much alone time necessarily. I just couldn't find anybody that was interested because my mind was splitting in a hundred directions. How could I possibly find somebody that wanted to flit in all the same directions that I did? How would you even keep up with me?*

*Now I just find that for at least a lot of people, you're light and transparent. There's not as much need to assess and guess at and wonder about what this person is up to or what they're thinking or would they be a good companion? I really hardly ever dated because the whole thing just looked like such a—it just all looked so opaque and unpleasant to me, but when I watched people try to do it, I'd think, "Hey, why would you go to all that trouble? Just hang out with people and do stuff if you feel like it."*

*Now I just find that there's a way where it's just easy to be with people that you want to be with, and you don't have to figure out whether you're going to enjoy them or not or whether they're going to be bored with you or whatever. I don't know. I'm ramping it up. I'm exploring.*

Laura: Yes, and with people as well as the wider universe.

Eric: *Right, I'm not "Eric alone with his thoughts" all the time. I can still go aside any time I want to ponder a thing or wonder about a thing and enjoy my own company without interruption, but I'm not–remember in the story of the last day of my time here I thought I was going to join up with people that were going to do something that we would all enjoy together? Then it turned out to be that everybody came with somebody they knew already, and I didn't know anybody there. They all were sort of paired off. Then walking along a physical trail, most trails are two abreast at most. Trails are not really easy places to keep a conversation going because somebody's behind you, or you're in front of them.*

*Now I can be on something. I can go exploring like we were that day, except it's not uncomfortable, and I'm with interesting people that want to be around me. We can talk. There are cool ways that people can know here. We're still like babies, I think, at least I am. I know that I'm probably only crawling, but I think I'm walking. I'm probably excited about the fact that I can put my foot in my mouth. Whatever it is, I know that I'll keep growing into more abilities and powers and possibilities, but for right now, I'm just happy to be exploring.*

Laura: That's wonderful, Eric.

Eric: *That's probably enough because I just heard the campus bells chiming over there, and there are other people waiting to talk with you. The guy in front of me said,* "There's somebody else at the door" *or* "Next!" *or something like that.*

Laura: Thanks so much, Eric. We're glad to hear this update.

Eric: *You've been very kind to me, and I'm grateful.*

Laura: We're grateful to you. Many blessings.

Eric: *Good luck with this book, too.*

Laura: Yes, thanks.

Eric: *I can hear him* [meaning me, Nathan]; *when he's praying sometimes he speaks to me and to the others whose stories he's planning to include in his book. He has sometimes asked all of us to pray for it. I wasn't really a praying person, but I think what he means is there's a way that you can send energy toward somebody that might be influential in opening a door for you or something like that. I'm doing whatever I can...I'm doing something to try to help because he asked me.*

Laura: Thank you. Thank you.

Eric: *All right, I'll see you.*

Laura: All right, take care.

Nathan: Glory be to the Father, and to the Son, and to the Holy Spirit, as it was in the beginning, is now, and will be forever. Amen.

Thanks for bringing me along on your explorations, Eric. I can't imagine not wanting to hang out with you and your new pal, Al. We're interested in a lot of the same things. So what if your mind does go in a hundred different directions? I won't feel obliged to keep up. If you turn out to be too much for me, I can always take one of the new things you've helped me explore and go off by myself for a while and ponder it. You know, kind of be alone with my thoughts.

## Chapter Fifteen
# Hal, Who Doesn't Need a Seat Belt Now

This is the last of the stories I'll share in this book. It's a simple story of a nice guy who died in a car crash, who relived it for a time and eventually crossed over. His name is Hal. I think you'll like him. I know I do. Hal is very down-to-earth and easy to talk to.

Though Hal died in the early 1970s, he only moved into my dreaming consciousness a few months ago. My steadfast prayer partner Laura and I recently helped him cross over. Since Laura and I no longer live in the same state, our protected prayer conversations with night visitors have this new wrinkle: we conduct them via a video conference call. Rather than let a backlog of night visitors accumulate between face-to-face visits, she suggested this technological solution. I was a little reluctant. I prefer real presence to the virtual kind, but on the other hand, I had learned that some of my night visitors do keep track of time and are aware of its passage. No one has complained to me about being kept waiting, but I thought this might keep things moving. I found right away that the process worked just fine.

Here is the dream I received:

*I was driving on a highway near my home. The cars were from the late sixties and early seventies. A section of the road turned from multi- to single-lane. The driver's side front of my sedan clipped a metal pole. I overcorrected. The driver's side front hit a bridge abutment. I awoke.*

At the appointed time, Laura and I looked at each other through our computer screens. After a few minutes of friendly conversation, we were ready to go into our protective prayer and get to work.

Nathan: In the name of the Father, and of the Son, and of the Holy Spirit. We call upon Michael the Archangel and ask, Michael, that you stand guard over us and keep us safe from any that would do us harm, on our own guardians, and we call on Sts. Benedict and Dominic, St. Francis, Holy Mary, St. Mary Magdalene, any of the other holy ones who would like to gather around us to secure the space and keep us safe. And then we're at the service of someone, I think a man, who was in a car crash and came in a dream, I think on the fourth of April of this year. We ask this through Christ, our Lord. Amen.

I closed my eyes, took a few deep breaths and made interior space for the person in the car crash to inhabit me.

Nathan: I think this person is male, and I think he was the only one in the car. There's no reference to anyone else. But that's all I got.
Laura: This is very much like another one that we did recently.
Nathan: The one who drove off the road into the swamp?
Laura: Yeah, the guy who tried to pass, cut across the highway, and flew off and ended up dead.
Nathan: Well, that one was earlier in the same month, about a week before. Anyway, we ask now in the Holy Spirit, if we can be heard by the person who brought this material in a dream? I'm Nathan, I'm with Laura by computer, by technology, but we're at your service. We want to help in any way we can.

We were still for a short time.

Laura: Are you sensing anyone coming?
Nathan: Not quite yet.
Laura: If the person from this dream is nearby, please come ahead and join us. Nathan is here so you can talk through him, and tell us what you'd like us to help with and what happened to you just before your death.
Nathan: There's beginning to be movement. It might have been raining in this scene or foggy.
Laura: If you're there, and you're the person who came to Nathan in his dream not long ago, please go ahead and connect with us.

Someone did, and spoke through me.

Guardian: *This is his guardian. We're here, and we're grateful for your presence, and we're doing some gathering and connecting. The one that I accompany, I think, is up to the task.*

Laura: Very good. Well, thanks for coming and for bringing him with you. We'll give him a minute to settle in and use Nathan's voice.

Guardian: *I've been waiting for this day for a long time and am grateful for your help.*

Laura: Good, we're glad you are here. Would you like to begin by telling us your name? [Laura thought it was the man, but it was still the guardian.]

Guardian: *I haven't spoken it in language in a long time.*

Laura: If you remember it, that's fine. If not, we'll just go ahead.

Guardian: *Nathan has been doing some work with names and etymologies, writing out peoples' names' meanings, and there are a lot of name meanings in his head. But mine sounds something—there's a Greek word, "Miel," that means honey or honeybee, and my name has some of that sound in it in the way that you talk. My name has to do with the sweetness of the Lord, "taste and see."*

Laura: That's lovely. Shall we call you Miel, then?

Guardian: *Yes, that will do, but I'm about to step aside so that my beloved one can do what's needed today. Thank you for your help.*

Laura: You're most welcome.

The man from the dream came forward.

Man: *Okay, I've never done this before, but I'll give it a try.*

Laura: Well, it's already working. I'm hearing you fine. You're using Nathan's voice, I'm Laura, and we're here to try to help you. Your guardian has brought you here, to see if you're ready to move on, and we'll do what we can to help facilitate that. Would you like to tell us a little bit about what's on your mind, what happened to you, and what's going on?

Man: *Well, you got a bit of a picture of what my last—the last things my eyes saw. And for some time afterward—I think you call it trauma-looping?*

Laura: Yes.

Man: *It took me some effort to make it stop doing that, so even going back into it is something I haven't done, but I know now I can turn it off. Still, I'm a little wary about looking at it, but I know I can turn it off. It doesn't have to do that. But the basics of it were, yes, I wasn't very far from home, and it was in the early 1970s and I was in my car—I think he called it a sedan. I was driving on a highway; they had widened it, but I guess they didn't have the money to redo the bridge. The bridge was an old one, and it was narrower than the rest of the roadway, and so probably they intended to replace it, but they hadn't done it yet. It was raining, not a terribly hard rain, but it was raining and it was beginning to move toward dusk. We were traveling at highway speeds, 50 to 60 miles per hour, something like that. And they had a sign, you know, "Road Narrows" or "Merge," but I think all of us were going too fast for what was safe. When it did come time for the merging to happen, there wasn't much room. There wasn't enough space, and I tried to move over to the left, and the front bumper clipped something. There was a median, like a railing, or street light, or something, and I tapped it, but I was going pretty fast, so I tried to steer the other way, and I overcorrected and skidded and the front of my car, right in front of me, the driver's side hit the abutment of the bridge. Then I went off the side and tumbled and then—you know, the next thing was I died. But the scene starts to shift, and you're not so much looking through your hands on the steering wheel, and it begins to be this other business going on. And then a little bit of what was happening was people coming running, and I don't even remember an ambulance, or police, or firemen, or anything like that, but at least the first few people who came running. And after that, it became other stuff, other, you know, I guess you'd say spirit people or something. And whatever all that was I was just not interested in it. I just didn't want—whatever that was, I just didn't want it.*

Laura: I understand. It was a shock to you, and at that time you needed some time to process it. Let's go back to what you said at the beginning. You said you'd kind of been in a loop where this was happening to you over and over. That's often what happens in a traumatic death like this, sudden, impacting you so terribly without any expectation, and everything changes forever at that point. And so you replay it and replay it, but it sounds as though you've really done well to move beyond that. Even though it's still in your mind—your consciousness, I should say—you're still able to stop the loop. That's a major thing.

Man: *Partly. I don't know if you remember that time. You were alive then, in the early 1970s, right?*

Laura: Yes.

Man: *They started putting seatbelts in cars, and they started to buzz and, I don't know, you had to override them, or keep them locked all the time so you didn't have to bother with it. And there were all these commercials for "buckle up for safety." I just didn't do that, and so when this happened, the loop I was in had me banging around inside the car as it flipped and rolled, that kind of thing. So for a long time I was a pinball, I was just spinning like I was inside a dryer, being bounced against the walls and the sides of the doors and whatnot. And that's why I died, because my body was flying around all different directions.*

Laura: So no seat belt. I remember particularly, because my father worked for the Chrysler Corporation, that Chrysler cars in those days had voices that would speak to you, telling you to put your seat belt on. It was kind of eerie, and a lot of people wouldn't wear them then. So maybe your car was one of those or something like that.

Man: *I'm inside this man, and he's remembering when he was a kid, there were sensors in the seat. If you sat on it and turned the key and the buzzer sounded, it meant somebody was sitting there without a seatbelt on. Anyway, I didn't wear a seatbelt. Would I have survived it if I had? I've spent a lot of years tumbling that around in my head: Why didn't you just wear the seatbelt? Well, so what. You gotta die of something, so just get on with it. And I understand that being here with you is part of getting on with it.*

Laura: It is, and it sounds as though you've resolved not only the looping part but also the feelings that you had about how this could have been avoided. It's happened; you've processed it enough.

Laura and the man discussed more of the details of the collision with the bridge, which occurred when the man was driving home from work.

Laura: About how old would you have been then?

Man: *I think I was thirty-seven.*

Laura: Did you have a family?

Man: *You'd think that was a simple question.*

Laura: A wife or a girlfriend?

Man: *I had been married and divorced, and so I was kind of a weekend dad.*

Laura: Well, so you were coming home from work, thinking about what was going to go on that evening, and all of a sudden this happened. You mentioned that you recall something about an ambulance or people being there. That was the last thing you remembered before—

Man: *No, I don't remember an ambulance. I would assume that one eventually came, but what I was saying was, there was music—I had the radio on—and that was weird because it kept playing, like the music kept going while the car flipped and crashed. That was weird. I think I remember that there were people who saw my car going off the bridge, off the side, and falling down the embankment. There were people that ran down there and tried to help.*

Laura: So that's all you remember.

Man: *I imagine the police came and an ambulance, or a fire department, or sheriff, or somebody, but I don't remember all that. I just remember people stopped and ran down this embankment to see, but that's all I remember. Then the rest of that scene began to be like spirit people.*

Laura: Let's go back to that. The spirit people came. Was there anyone in that group you recognized?

Man: *No.*

Laura: Then they may have been people who died in accidents or people who were just willing to come…

Man: *Maybe, but all I had was a glance at them, and I wanted no part of that. I didn't give that a shot. I just said no to it.*

Laura: Do you know why you said no?

Man: *I think I was just overwhelmed, scared, shocked, and angry. I don't know. In the moment I just said no.*

Laura: So the spirit people left. Did others try?

Man: *So you recall my little guy, what did he call his name? Honey?*

Laura: Miel?

Man: *Miel Something. Or Something Miel. Yeah, he's a nice guy. We've talked a little bit more lately. He's different. I think he's an angel, but not with wings, and not pink and mostly naked like in paintings. I think he can make himself be more like me to make me be comfortable talking with him.*

Laura: So he's been helpful to you in kind of getting you ready to move on?

Man: *Well, he's just been at his post, I think, hanging around me and then when it came time to come in this dream, he showed me and coached me a little on how to do that.*

Laura: Can you tell us a little more about that? What kinds of things did he show you that were helpful?

Man: *Well, I'm having to connect deeper, like screwing in a light bulb.*

Laura: Yes, it is like that.

Have you noticed that in many of these accounts there comes a moment like this? When conversation moves from light and informative to emotionally difficult or intimate, folks often have to pause and find a way to connect more deeply. They use mechanical metaphors like dials or sockets. You've been in conversations like that, haven't you? You're in a conversation that turns in a way that requires deeper vulnerability and deeper trust. You may both need to focus more, maybe to lean in. That's what this feels like.

Man: *Turning something. Well, I don't know how it works, but when I guess, you know, when you're asleep, your brain is still firing all over the place, and some of it's nonsense dreaming, and others of it is more like organized dreaming. You've got all kind of thoughts in your head, and I don't know. Is it like filing in the night? Whatever your consciousness is doing, it's finishing up yesterday and getting ready for tomorrow somehow, and taking all these experiences and organizing them. Anyway, my guardian friend showed me how there's sort of a flow about it, sort of like radio waves, or like thoughts, or kind of like a wave. I'm thinking like radio waves, they can carry messages, like music. And what you put on it is kind of like floating downstream, but you have to launch the boat. And so Miel showed me how it's done. "This man is asleep but his stream of consciousness is right here, and all you have to do is step off the bank and into the flow and then show him the basics of what the last things you saw were, what happened to you." So that's all it was. It didn't take very long. The whole accident didn't take very long when it happened in the first place.*

I love how this night visitor can make this complex metaphysical action seem so simple. You just have to "launch the boat."

> Laura: And when you look around you, how would you describe where you are now? Can you give us any insight into that?
> Man: *There's not much to say. It's just land.*
> Laura: Not where you were on earth, but some other place.
> Man: *I didn't stay next to the car in the ditch, if that's what you mean. No, I didn't do anything like that. I don't know that I chose it but maybe failed to choose it. It reminds me of the DMV, some government office where they didn't put any effort into putting anything on the wall, or maybe some plastic plant. It's just some space. Yes, it's a space, but not a space anyone would want to go out of their way to stay in for very long.*
> Laura: Kind of a gray place?
> Man: *More like a tan place, but bland.*

This is consistent with how many others have described their "stuck" surroundings: dull, boring, nondescript. Comparing them to a tan DMV office with a plastic plant, that's a nice touch.

> Laura: Well, you remembered quite a lot about what happened. I wonder if you could share your name with us so we would know what to call you.
> Man: *Hal.*
> Laura: Well, Hal, you've been kind enough to share so much of your experience with us. We'd like to help you move on to the next stage of your afterlife.
> Hal: *That's kind of the point, isn't it?*

Laura: It is. If there is someone or some group of spirit people you would like to call in to accompany you to the next place, you can do that now. Or if you don't have anyone in particular in mind—

Hal: *I don't think so. I feel like I've climbed up on the high dive and it's time for me to jump off, but I don't have a person in mind, that I would say, "I'd like to see so-and-so." I'd rather just see who comes. There were people who came for me the first time, and I told them to go away. I didn't really know what I was doing, but that was the result of it. I'm wondering if there's anybody who came the first time who would come this time.*

Laura: Why don't you ask? Ask for anyone who came the first time, if they're available to come be with you?

Hal: *Do I ask God? God, bring me the right person, whoever is the right person or people. I think some people tried to come for me, and I just wasn't ready. I didn't mean to offend. I was, in the moment, not ready. If there's somebody you think is the right one or the right ones, I'm asking.*

Laura: Now, look around you and see if there's a group of people coming toward you.

Hal: *My angel is telling me they're already here: "You're the one who just needs to let yourself be still and see around you." So I'm going to be still for a bit. He's saying, "They've been here all along, but you just weren't able to see them." You know, Nathan has a lot of Wizard of Oz thoughts in his head.*

Laura: Yes, he does.

Hal: *And there's the scene of the little girl, Dorothy, waking up at the end of the movie. When she opens her eyes there's all these people hovering? So I think I'm opening my eyes. Hang on a bit…I can feel them…There's a young woman named Stella.*

Laura: Is she the spokesperson for the group?

Hal: *She was from my high school. She died in a car crash. I didn't know her very well, but we had a service for her in the gym, and we planted a tree for her.*

Laura: So she's come for you.

Hal: *I don't know why her, but she did die in a car crash. I thought she was gentle, and she's nice, she's quiet. She wasn't the cheerleader or, you know, when you're in a high school there's always a whole bunch of people that are not the cool kids. She was just some gal who died in a car crash.*

Laura: Now it sounds as if she's a special person and always will be for you, since she's come to help you move on to the next stage.

Hal: *She must have learned how to do that.*

Laura: Is she inviting you to go with her, holding her hand out?

Hal: *I don't think she needs to hold her hand out. She's just standing there making me know that this is her job, that she's learned how to be a hall monitor, or something. She's an usher, or somebody that's in a corridor or a doorway that belongs there and welcomes you and opens the door.*

Laura: That's great that she's come for you. If you're ready now, Hal, we'll just bid you farewell and thank you for sharing your story with us.

Hal: *I think whatever next happens, I'll be leaving the two of you. So thank you for your unusual work.*

Laura: You're very welcome.

Hal: *God bless you.*

Laura: God bless you as well. Goodbye now.

Hal: *Bye.*

Nathan: Glory be to the Father, and to the Son, and to the Holy Spirit, as it was in the beginning, is now, and will be forever. Amen.

Did you notice that a big change had taken place between the time of Hal's accident and his appearance in my dream, and our prayer conversation? He had spent a long time in a trauma–loop. Besides the bouncing around he did inside that looping scene in his tumbling car, he kept thinking about his unbuckled seat belt. Maybe if he buckled up like those commercials said to do....

At some point Hal learned to stop looping. He didn't say how that happened or what help he might have received in doing so. It was clear that that needed to happen before he could move forward. By the time we met him he could say, "Well, so what. You gotta die of something, so just get on with it. And I understand that being here with you is part of getting on with it." God bless everyone who helps traumatized persons put that kind of looping behind them.

As always, we thought it important to get permission to include his story in this book. We wondered if Hal would have much of an update for us; he'd only crossed over a few weeks ago. But Laura and I got together, again by video conference call, and went into protective prayer.

Nathan: [We begin with opening prayer asking St. Michael, our angels and guides] to keep us safe one more time. We call on our own guardians: St. Dominic, Holy Mary, St. Thomas Aquinas, Paulus, Mary Magdalene, St. Benedict, Francis, St. Maximillian, St. Rose of Lima. Please stand guard over us and help us with what might be a brief conversation with our new friend, Hal, that we were assisting a short time ago. We ask this through Christ, our Lord. Amen. And so in the Holy Spirit of Jesus Christ, we ask if we could be allowed to speak to Hal, who died in a car crash in the early seventies. Hal, we won't be long, but we have something to ask of you.

Laura: I feel something coming in already.

Nathan: Okay, Hal, you remember how to launch the boat?

Happily Hal did remember and came in quite quickly

Hal: *Hey, Hal, here. It's good to be back with you.*

Laura: Thanks for coming. It's good to hear your voice.

Hal: *Well, this is an unexpected pleasure.*

Laura: Thanks.

Hal: *You want me to help you somehow.*

Laura: Yes, we don't want to interrupt what's going on with you now, but at the same time, Father Nathan is getting ready to complete the book that he's writing about these Interrupted Death Experiences similar to yours, and there are some things about your story that he really liked and found interesting, and he thought other people would find them interesting, too. So we wanted to ask if you might be willing to have him share your story in his book.

Hal: *So you want to make me famous?*

Laura: [laughs] Well, we'd like to tell your story. We'll see how it goes.

Hal: *It's a little late to make me famous, but, sure, I'd be happy to have my story shared. There's nothing in it, nothing embarrassing in it, and it happened a long time ago. If it turned out that family members discovered the book and recognized me in it, there's nothing in it that would harm anybody, do you think?*

Laura: No, not at all. You did mention that you had children, or at least that you were a weekend dad, so there—

Hal: *Yeah, and if they are—or any friends or anything—for one thing it's been an awfully long time. And then, you know, I wasn't doing anything wrong except driving seven to ten miles over the speed limit. There's no shame in there, and I can't think of any reason why if they read this it would break somebody's heart or rip open an old wound or anything.*

Laura: No, there's nothing like that. Some of the things we found interesting were the way that you told your story, the way in which you helped us to understand a little bit about how people like you come to Nathan in his dreams. Also, how, when you come to talk about your feelings, you kind of adjust the wavelength and go a little deeper, so those things I think would be interesting to others besides us.

Hal: *Yeah, and you know, even there on the earth you can be in a conversation that*

182                    Afterlife, *Interrupted*

*then begins to get more emotional, and even have to do something like that here. You have to take a deep breath, or maybe leave the room and come back, or with some interplay of gestures or looks or something indicate to a person that you want to go deeper. Or maybe you say it: "I have something I'd like to tell you, and I'm nervous about it." Or "I'd like to share a confidence with you." Sometimes you might even say, "If I say this to you, would you promise to keep it in confidence?"—that kind of thing. There's a way in conversations here, where that same descent or ascent happens, and you kind of have to renegotiate or plug into each other at a deeper level.*

Laura: Well, that's interesting. It's been such a short while since we've talked, we didn't know how it would feel to you to be coming back and connecting with us so soon, but it sounds as though some things are going on that are helpful to you. We hope so.

Hal: *Yeah. I'm not a very complicated guy. You know, I tumbled down that embankment, and I tumbled inside the car. The car was tumbling, and I was tumbling inside of it, and for a long while I lived in a tumbler. I just—my thoughts were circular and kind of bumpy and confused, but I think the people who took care of me from that day forward until the time that we met were watching me, and my little honey bee dude…*

Laura: Miel.

Hal: *Yes, Miel. He was a good kind of coach, and I think I told you he could make himself be like me enough to make me feel he was a buddy, which was a really good idea on his part. He kind of made me feel like I was with somebody I had hung out with in school or on a job or something, somebody a little bit older and a little bit wiser. Whatever he did he did it well. And, of course, he helped me figure out how to do this at all.*

Laura: Sounds like he was a good companion for you.

Hal: *Still is. He hasn't split. He explained to me that now some of his biggest jobs are over where I'm concerned, and he doesn't have to protect me quite the way he did before, but he doesn't intend to just disappear from my life. He might just get recycled and get a new earth person to take care of, but for right now he's sort of between jobs.*

Laura: I see. Well, and what about Stella who took you on to the next stage? Is she still around, or—

Hal: *I suppose if I called her back she would be, but no. Remember, we really didn't know each other very well to begin with. I mean, she recognized me and obviously she came for me, and I recognized her. But we'd never had a conversation of any length even though we were going to the same high school. I doubt that we will hang around each other. We didn't before, and she did the thing she knows how to do and I needed* done. So weren't you just talking about something like that?

Laura: Yeah. What we were saying was that sometimes the person who comes to escort someone like you on is not at all the one you might expect—a loved one from the past, a grandmother, or something—but there's always a kind of a logic to it. It makes sense.

Hal: *Yeah, and, if you recall, you gave me the option of calling on a specific person, and I passed on it. I just asked God to send the right person, and I think I suggested that it could be somebody who came for me the first time that I'd said no to. That made sense to me.*

Laura: Yes, and whether Stella was in that group or not we don't know, but at least she was the one who came, and there's a logic to that. You had known each other slightly and had something in common.

Hal: *I think just before I got here you and he were talking, and wasn't he just finishing writing a chapter about people in a plane crash?*

Laura: Yes.

Hal: *And I think you were saying—there are still kind of remnants in here—that the two ladies that you talked to were not people that he would likely have an ongoing relationship with?*

Laura: Yes.

Hal: *And that some of the other people that will be in your book, you met them and you want to stay in touch?*

Laura: That's right.

Hal: *Well, that's kinda normal, isn't it? Whether you're here or there, you know there are some people you just hit it off with and others that you thank for their service and probably don't see again unless you need the same thing twice. Based on that, I won't be needing that again, going down that corridor the hall monitor knew how to coach me or walk through.*

Laura: Yes, so Stella came for that purpose. Maybe you'll see her again and maybe you won't, but thank God she came when she was needed.

Hal: *Yeah. Correct. So, yeah, you've got my go-ahead. I'd be honored to be part of the book, and I think I knew that you were thinking this way. Somebody tipped me off. And I understand that you've asked the other ones to be a kind of prayer team or circle for you?*

Laura: Would you be willing to do that?

Hal: *I would. There's a young woman here from India. I think her name is Rani.*

Laura: Oh, yes. We know Rani.

Hal: *Well, she said that you—between the two of you, you kind of gave her a special*

Afterlife, *Interrupted*

*job on this team because she also wants to write a book.*

Laura: Yes, uh–huh.

Hal: *And you kind of told her that out of all the other ones that are in the book—I think he told her that he'd like her to be a kind of an apprentice and take a larger role than the others since this might be something she had a particular interest in. So, anyway, she found me out and told me one of the jobs is to pray for you, whatever you think that is and however you do it.*

Laura: Oh, well, thank Rani for us and tell her hello for us.

Hal: *She's probably listening in, but, sure, I will. You're getting to the point in the project where our prayers might be helpful to point things in the right direction.*

Laura: Yes, to give the book wings.

Hal: [laughs] *I like that.*

Laura: Well, and thank you for your willingness not only to share your story but also to be part of that posse, as Nathan would say.

Hal: *Well, put me in the column of people who would like to hang out with you whenever you make your journey over this way.*

Laura: Well, great. We'll look for you when we arrive.

Hal: *By that time I'll be all cleaned up, and you'll be seeing me at my best.*

Laura: Very good, Hal. Many blessings to you, and thanks so very much for this.

Hal: *All right. God bless you right back.*

Laura: Thank you. You, too. Bye-bye.

Nathan: Glory be to the Father, and to the Son, and to the Holy Spirit, as it was in the beginning, is now, and will be forever. Amen.

Whenever I sit down to write, and before I go to sleep at night, I now call out to my "book friends," all the folks whose stories you've heard here. Even when I'm alone, the room gets crowded. It's true, in prayer I did promote Rani to Afterlife Assistant Editor and asked her to take the afterlife lead in praying this book project all the way home. So the writing is nearly done, but production and marketing and publicity and a lot of other things I've never done and don't know how to do must now happen quickly. My night visitors turned book friends all have plenty of experience of having to figure out how to do new things, even to become a new version of themselves. I can't think of a better group of coworkers to help, borrowing Laura's phrase, "give the book wings."

# Epilogue,

## But Not a Conclusion

*"Rejoice always, pray without ceasing;*
*give thanks in all circumstances."*
St. Paul

First Thessalonians 5: 16–17a

The headline at the top of this page could have been *conclusion* because this is the end of the book. I'm glad I looked up the word conclude. I love etymology, the meaning of words. This one surprised me. I knew the prefixes *co, com,* and, in this case, *con,* meant *with.* But the Latin *claudere* means *to shut up, to close, even to slam.* Hmm. So there can be an end of a contentious conversation that you want to conclude in a way that shuts up the opponent and declares you the victor. Well, that being the case, I'm not writing a conclusion, I'll tell you that.

How about *epilogue? Epilogue* just means *an added word.* Of course, it's an added word that's at the end of a lot of other words. But I like that a lot better. I'm only adding a word here. I want to summarize some of what has already been written but to do so at the end to give a few ideas a deeper resonance.

I'm looking back at the prologue. In it, I had a bullet point list of a few key ideas. I think I'll return to that here. The first point is still the first thing I want readers to understand. Most people who die traumatically quickly complete their transition into the afterlife. Only a few need the assistance my prayer partners and I have been asked to provide.

Please hear this: If you have suffered the loss of a loved one to a violent, sudden, traumatic death, don't assume that they were stuck and needed the services of someone like my prayer partners and me. Most people don't. I think it's a pretty rare experience when people have their death interrupted and slide off to the side for a time. Most people, I think, are greeted at the time of their sudden death, go with the greeters, and transition smoothly, even if unexpectedly, from this life to the next.

The next point is critically important too. All human beings who die survive their deaths. You're eternal. You always have been since you came into existence. You will always be. As a Catholic Christian, I was taught this at an early age. It's still true. Everybody is eternal because everybody is marvelously made. It doesn't have to do with being good girls or bad boys. It's not about whether you practiced a religion or you didn't. It's not about whether you've lived a morally, ethically, upright existence or not. You're just the kind of being that, once it comes into being. will never stop being. That's just a truth of the universe. You will always be.

I remember on Easter Sunday this past spring, I was preaching before a congregation. I looked into eyes of a young woman only a few feet away and asked, "When your life here is done, what should we do with you? Do you belong in the trash or in the recycling?" She laughed, and so did everyone around her. We laughed because it's a laughable idea. But which are you?

Are you something that is just rubbish that should go in a landfill? Or are you the kind of thing that has ongoing value and the ability to become something that you haven't been yet? Could you be recyclable? Well, in fact, your body, if it's allowed to decay and return to the earth whence it came, begins to become something else. Those ashes, that dust, become something new on the earth. The part of us that doesn't stay earthbound is doing the same thing. We're becoming something new. We take part in our transformation. We have a redemption value. I'm convinced of that.

Your individual consciousnesses will survive. You will be you. I've lived all of these stories of people being reunited with loved ones, sometimes very surprising loved ones, who came for them. You and those you love will retain your stories in all their detail. You will be you after you pass. You won't have to be any kind of version of you that drags you down or saddens you. You'll have the opportunity to shed pieces of your own story and try on new things; you'll be helped to heal from one thing and grow into the next. If you've read these stories, you know that even through this little cosmic peephole, we've seen people growing right before our eyes.

No one dies alone. Even some of these people who died terrible traumatic deaths, sometimes apparently alone, were at the least accompanied by their guardian. We all have one. You don't have to think of a guardian angel as being a winged creature or cherub or any other silly depiction. Your guardian is a spirit being, a being of light, who simply loves you and has been at your side because your creator wanted you to be accompanied through this life and into the next. We all have a guardian; you've seen how faithful they are. They stay with people who thought they wanted to be utterly isolated. The guardians respect that

Afterlife, *Interrupted*

decision as best they're able. They go off to the far edge of whatever territory their beloved creates, but they stay at their post, and they help when they're able.

You will be greeted and welcomed by loving helpers when it comes your time to pass. When it was time for you to leave the womb, you weren't just plopped onto a table or onto the ground. You were accompanied by people who helped you leave the womb. You were received into the arms of people who knew what to do with a newborn. That's the way it works. When you pass from this life to the next, there will be others who will be there who are experienced and know how to help you.

You will be respected. I love that word. It means to be looked at again. Respecting—choosing to respect another person—is a humble act because you're saying you're willing to look at them again, presumably because you might have overlooked something important the first time you viewed them. People are respected in the afterlife. And if you want to go into the afterlife disrespecting yourself, that will only be allowed to a point, because truth is essential. Even those in the habit of thinking badly of themselves are coached that they have to stay in the truth. It's important to be true because only what is true is real. Everything else is an illusion. It may take you a while to be able to do that. You grow at your own pace.

That brings us to another thing: the way time behaves. People who have died are not inside of time, exactly. At first, I thought that, after they passed, nobody was really even aware of time. My earliest night visitors couldn't answer the question of how old they were, or in what year they died, without having to really labor at it. I thought it just must be that once they're outside of time, they pay no attention to it.

But then I found that others absolutely paid attention to time and earthly events. Remember the story of Cheryl Lynn, who came to us in early February of 2018 and immediately referenced the upcoming Winter Olympics? She was still paying attention to time. I don't know whether it was she, her guardian, or someone else who knew the amount of time that had lapsed between when her story entered into my dream and when my prayer partner and I got around to dealing with her. I understand only that time behaves differently in the afterlife.

There are all kinds of opportunities to learn things in the next life. I was a student who looked forward to the start of school at the end of the summer. That's because I had lots of friends at school that I didn't see during the summertime. You too have gone off to school with other people. One of the blessings of schooling is the ability to be in the company of others who are trying to learn the same things you want to learn.

In these afterlife schools I've seen, everyone is in the school they really want to be in. There are lessons they crave to learn. They seek some knowledge that they really long to possess so they can use it to improve their circumstances. They get to be with other people who have the same craving, and presumably others who know plenty about what needs to be taught. It doesn't surprise me at all that, especially at the very beginning of the afterlife, there would be all kinds of things to learn and all kinds of joyful opportunities to learn them with other people.

I think of the afterlife schools as Montessori schools. You might not be placed in straight rows, forced to sit up straight and not talk out of turn. There are places where all kinds of cool things are placed in your environment, all of which can teach you something. No one is scolding you to keep up with the rest of the class or to keep on a pre-arranged schedule.

That brings us to the non-judgmental zone of the afterlife. So many of those we've helped have commented upon this: judgment falls away. The griping, sniping, unnecessary type of judgment that we receive from others, and foist upon others, and that is all too often in the air we breathe, is not tolerated in the afterlife. That is the biggest joy and the deepest relief I've seen in the lives of the people I've helped. They're so happy to live in a place where they don't have to deal with the harsh, critical judgment of other people. It raises a question for this life: could we all just lighten up and let each other be? Could we reserve our judgments for those circumstances where they are really and truly called for rather than having an opinion about anything and everything that comes along?

You'll leave behind physical pain. I tell dying people, cancer patients in particular, that the moment is coming when you're going to be released from this pain. It's the truth. The same is true for the alcoholic or drug-addicted person who gets to leave behind a body that, for reasons they might not understand, craves an addictive substance that only makes their life worse. That will go away at death. What remains then is the opportunity to focus on these questions: who did I hurt while I was under the influence? How did I hurt them? What opportunities for growth did I miss? How can I change?

We all have some kind of body that others recognize as us. You know how, in the course of a week or a month, you might have lots of different human interactions that call for you to show others different versions of yourself? You might want to look your best when getting dressed up for a wedding or a funeral, for example. Or when you're going for a job interview, or maybe out on a date with your fiancé's parents. Later, you might look very different, putting on a t-shirt and sweats to watch the game. You might show another version of yourself when hanging out with old friends. We have different faces of ourselves that we routinely show the world, depending upon the circumstance.

In the afterlife, we can change not only our clothing, but how our bodies manifest. People who died in old age show up looking as they did in their wedding pictures or in their army uniform. Do you remember in Dwight's case, how he was so ashamed of the way he died? His entire clan showed up; he said that they were translucent enough so that he could see their "stuff," the things they were once ashamed of. They didn't just jettison their stuff. They somehow contextualized it. They incorporated it; they found room for it, because it was part of their story. But they held that part of their story in a way that was helpful to

Dwight. In the Christian tradition, we have many paintings and depictions of Jesus risen from the dead. These often show Jesus in a white robe, but with his hands and his feet showing so you can see the nail marks from the crucifixion. Often beams of light, rays that are white and gold, are shown streaming through the nail marks. "Look at the worst of what befell me. It's okay. It all belongs." Even this horrible, violent, bloody mess that was once his body is now transformed. Those experiences are still part of the whole of Jesus. He can empathize with everyone who's been through anything horrible. And, certainly, Dwight saw that compassion during the visits with Jesus that he described.

In the afterlife you can visit or look in on loved ones here on earth. This is really important. I want you to know that if you've lost loved ones to death, you can still talk to them. I do it all the time. They will hear what you receive. Now, whether you're able to receive what they might send back, that can vary an awful lot. Some people do seem more sensitive to receiving messages from their dead loved ones than others are. Nevertheless, you can send messages of love to the people that you love and know they are heard.

I recommend doing that because of my practice as a Catholic Christian. Specify who you want to speak to in prayer. We Catholics do that with the sign of the cross. You've seen it, haven't you? We touch the fingers to the forehead, the chest, and each shoulder, making the shape of a cross over our body, mind, and spirit, bringing the whole of ourselves into a conversation and saying, within this body of the risen Christ, I want to speak to so and so.

Now, you might adapt that to your own uses if you're not a Catholic or a Christian. I believe that we're blessed when we study each other's religious practices and, wherever we see something that rings true to us, find a way to incorporate it. I think that your loved ones will hear you if you speak to them. And they might be able to get a message through to you in a way that you can receive.

What did you think about the surprising breadth of the escorts, the people who came to help someone finish crossing over? Most of the time, I've simply asked, "Can you remember anybody who loved you who died before you did?" Can this frightened, traumatized, stuck person remember being loved by someone? Just the memory of being loved can be calming and can give confidence. So I've often asked that question and found that, as soon as the person names someone who they knew had died but who loved them, that loving person appears. They simply come in a way that shows that they're present and available if needed.

Often they are grandmothers, moms, teachers, aunts, and uncles. I've seen many more women than men. Whoever they are, they've often been the ones to escort a person and help them cross over. Some of the time, people have simply asked for the right person to be sent. Some have called it "taking the luck of the draw." They just say (sometimes to God), "Please send me the right person." When that has happened, there have been a surprising number of early childhood acquaintances. I think there's just something about the purity of our spirits when we're young, that can help even older people who got stuck in the crossing over. Often it's someone they knew on the playground, a school teacher, or a neighbor lady who made cookies and gave them out to the kids. Sweet church ladies, Cub Scout leaders, coaches, and high school shop teachers: these are only some of those who end up being these cosmic crossing guards. All these odd little characters who weren't at all stars in your show, but simply in the background in your larger life story, end up in this crossing–over role.

I did include some stories here that feature celebrities. (I didn't load the book up with them because this topic can seem outlandish enough without adding the celebrity angle.) Some of the celebrities I've dealt with have been people of heroic virtue and courage whom others felt like they would trust. Sometimes they have been, as in Dwight's case, the famous person he was named after. When a celebrity shows up, as Einstein did for Eric, it's because Eric asked. For him specifically. And remember how pleased Dwight was to be able to have lunch with President Eisenhower because he invited him? Having access to each other in the afterlife, regardless of how we perceive their stature in life, sounds like one of the delights of the experience.

What constitutes readiness for a person to move along? As I got more and more involved in this work, I did start to ask my night visitors, "How did you find me?" And very often what I heard back was, "I don't know; someone brought me here." Well, who would that someone be? It's someone who seems to be in a healing role who has insight into the status of the person that they're bringing along.

Over time, I began to feel more and more like I was involved in coordinated healthcare. I was involved in some sort of trauma care, but not at the front end. Someone else was there to help the traumatized person through the trauma itself. There was some sort of oversight during a dormant period that reminded me of the way that you might be unconscious when you were brought in by ambulance, or put into the ICU while lots of conscious souls around you were seeing to your healthcare.

As healing progresses, and the stuck person is able to begin to awaken to their circumstance, there comes a moment when they're ready to transition from that status to something and someplace else. I began to understand myself as somehow helping in that movement, which included completing the death experience that had been interrupted.

This whole experience is all about love. Which brings me to a point that Catholic and other Christian readers might well wonder. Why would you bother asking for all these other relatives and schoolteachers and celebrities to come and help a stuck soul? Why wouldn't you just ask Jesus? Well, I believe God is love and that whoever has been the most loving person in your life has been the person who has most revealed the presence of God to you. I believe it's the incarnation. Whatever flesh–and–blood person has helped you know how loved you are is God's most effective agent in your life.

I was warned that printing this book might encourage some people to dabble in the occult. What if some people might be intrigued with spiritual gifts and want to have seances or use Ouija boards, or tarot cards, or whatever to dabble into spiritual, spooky, unknown things? I'm not advocating any such thing.

If you want to be involved in trying to help people who might still be stuck, in the Catholic church there's a really simple process that anybody can take part in. It's called praying for the souls in purgatory. You don't need to know the specific needs of souls who have died. You can simply pray for them and send them sacred energy. Ask God to give them the same. As you know, I was doing that as a little kid, and I'm still doing that now. If you'd like to somehow be supportive and helpful to people who might have died and not crossed well, just start praying for them. So if you want to be involved in a spiritual practice that expands what you have been doing because you read this book, that's what I'd recommend. In whatever way it makes sense to you, pray for those who've died and pray that because of your love for them and your concern for them, you are sending them aid. When we donate money to a health charity, we don't have to know every last recipient of the cancer treatment that our money helped recover. When you give blood, you don't have to know the person who receives the transfusion. There are times when, yes, you can donate a kidney to a relative or someone you know, but lots of our benevolent work involving healing is done for people that we don't explicitly know. You can pray for the good of people that you don't know if you'd like to.

I was taught to pray as I moved into sleep when I was very young. My Mawmaw napped during the day and had a rosary hanging from a cup hook next to the daybed where she slept. She told me, "If you fall asleep before finishing your rosary, your guardian angel will finish it for you." Even private prayer is shared. We're never absolutely on our own.

As I grew, I learned more about how our bodies work. I learned that it only looks like we're doing nothing when we're asleep. Our creator gave us bodies that are designed to be unconscious about a third of the time. Our sleep is cleansing and restorative. We don't have to remind our bodies to breathe during sleep; they know how to do that while we're unconscious. And when we breathe, what happens? Simply put, it's "in with the good, out with the bad." One complete breath, inhaling and exhaling, or inspiring and expiring, both nourishes and cleanses us.

I learned early on that we can join ourselves to others in lots of loving ways. Prayer, even prayer while asleep, is just one of them. I knew from an early age that "purgatory" meant "cleansing place;" and I knew that half of what every breath did was cleanse. So, after I'd learned all about breathing, I began consecrating my breathing before going to sleep. That way, I figured, my breath could be cleansing me and someone in purgatory at the same time. I've done this all my life.

I do a dedication of my breathing before sleep. You know how people will call into a radio music program and ask the disc jockey to play a particular song for a loved one? That's often called having a song "dedicated." Well, right before sleep, I think of a particular person who has died and dedicate that night's breathing for them. I ask God the DJ to bless and cleanse them of anything still in them that's spent and toxic. It's easy.

Remember, too, that one of the names of God is Holy Spirit, which just means Whole Breath. One more thing: When we do things for others, goodness often rebounds back to us. I might lie awake thinking of something upsetting that's destroying my ease and want to pray about that. I wouldn't recommend that as promoting restful sleep. Allowing your thoughts to focus on another and their healing might just send a restful, healing grace back your way.

There's a line from one of the Hebrew psalms that says something like "The Lord gives gifts to his beloved while they slumber." I try to join my giving heart to God's inexhaustible love as I sleep. I don't need to know how this all works. I just know that it does. If you want to do this but don't believe in the word purgatory, well, come up with another word. Again, the word *purge* really only means *to cleanse.* Some of the stories in this book have had plenty of cleansing in them. Recall how Don talked about needing to get cleaned up, to get dressed up. For him, that cleansing metaphor was apt. Rani spoke of stepping out of dirty clothes. Purgatory is simply the name for a place that supports us in shedding what doesn't serve us.

Many of these stories have enough detail in them that surviving loved ones may recognize their beloved one. That's why I went to each of my night visitors and asked permission to use their story. As you know, in one case, we changed a name because one night visitor didn't want it known that she had been a murder victim. She didn't feel that her children needed to know that.

Here I'm addressing myself to loved ones of any of the night visitors who allowed their stories to be included in this book: I love you even though I haven't met you. I'm sorry the one you loved died so abruptly. *Abrupt, rupture, interrupted:* these words involve ripping and tearing. Your loved one's death may have left you heartbroken. We now share in common a love for the same person whom I met in a different way from how you knew them. I apologize in advance if anything that I've brought up or written wounds you. If you'd like to be in touch with me, that can be done through my website. I would welcome contact with any who are relatives or friends of any of the people who are in this book, if you would find that helpful.

Now, remember I'm not concluding. That is, I'm not telling anybody to shut up. And in fact, it's my hope that this whole book really opens a conversation rather than concludes one.

Godbless,
Father Nathan

# Afterword

Remember that I am, first of all, a preacher. Much of my preaching takes place within a Catholic Mass. I usually begin with a story, maybe about a guy named "Bob," segue into a reference to the Scripture passages selected for that day, and move toward a conclusion, often a call to action. But I have a bad habit. Sometimes I get people all involved in a story, shift away from it, and leave them hanging without knowing I've even done so. Often, at the end of the service, on the church steps, some poor soul is left asking, "But Father Nathan, what happened to Bob?"

Back in Chapter One, I told you this part of a story about my dad's mom, Mawmaw: Mawmaw leaned close to me to whisper to me. "Robert, would you like to know the secret of the happy death I'm asking for? Pawpaw needs me, and he's much older, so I need to outlive him. But not by much," she told me, because then her main work would be done. Once he had died, she said, "I'll be ready to go, too, right behind him."

Here's how that story ended.

I was home from college on a break when we got the call from the nursing home where they shared a room. Mawmaw was dying. While we were in her room waiting for some medical paperwork to be done, and while my back was turned, Pawpaw breathed his last. His daughter, my aunt Sister Maximus, was watching. She said she saw him leave his body. Mawmaw left her body fifteen hours later. After sixty-four years of marriage, their two caskets were wheeled up the aisle of our church, as we prayed them on their afterlife journeys. Mawmaw had gotten the happy death she'd asked for.

# Acknowledgments,
# Or Many Hands Make Light Work

**D**o you remember the song "He's Got the Whole World in His Hands"? I can picture where I was standing, singing it in kindergarten. After starting with "little bitty babies" and moving through a list of others, it concludes with, "He's got everybody here." I'd add hereafter, too.

I told my baby sister and publisher, Cathryn, that on this book's cover I wanted hands reaching out to other hands. I had in mind those Sistine Chapel hands, God's and Adam's, that are almost touching. The work of helping stuck souls cross over is made lighter because, as you've read here, there are so many helpers.

In the industry, mine is called a self–published book. In truth, it is the work of very many selves, some here, some hereafter.

Let's start here with this trinity: Cathryn Castle Garcia, Laura Dunham, and Betsy Rapoport.

Cathryn has gotten this book all the way to the finish line by doing too many tasks to mention, all while writing her own book* with her husband, Gui. Laura was a gifted gift from God who came on the scene just when she was needed. She helped craft the outline, choose the stories we'd tell and participate in many prayer sessions where we did the work of helping my night visitors. Laura, too, has a new book out.** Betsy is the pro who knew how to help us shape this story. She has a gift for anticipating what readers want to know and drawing that out of an author like me.

Many other hands have left a loving fingerprint on *Afterlife, Interrupted*. My Dominican community has provided me with a way of life with room for contemplation and writing. Mark, Jude, John Paul, Bryan, and Bart, I'm especially grateful for your fraternal support. You, too, Michael, Xavier, Francis, and Garry. Thanks for listening with love to my wild and wooly experiences. More recently, Tom, Emmanuel, Angelica and Mary V. have had my back.

Let's put our hands together for all of the prayer partners: John and Mimi, who show up here, and Barbara, Bova, Katie, Colleen, and so many others who helped in that holy work over the years.

Thanks to all my early readers who are helping this message to be known. We have good news to share.

The folks at the International Association for Near–Death Studies (IANDS) have been calling the world's attention to the conscious survival of bodily death for decades now. I look forward to working with you on this mission.

Steve Harrison and his Quantum Leap team and Jack Canfield and his, I'm so grateful for the mentoring you've provided.

Let's give a hand to all the afterlife folks, starting with the officially sainted ones: Holy Mary, Joseph, Andrew and Peter, Paulus and family, Mary Magdalene, Archangel Michael and Phillip James, Benedict, Dominic and Francis, Carlo, Maximillian, Rose, and Aleydis. Take a bow, Jack and Jacqueline, Dwight, Albert, Judy, Frank, and Louis. All you greeters who came when someone needed you, and all those ancestors who made a scared soul know they belonged to a people, thank you.

And now those of you I've addressed in prayer as my "book people," Ray, Rani (my *Afterlife* Assistant Editor), Buddy, Cheryl Lynn, Don (and Ralph), Shelby, Paul, Sophia*, Shelley, Dwight, The Plane Passengers, Vicky (and Patrick), Eric, and Hal: you came through hell-and-back, and so generously gave us permission to share your stories of death and rebirth. A profound thank you.

Jesus said to his closest followers just before his death, "I call you friends because I have told you everything on my heart." Richard, you heard my heart when I was afraid to speak of these experiences at all. I couldn't ask for a better friend.

Finally, Friend of My Heart, thanks for creating and loving me, and all of the above.

Nathan G. Castle, OP
September, 2018

*Ocean Metaphor: Unexpected Life Lessons From the Sea*
**Extraordinary Time: Spiritual Reflections from a Season with Cancer, Death and Transition (Cascade Books, 2018)*

# About the Author

Nathan G. Castle has been a Catholic priest of the semi–contemplative Dominican Order since 1979. Father Nathan has served as a campus minister at Arizona State University, the University of California, Riverside, and Stanford University. Currently, he lives in a community of Dominican men and women serving the University of Arizona in Tucson.

Father Nathan has prayed for deceased souls since childhood and has helped stuck souls cross over for almost twenty years. He has used his first book, *And Toto, Too: The Wizard of Oz as a Spiritual Adventure,* as the basis for healing of trauma retreats for spiritual groups and survivors of natural disasters.

Available for speaking engagements and retreats, Father Nathan can be contacted through his website, nathan-castle.com.

Printed in Great Britain
by Amazon

61804496R00115